THE LOOSHAUS

THE LOOSHAUS

CHRISTOPHER LONG

YALE UNIVERSITY PRESS NEW HAVEN AND LONDON

Published with assistance from the foundation
established in memory of Calvin Chapin of the
Class of 1788, Yale College, and from the Martin
S. Kermacy Endowment, School of Architecture,
University of Texas at Austin.

yalebooks.com

Designed by Jena Sher
Set in type by Amy Storm
Printed in China through Oceanic Graphic Printing,
Inc.

Library of Congress Cataloging-in-Publication Data
Long, Christopher (Christopher Alan), 1957–
    The Looshaus / Christopher Long.
        p. cm.
    Includes bibliographical references and index.
    ISBN 978-0-300-17453-3 (cloth : alk. paper)
1. Looshaus (Vienna, Austria). 2. Loos, Adolf,
1870–1933—Criticism and interpretation. 3. Modern
movement (Architecture)—Austria—Vienna. 4. Vienna
(Austria)—Buildings, structures, etc. I. Title.
    NA4178.V54L66 2011
    725'.230943613—dc22   2011014919

A catalogue record for this book is available from
the British Library.

10 9 8 7 6 5 4 3 2 1

P. viii: Looshaus, c. 1930. Photo by Martin Gerlach.
Bildarchiv der österreichischen Nationalbibliothek, Vienna.
Jacket illustrations: (*front*) Looshaus, 1911 (fig. 84)
(*back*) detail of Looshaus (fig. 91)

FOR MARTIN

CONTENTS

PREFACE

I remember vividly the first time I saw the Looshaus. It was 1976. I was eighteen, in my first year at university, and I was visiting Vienna with my friend Martin Enge. We had gone together to meet one of his cousins for breakfast at the Café Bräunerhof in the inner city. Striding across the Michaelerplatz that sunlit early summer morning, I looked up and glimpsed it suddenly. From my reading on the Viennese fin de siècle, I knew a little about the building and the controversy that had once swirled around it. But I had not expected to see it, and it startled me.

I was most surprised by its ordinariness. To my untutored eye, it seemed unremarkable: simple, forthright, scarcely different from many of the older surviving buildings in the city. I was unaware at the time that my first, unaffected impression was precisely as Loos had intended: his "Haus am Michaelerplatz" was an extension of Viennese tradition, not a disavowal of it. The building, once so celebrated or despised, was in part a summons to learn from the old, a fervent profession of Loos's veneration of Biedermeier culture and his conviction that the new modernism should be grafted onto a time before the corrupting influence of nineteenth-century historical revivalism. But all this I was to understand only years later.

In his own time, Loos had sought to explain his ideas, but not many of his detractors — and, even, few of his supporters — grasped his message fully. They saw in the building what they wanted to see: a bold statement of modernist purity or a radical rejection of established values. It was both and much more.

I began research for this book while teaching in Prague in the mid-1990s, and over the years I have incurred obligations to many people. Anyone now writing about the Looshaus is indebted to Hermann Czech and Wolfgang Mistelbauer, who wrote the first book about it, and to Burkhardt Rukschcio and Roland Schachel for their groundbreaking research on Loos's life and work. Together, they provide the essential basis for every scholar researching Loos and the Looshaus.

For assisting me with locating information and photographs, I would like to thank Therese Muxeneder at the Arnold Schönberg Center, Vienna; Danielle Kovacs at the Special Collections and Archives of the W. E. B. Du Bois Library, University of Massachusetts, Amherst; Markus Kristan and Ingrid Kastel, at the

Graphische Sammlung Albertina, Vienna; and Helmut Selzer of the Wien Museum, Vienna. In addition, I want to express my gratitude to the librarians, archivists, and staff members at the Avery Architectural and Fine Arts Library, Columbia University, New York; Baupolizei (MA 37), Vienna; Library of Congress, Washington, D.C.; New York Public Library; Österreichische Nationalbibliothek — Bildarchiv, Vienna; and Wien Bibliothek, Vienna. Once more, I am thankful to the staff of the Architecture and Planning Library at the University of Texas at Austin, especially Martha González Palacios and Daniel Orozco, for their gracious and expert assistance. For assisting me with information and photographs, I would like to thank Maria Makela, Peter Jelavich, Sherwin Simmons, Josef Strasser, Otto M. Urban, and Jindřich Vybíral. I owe a great obligation to the two anony-mous readers of my manuscript and, especially, to Hermann Czech, who read the final draft and made numerous suggestions for its improvement. They corrected a number of errors and cleared up some misunderstandings. I am also grateful to John W. Boyer, who kindly spent time helping me understand the intricacies of Viennese municipal politics. Any errors that remain are, of course, my own.

I want to acknowledge my very able research assistants, Barbara Ellen Brown and Laura McGuire, for their help over many years. Isben Önen aided me during the last phase of my search for material and made a particularly valuable contribution. I owe a special debt of thanks to Elana Shapira, who helped me track down a number of articles, photographs, and documents in Vienna that were central to this story. She also generously shared with me her research on the Goldman family and their role in building the Looshaus.

Mirka Beneš, Richard Cleary, Francesco Passanti, and Wilfried Wang, my colleagues in the School of Architecture at the University of Texas at Austin, offered the stimulus of their ideas and suggested possible avenues of research. I remain deeply grateful to them for their insight and support. Vincent Snyder generously provided the two drawings of the Michaelerplatz. I would also like to acknowledge my former students Vladimir Kulić and Monica Penick for their aid and suggestions.

Grants from the vice president for research and the Martin S. Kermacy Endowment at the University of Texas at Austin helped to offset the costs of the photographs and allowed me to undertake several research trips. I am grateful to Frederick Steiner, dean of the School of Architecture, for his continued support.

I would like to thank Michelle Komie, Heidi Downey, Katherine Boller, Mary Mayer, and Jena Sher at Yale University Press, who with skill and patience worked to make this book a reality. I am also indebted to Tano Bojankin, who aided me with last-minute research and details in Vienna; to Wolfgang Thaler, who provided the superb color photographs of the Looshaus; to the Raiffeisenbank, Vienna, current owner of the building, for permission to access and photograph the interior; and to Reinhard Pühringer, the bank's liaison.

I cannot end without mentioning my dear friend Martin Enge, who opened my eyes to Austria and its culture and has been my willing and inspiring guide to its inner workings for nearly four decades.

Finally, I want to thank my wife, Gia Marie Houck, and my father, Harry Long, for their unceasing love and support.

PROLOGUE

"Vienna, spring 1911," the architect Robert Hlawatsch recalled decades after his first confrontation with the Looshaus: "My father and I—I was then eleven—strolled through the inner courtyard of the imperial palace, entered the Michaeler-platz, and walked toward the building of the gentlemen's tailor firm Goldman & Salatsch. I was shocked by the bare, unadorned upper stories. 'Papa, what is that? Who designed that?'" His father replied: "'The architect Adolf Loos built this building; the experts say it is something special.'" The young boy was unimpressed: "'Papa, if I were to meet this man, I would not shake his hand.'"[1]

Hlawatsch's childhood memory of his own shock and disquiet and his unsparing verdict was not an uncommon response. For most Viennese, accustomed to the florid surfaces of the late Neo-Baroque or the new Jugendstil, the building—especially the cold blast of plainness from its upper façades—seemed alien and unwelcome. The controversy that raged for nearly a year and a half after the exterior walls were plastered was virulent and unremitting. During the course of a very public debate about the work's merits—or, in the eyes of many, the absence of them—Loos would suffer a mental and physical collapse, leaving him incapacitated for weeks. His friends and supporters rallied to his defense, attempting to salvage his reputation and his design. And his opponents, equally determined, sought not only to ruin him and remedy his aesthetic "errors" but to assail the very principles of his vision of the new architecture.

The dispute over the Looshaus, as the building was soon dubbed, was more than a quarrel about Loos, his ideas, or his startling design. It was a challenge, on Loos's part, to late historicism and the Jugendstil—to what he deemed a misguided revivalism on the one hand and a contrived and inauthentic modernism on the other. The Looshaus, in his eyes, was an effort to correct the mistakes of recent architecture and design, to show the Viennese and the world a true and fitting modern language. For his foes, the building reflected all that was wrong with the new architecture: in the stark upper façades they saw not an affirmation of modern life but a debased and frightening austerity.

The controversy over the Looshaus laid bare a widening divide within the modernist camp in Vienna: among Loos's critics were not only conservatives, but some of the city's leading reformers. In spite of having shared enemies, the

Viennese modernists were never a cohesive group; they were, in fact, no more united than the establishment they were fighting. Loos detested many of the leaders of the reform movement, and they, in turn, assailed or ignored him with equal disdain.

The controversy was a symptom, too, of political turmoil and social restlessness. Many of those outside the world of architecture and design viewed the building as an omen of uninvited change, a brash intrusion into stability and order. It was an unavoidable sign of the separation of the young from the old, of those who embraced the new age and those who resisted it.

Above all, the Looshaus debate raised questions of aesthetic and cultural meaning. What was the proper stylistic expression for modern times? What role should the architecture of the past play? How should architects respond to new materials and building techniques? How should buildings meet the demands of modern life? Loos's answers to those questions repeated in high relief the lines of his own philosophy of design and cultural progress. The Looshaus, as one younger Viennese architect observed, was a "built idea — an almost verbatim essay, in concrete, stone, stucco, and wood, of his architectural principles.[2] Perhaps more than any other architect of his day, Loos built what he said and what he believed, though deciphering his intentions sometimes requires great effort.

This book is an attempt to recount the Looshaus's remarkable story; to excavate Loos's ideas for the building; and to probe its meanings. It is an attempt to give the building back to its age; to dispel some of the myths that still surround it; to see its place in the early days of the new architecture; and to understand its part in forming the look of modernism. As built object and idea, the Looshaus offers a special portal into Loos's early work and the story of the Viennese *Moderne*. To reopen it is to reveal fresh vistas on him and his time.

1

THE COMPETITION

In May 1909, Leopold Goldman and Emanuel Aufricht, owners of the gentlemen's tailor and outfitter firm Goldman & Salatsch, announced a competition to design their new building on Michaelerplatz — St. Michael's Square — in Vienna's inner city.[1] The venerable firm of Goldman & Salatsch was among the preeminent outlets for men's clothing in Vienna (fig. 1). A decade before, it had acquired the coveted title of "supplier to the imperial and royal court." It was also the official tailor of the Archbishop of Vienna, the Bavarian court, the Austrian Automobile Club, and the imperial yacht fleet. The company exported its finished wares throughout Europe — even to China and South America — and its clientele included members not only of the Austrian royal family but also of the "highest circles of society and of the aristocracy in Germany, Russia, France, Switzerland, Italy, Spain, Bulgaria, and Romania."[2]

Goldman's father, Michael Goldmann, a Jewish tailor from Moravia, had founded the company in 1878 with Josef Salatsch, a Catholic immigrant from Bohemia. The two first operated their salon on the Schottenring section of the Ringstrasse. After Salatsch left the partnership, in 1896, Goldman moved the shop to the Graben, then most fashionable shopping area in central Vienna. By that time he had dropped the second "n" from his name, using, it seems, the anglicized version to underscore his ties with the fashion scene in England. In 1903, his son Leopold and son-in-law Emanuel Aufricht became partners in the firm; they took over the running of the company after Michael's death in 1909.[3]

The site for the new building was on the northeast side of the square, directly across from the Hofburg, the imperial palace, where two major streets, Kohlmarkt and Herrengasse, intersected. The Michaelerplatz already had a very long history. In the first century it had been the site of Cannabae, a settlement for the consorts and children of the Roman soldiers stationed at the adjacent castrum of Vindobona, one of the dense network of military installations and settlements the empire constructed along the Danube, then the northeastern frontier of the Roman world. Roman legionnaires were forbidden to marry, but many spent their free time with their families in the houses there. The district, just outside the fortress walls, was a ramshackle collection of dwellings, shops, taverns, and a number of bordellos. Two important roads crossed at the gate into the city: one from the south and one that extended along the *limes,* or defensive line, paralleling the course of the Danube and the western and southern walls.[4]

Much of the area appears to have burned in the early fifth century, but a small settlement remained. The streets and houses of early medieval Vienna followed the former Roman walls. Near where the gate had stood an open space was preserved — first known as Widmarkt, later Kohlenmarkt — that served as a marketplace. The Michaelerkirche, the church of St. Michael, was built on the east side of the square at the beginning of the thirteenth century; a few decades later, under the last of the Babenberg kings, construction of the Hofburg began along its southern edge. Over time the palace was expanded, and by the beginning of the eighteenth century, five- and six-story residential buildings had replaced the original medieval houses framing the remainder of the square. The resultant space, however, was narrow and irregularly shaped, ill suited to serve as a formal entry to the palace (figs. 2, 3).[5]

Throughout the course of the eighteenth century, various architects, including Joseph Emanuel Fischer von Erlach, son of the great Viennese Baroque architect Johann Bernhard Fischer von Erlach, put forward proposals to raze some of the old apartment buildings and stores on the north and south edges of the square and rebuild the front of the palace, but little, aside from the construction of the court theater, was accomplished until the late 1880s. Finally, in 1888, the "Stöckel" (literally, the "little housing block"), a row of three buildings that jutted into the center of the Michaelerplatz, was demolished, and in 1893, court architect Ferdinand Kirschner completed the rebuilding of the east façade of the palace based on the earlier plans of the younger Fischer von Erlach and the late eighteenth-century architect Ferdinand von Hohenberg (figs. 4, 5). A few years later, one of the last remaining old buildings on the north side of the square, the Griensteidl-Haus, was torn down and replaced with the Neo-Baroque Palais Herberstein (figs. 6 – 8).[6]

FIG. 1 Advertisement for Goldman & Salatsch. *Der Ruf,* February 1912.

The changes transformed the Michaelerplatz, recasting what had once been a middle- and lower-middle-class residential area into a formal approach to the Hofburg framed by expensive shops, offices, and apartments.

The remaking of the square was part of a wider rebuilding effort that had commenced in the 1850s. In 1857, Emperor Franz Joseph had decreed the razing of the city walls and the construction of the new Ringstrasse. The swift growth of Vienna in the second half of the century brought other changes to the inner city.

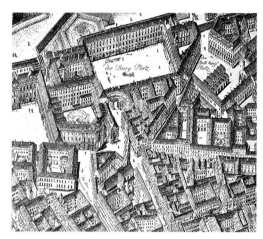

FIG. 2 Bird's-eye view of Michaelerplatz. Detail of an etching by Joseph Daniel von Huber, c. 1774. Moriz Dreger, *Baugeschichte der k.k. Hofburg in Wien bis zum XIX. Jahrhundert*e (Vienna, 1914).

FIG. 3 L. Thüming after J. M. Bayrer, view of the Michaelerplatz and Kohlmarkt, early nineteenth century. Author's collection.

FIG. 4 Michaelerplatz, late nineteenth century. Left, the "Stöckel"; in the center, the Dreilauferhaus. Wien Museum.

FIG. 5 Ferdinand Kirschner, after Joseph Emanuel Fischer von Erlach and Ferdinand von Hohenberg, completion of the Michaelertrakt entry to the Hofburg, 1889–93. Bildarchiv Foto Marburg.

FIG. 6 Griensteidl-Haus, Herrengasse 1–3, Vienna, c. 1895, shortly before it was razed to make way for the Palais Herberstein. Wien Museum.

Throughout what had once been the medieval town, scores of modest residential buildings and shops were leveled to make way for much grander structures, many of them offices for the empire's leading companies.[7] Simple apartment houses gave way to monumental edifices mimicking the old *Adelspaläste,* the aristocratic palaces of the Baroque.

The physical transformation of the inner city echoed its changing social structure. Where once all of Vienna's social classes had lived side by side, by 1909 only the aristocracy and the upper middle class remained; the petite bourgeoisie and artisans had been forced out to the *Vorstädte*—the adjacent suburbs—and the proletariat to its outer edges. The modernization of the city also brought an alteration of the relationship between residence and workplace: in the inner city, living and labor, domicile and shop or office, had become divided. The new buildings still integrated commercial space and housing, but those who lived in them more and more often worked elsewhere.[8]

In June 1909, the parcel of land that Goldman and Aufricht had acquired was still occupied by two buildings, the Dreilauferhaus (House of the Three Runners), built in 1797, and a smaller adjacent residential and commercial building at Herrengasse 4 (figs. 9, 10). The *Wiener Bauindustrie-Zeitung,* the leading organ of the construction industry in the city, announced in early May that these buildings and several others nearby were slated for demolition.[9]

By then, the widening threat to the historic fabric of the city had begun to stir protest. The art historian Hans Tietze wrote that demolition of the Griensteidl-Haus, a building of "salutary simplicity and middle-class modesty" and its replacement by a "monstrous representational edifice" had "completely destroyed the character of the old square."[10] Tietze reserved his sharpest condemnation for the destruction of the adjacent Dreilauferhaus "to make way for a more lucrative new structure"; it was, he wrote, an "aesthetic wound."[11]

Goldman and Aufricht viewed their project not as a faithless act of civic assault but as a donation to Vienna's urban health. They recognized the potential profit in constructing a new building on the Michaelerplatz, but they also believed that they were contributing to the city's renewal. The municipal authorities likewise saw the project as an opportunity to enlarge and revitalize the square. The new site occupied a much smaller footprint than the Dreilauferhaus; rebuilding the northern edge of the Michaelerplatz would yield new public space and provide more direct connections to and from the surrounding streets.

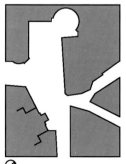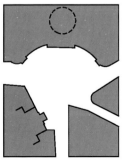

FIG. 7 Carl König, Palais Herberstein, Michaelerplatz 2, 1896 – 97. Visible on the left is the north corner of the recently completed entry wing of the Hofburg. Author's collection.

FIG. 8 Plan of Michaelerplatz, c. 1888 – 90 (left) and 1898 – 1909 (right), showing the changes to the square after the demolition of the "Stöckel" and the completion of the new entry to the Hofburg. Drawing by Vincent Snyder.

The sensitivity of the site — especially its location directly across from the Hofburg — and the controversy surrounding the destruction of the old Dreilauferhaus were undoubtedly what prompted Goldman and Aufricht to undertake a competition for the new building's design. The strategy was a sound one and might have aided in deflecting criticism had the two men opted to undertake a public competition rather than a private one. But they decided, apparently in an effort to retain full control of the process, to invite the architects themselves and to judge the entries without an outside jury. They neither made announcements in the Viennese newspapers nor enlisted the aid of the Austrian Federation of Architects.[12]

Because Goldman and Aufricht allowed no outsiders to take part, the details of the competition remain obscure. All we know about it comes from Loos himself, who later recounted what had purportedly happened:

When the firm of Goldman and Salatsch undertook to build a new store, they announced a limited competition for eight architects. I was supposed to be the ninth. But I alone declined. I know very well that competitions are the cancer of present-day architecture. I know that the best architect is never awarded first prize; the winning entry is always the one that most closely approximates the fad of the moment. Competitions make good sense for women's hairstyles and hats. Five years later one would undoubtedly choose a different winner from among the entries. The same would happen in our architectural competitions. But then it is too late. The architect who is five years ahead of his time has no chance in competitions.[13]

FIG. 9 Michaelerplatz, with the Dreilauferhaus (left), c. 1900. Author's collection.

Of the eight architects Loos mentions, the names of only three are known, and that is because he happened to preserve their entry drawings among his papers. They were a remarkably undistinguished group. The oldest and best known of the three was Karl (or sometimes Carl) Stephann. He had a long and productive career behind him and was the designer of more than thirty buildings, most of them commercial and residential structures.[14] None of these works was particularly successful, however, and Stephann certainly did not belong to the first rank of the city's architects. His submission, which brought together elements of the Neo-Baroque, the German romantic "Alt-Deutsch" look, and Biedermeier neoclassicism, was a more or less customary expression of Viennese historicism (fig. 11). Though it was better elaborated than most of Stephann's buildings (presumably in response to its site on the Michaelerplatz), it was unresolved and awkward. It would have fallen far short of establishing a monumental presence.[15]

FIG. 10 Dreilauferhaus shortly before being razed, c. 1909. Wien Museum.

FIG. 11 Karl Stephann, competition project for the Goldman & Salatsch Building, June 1909, perspective. Black ink and photograph on paper, 22 7/8 × 26 1/2 in. (58.1 × 68.4 cm). Graphische Sammlung Albertina, Vienna, Adolf Loos Archiv (hereafter ALA) 225.

The second of the known entrants, Alois Augenfeld, had an even less impressive record. He had begun to practice in the mid-1890s after completing his studies at the Vienna Technical University, and he had fared well in several competitions. But he had built almost nothing prior to 1909. His entry, too, was a more or less conventional exercise, a competent, if uninspired, version of late historicism. Still, Augenfeld's handling of the massing and site were more assured than Stephann's; despite his recourse to the language of the Neo-Baroque (borrowed, it seems, from the adjacent Palais Herberstein), the project had a more modern cast (fig. 12).

Much less can be said about the submission of the third of the known entrants, Ernst Epstein. Like Augenfeld, Epstein, who was only twenty-seven at the time, was still young and unknown. He had managed to erect a handful of apartment buildings for a wealthy developer on the city's western edge, but he was not a highly regarded designer.[16] Most of his executed works reflected a modernized version of late historicism, though a few, like his residential and retail building at Hütteldorfer Straße 206, drew from the Jugendstil.

Unlike Stephann and Augenfeld, Epstein, it seems, did not prepare a full set of drawings. Only a single ground plan of his project exists — for one of the upper residential floors — and it provides few clues about the appearance of the exterior or his intentions for the store (fig. 13).[17]

One other façade design from the competition has survived, from an unnamed entrant (fig. 14). The drawing, a frenzied pastiche of historical elements, was later published in one of the Viennese newspapers under the heading "Baustiljammer" — "stylistic distress." It almost certainly came from among those Goldman and Aufricht had passed on to Loos, who in turn supplied it (and evidently also the title) to the press, apparently hoping to deride such architecture and draw a contrast between his design and the other proposals.[18]

Nothing is known about the other entrants. Loos later mentioned in passing that Friedrich Ohmann, a prominent architect who occupied one of the two chairs for architecture at the Academy of Fine Arts, had been invited to submit a design but declined to take part (a statement that contradicted his later claim that he alone had declined the invitation to submit an entry).[19] Whether any other architects invited by Goldman and Aufricht turned down the opportunity is unclear.

The unimpressive caliber of the three architects who have been identified raises a number of questions. What were Goldman and Aufricht's intentions?

FIG. 12 Alois Augenfeld, competition project for the Goldman & Salatsch Building, August 1909, perspective. Pencil and colored pencil on paper, 19 ³/₄ × 25 ³/₄ in. (50.2 × 65.3 cm). Graphische Sammlung Albertina, Vienna, ALA 228.

Why, for such an important commission, did they not approach the city's leading designers? Why did they not undertake a more visible competition?

In their book on Epstein, Karlheinz Gruber, Sabine Höller-Alber, and Markus Kristan have suggested that the competition may have been held only for the sake of appearances, to placate the city's architects and head off potential criticism from the authorities and the public: Goldman and Aufricht's intention all along was to give the commission to Loos.[20] This was why they invited such mediocre or young architects as Stephann and Augenfeld. Gruber, Höller-Alber, and Kristan also claim that Epstein, who had previously worked for the Goldman family, was aware from the outset that the competition was a sham, and that the evidence for this is the fact that Epstein's only surviving drawing, which appears to have been executed in some haste, was in the form of a blueprint and not on a presentation board, something that would have been highly unusual for Viennese competitions of the day.[21]

This might explain why Goldman and Aufricht had decided to hold a private competition. A public competition would have been much more difficult to control. But if the men thought that a competition was a means to deflect criticism, why would they not have released the names of all of the competitors and publicly announced the winner? It is telling that neither the clients nor Loos ever revealed the identities of the other entrants. What did they wish to conceal?

If Loos is to be believed and Friedrich Ohmann was indeed asked to submit an entry (a statement he made publicly and thus not likely to be false), this also calls into question the assertion that, aside from Loos, only mediocre or inexperienced architects were included. Ohmann was among the leading modernists in Vienna; he undoubtedly would have prepared an acceptable design — one in all likelihood less controversial than Loos's. Ohmann's previous works, including additions to the Hofburg and a scheme for the city park, relied on a lively admixture of monumental Baroque and Secessionist elements, and they had generally met with praise from the critics and authorities. If the competition were set up to fail, why did they approach Ohmann?

On the other hand, if Goldman and Aufricht were serious about finding an appropriate design for their building, why did they not at least consult with some of Vienna's eminent architects? Otto Wagner, the most visible of the city's modernists, may not have been an easy choice because he remained a controversial figure. But there were many others they might have approached. Given the many renowned architects in Vienna, why invite a figure like Augenfeld, who had so little experience?

It is possible, in the cases of Augenfeld and Epstein, that Goldman and Aufricht may have wanted to support young Jewish architects. And the choice of Stephann may have been an attempt to engage a more experienced figure. But all this remains conjecture.

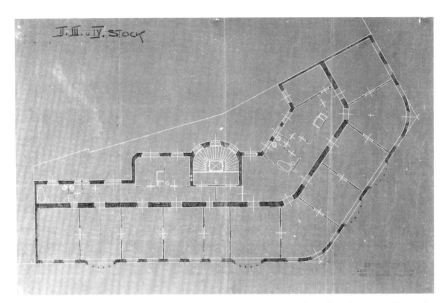

Baustiljammer.

FIG. 13 Ernst Epstein, competition project for the Goldman & Salatsch Building, n.d. [May 1909?], ground plan for the second, third, and fourth floors. Print. Graphische Sammlung Albertina, Vienna, ALA 350.

FIG. 14 Architect unknown, competition project for the Goldman & Salatsch Building, 1909, front façade. *Der Morgen,* December 11, 1911.

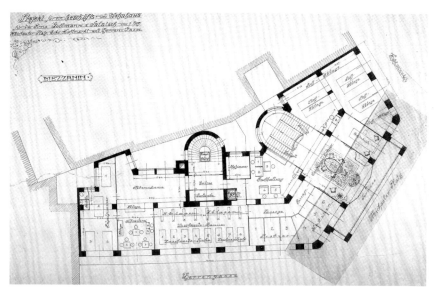

FIG. 15 Karl Stephann, competition project for the Goldman & Salatsch Building, May 1909, plan of the mezzanine. Black ink on paper, 19 ⅜ × 26 ¹/₁₆ in. (49.2 × 66.2 cm). Graphische Sammlung Albertina, Vienna, ALA 348.

That there is no information about the other designs makes it difficult even to guess about the competition or the motives of the clients. It may have been that one or more of the other four submitted designs — perhaps all of them — were quite accomplished and that the clients concealed them in order not to challenge Loos's design; revealing only the poorer designs would have made their decision to engage him easier to defend.

It is possible, too, that the issue for the clients never had to do with the exterior appearance of the building at all. Perhaps none of the submitted designs offered an optimal solution for the arrangement of the new store's interiors, which would have been their primary concern. Stephann's drawing of the mezzanine floor, which was intended to house the shop's fitting, work, and storage spaces, is poorly thought out and impractical; it seems wholly inappropriate for one of Vienna's elite gentlemen's tailors (fig. 15). Perhaps Goldman and Aufricht turned to Loos because he was able to convince them that he could provide more workable and elegant spaces.

In the end, there is too little evidence to support either conclusion — that the competition produced no satisfactory design and the clients decided to turn to Loos, or that the competition was a sham intended to make Loos appear to be the appropriate and obvious choice to design the building.

All that is certain is that sometime during the summer of 1909 Goldman and Aufricht charged Loos with designing their new building.

2

AN ISOLATED FIGURE
IN THE FOREGROUND

It was not an obvious decision that the commission for the new building should have gone to Loos. He was not yet a famous architect. Although he was known to the city's cultural cognoscenti, his name was still unfamiliar to most Viennese (fig. 16).[1] He had attracted notice for his reviews in the city's newspapers in the late 1890s, but most of his realized designs were for residential interiors and therefore out of public view. His best-known work, the Café Museum on Karlsplatz, had been completed a full decade before.

Loos was thirty-eight years old in the summer of 1909. He had yet to build a single building. "He is an architect," his friend the critic Richard Schaukal wrote at the time, "who has no buildings to build, an eloquent teacher without students, an enthusiastic fighter whose foes go far out of their way on their daily rounds to avoid him . . . a clear voice whose echo has been muted."[2] Within the architectural profession, he remained a resolute outsider — in Schaukal's lyrical phrase, an "isolated figure in the foreground" of Vienna's cultural landscape.

All that would change in the space of little more than a year.

Adolf Loos was not a native Viennese. He was born in 1870 in the provinces, in the Moravian city of Brno. His father, also named Adolf Loos, was a master stonemason. The elder Loos had studied painting at the Academy of Fine Arts in Vienna before entering the newly founded class in sculpture.[3] Afterward, in the early 1860s, he moved to Brno and purchased a house and adjoining workshop. He married Maria Hertl, the daughter of a local government official, and within a short time he established himself as the town's foremost fabricator of grave markers and decorative stone objects.

The younger Loos's early years were spent in the workshop observing and, as much as possible, participating in the activities of his father and the journeymen and apprentices who worked for him. Often he played with the fragments he found on the floor, "building little houses about the stone and wood." One day, when it was raining too hard for him to cross back into the house, his father allowed him stay in the workshop. He made a plaster cast of his son's tiny hand. Loos treasured it. It was among the few possessions he took with him when he left home.[4]

The great tragedy of Loos's early life was the death of his father in 1879, at the age of forty-eight. Loos, not yet nine, was devastated. His mother, with whom he had a strained relationship at best, sent him off to one boarding school after the next — to Brno and Jihlava, in Moravia, and Melk, in Lower Austria. Loos had difficulties fitting in, in part because, around age twelve, he began to exhibit hearing problems that would leave him nearly completely deaf by the end of his life. He displayed neither aptitude for nor interest in academic study.

FIG. 16 Adolf Loos, c. 1903. Wien Museum.

Still undecided about his future, he enrolled at the Staatsgewerbeschule (State Trades School) in Reichenberg, in Bohemia (now Liberec, Czech Republic), in 1885. He first studied machine building but, the following year, transferred to the architecture department. The next year he transferred again, to the Staatsgewerbeschule in Brno. Among his classmates there were several other young Moravians soon to launch important careers in Vienna: Josef Hoffmann, Leopold Bauer, and Hubert Gessner. He managed to complete the last of his coursework in the early summer of 1889, but it would take him nearly another year to achieve satisfactory scores on all of his examinations.[5]

That fall he entered the Technical University in Dresden. He failed to pass his examinations at the end of the second term and spent the next year in the Austrian army fulfilling his required military service.

Liberated from his mother's influence, he embraced his freedom. His new-found appetite to experience the world left him with a case of syphilis. Appalled, his mother allowed him to return home to seek treatment; the cure rendered him no longer infectious but left him sterile.[6] Afterward, he applied, without success, to the Academy of Fine Arts in Vienna. With few options open to him, he returned to the university in Dresden but left again before the end of the summer semester to take part in maneuvers with his army reserve unit.[7]

With little to show for his time at university, Loos resolved — suddenly — to travel to the United States to visit the World's Columbian Exhibition in Chicago. His decision to go to America was doubtless a means to find an exit from his hopeless education and his mother's control; it marked the end of his formal studies and his relationship with her. She gave him the money for his passage on the condition that he would waive the right to his inheritance and never return to Brno. Armed with twelve hours of instruction in English from the Berlitz school in Dresden and fifty dollars, he set off.[8]

Loos spent the next three years in America. They would become the most important formative experience of his life. His training in Brno and Dresden had opened him to the discipline of architecture, but his journey to the New World made him.

He spent his first days in New York and then visited an uncle in Philadelphia before continuing on to St. Louis and Chicago. What impressed him were not the latest building trends but the social and cultural features of American life. Americans, he later told Richard Neutra, "had reverted to a sound attitude which had been lost in the old country."[9] He detected a new spirit in America, he would recount to his friend Robert Scheu, an energy and openness to new ideas, new possibilities: "It is indeed a very young country that applies the new iron technology resolutely and without worry, a land in which the trees of a primeval forest are felled and laid crossways on the railroad tracks. Human labor extends the steel rails over precipices and waterfalls, and draws telegraph lines across the prairies. And it is beautiful. A brilliant beauty, a unique collision of an advanced technical economy with the green, wild earth, in a single word — style."[10]

Loos's moment of epiphany, he revealed to Scheu, had come after he had returned to New York, where he spent nearly a year eking out a living among the city's impoverished immigrants. One day he saw a suitcase in a store window, a simple, unadorned leather suitcase with copper banding. The next morning it struck him, with sudden and inescapable force: this was the modern style.[11]

The idea that the new aesthetic was bound up with the most direct expression of an article or a building was to become a leitmotif in Loos's thinking. He "has made it his life's work," Scheu wrote, "to show that a chair is a chair, a fork a fork, a house a house. A thing should simply be what it is."[12]

The plain suitcase in New York presented Loos with another crucial insight: the modern style already existed. It was a frank expression of modern society, a logical and necessary outcome of the experience of contemporary life. Modernism, he came to believe, did not need to be invented; it could be found wherever craftspeople or manufacturers had made an honest attempt to solve everyday problems, without resorting to artifice. He began to question the prevailing belief in adapting past models for the present: "We were always told to look back, to adopt some other era as our model. This mountain has been swept from my sight. Indeed, the age in which we are now living is beautiful, so beautiful that I would not want to live in any other."[13]

Loos returned to Austria in the late spring of 1896 to take part once more in maneuvers with his army unit. Along the way he stopped in London. His time there only confirmed for him his belief in the superiority of Anglo-Saxon culture. The British and American capacity for producing honest and unassuming modern articles, he thought, was a sign of health for a society. It became the standard against which he weighed and criticized the cultural conditions of his homeland.[14]

Loos's early days in Vienna were far from easy. As a son of the provinces, with no connections and few prospects, he was at a decided disadvantage. In a city brimming with young and ambitious architects, he was fortunate to find temporary employment in the office of Carl Mayreder.

Mayreder taught at the Technical University, where he provided instruction in perspective, architectural drawing, and urban planning. He was a well-regarded and successful practitioner, and, importantly for Loos, open to new ideas. He possessed, too, an abiding love for the architecture of classical antiquity. (In the 1920s, he would assume the university's chair for "Classical building.")

Almost nothing is known about Loos's time in Mayreder's office. Mayreder was involved then with several building projects and competitions, including a new parish house for Fischer von Erlach's Karlskirche, two apartment houses, and a regulation plan for the city. Whether Loos worked on any of these projects other than the parish house (for which he later claimed he had provided some of the detailing) is uncertain. After leaving Mayreder's office, he penned a scathing review of the building, calling it a "bad example of a thoroughly bad Baroque copy."[15] But Loos doubtless learned much from the experience about the practice of architecture and urban planning, and about developments in construction and materials.

FIG. 17 Peter Altenberg in the Café Central, Vienna, 1907. Wien Museum.

The period spanning Loos's return from America and his departure from Mayreder's office saw the first glimmers of the modernist revolt in Vienna. In April 1897, a few months before Loos left again for summer maneuvers with his army unit, Gustav Klimt and a band of younger artists, architects, and designers — chief among them Josef Hoffmann, Koloman Moser, and Joseph Maria Olbrich — resigned from the conservative Künstlergenossenschaft, Austria's principal artists' association, and founded the Vienna Secession. (Otto Wagner, who was not a founding member, joined later.)

At first Loos found common cause with the Secessionists: he published his essays "Die potemkin'sche Stadt" (The Potemkin City) and "Unseren jungen Architekten" (Our Young Architects) in the July issue of their journal, *Ver Sacrum*. Soon, though, he broke with them. One reason was his anger over Hoffmann's re-fusal of his offer to design one of the rooms for the Secessionists' newly erected exhibition hall on Karlsplatz. But the bigger cause was his mounting disquiet over their aims and methods. He remained convinced that the route to a modern aesthetic lay through the crafts, through the effort to fill a practical need, without artistic pretention.

His position left him isolated, allied neither with the conservatives nor with the young *revoltés*. "He was too modern for the Künstlerhaus and too English for the Secession," one reviewer commented. "He has even more enemies in the latter than in the former. He utters contempt for every sort of plush, precious, or academic ornament." It is an "attitude diametrically opposed to artists like Hoffmann and Olbrich, with their delight in color and form."[16]

More meaningful for Loos were two contacts he made not long after his return from America. On his nightly haunts of Vienna's cafés and bars, he met the writer Peter Altenberg (fig. 17). Altenberg was a legendary — even heroic — fig-ure to the younger artists and writers in the city. Born Richard Engländer, the son of a middle-class Jewish family, he had studied law and medicine before dropping out to devote himself to writing. He was the very embodiment of the disreputable coffeehouse poet — cultured, intelligent, and louche in nearly equal measure, surrounded by a throng of admirers. Although his moist doe eyes and drooping mustache lent him the look of a contented walrus, he was a ferocious critic and a tireless champion of the new.

Altenberg belonged at the time to a group of writers called Jung Wien — Young Vienna — that met at the Café Griensteidl on Michaelerplatz and the nearby Café Central. It counted among its members the critic Hermann Bahr, Felix Salten (author of both *Bambi* and, reputedly, the notorious pornographic novel *Josefine Mutzenbacher,* the fictional autobiography of a teenage Vienna prostitute), Arthur Schnitzler, Hugo von Hoffmannsthal, and Stefan Zweig.

After the demolition of the Griensteidl-Haus, Altenberg held court in the Münchener-Löwenbräu Restaurant. Loos became a regular at his table. He was fascinated with Altenberg's bohemian lifestyle — his ability to cultivate patrons to supplement his meager income and pay for his meals and drinks.[17] Loos was also taken with his ideas about confronting the realities of modern life. In his writings, Altenberg made a plea for capturing the "essence in art"; his texts — mostly short, almost word-for-word sketches of Viennese life and morals — merged prose and poetry, striving to move away from conventional literary tropes in an effort to find a more pure and direct expression. He believed in the importance of uniting life and culture: literature, he insisted, should disclose the truth about how people lived and what they actually experienced. Altenberg proved to be a master of his own version of the artistic life: he became as renowned for his wayward behavior as for his impressionistic prose poems.

It was through Altenberg that Loos met the other central figure of his early years, the writer Karl Kraus (fig. 18). Four years younger than Loos, Kraus had first studied law before changing to philosophy and German literature. He left the university without his diploma and began working as an actor and director. He joined the Jung Wien group in 1896 but split with it the following year, afterward writing an acid satire, *Die demolirte Literatur* (Demolished Literature), pillorying its leading members and sparing only his friend Altenberg. (The piece brought Kraus both fame and a physical attack from Salten.) Two years later he founded the satirical — and wildly popular — culture magazine *Die Fackel* (The Torch), which he continued to publish — and, after 1911, write entirely by himself — until the 1930s.

Even as a young man Kraus was intense and temperamental, though among friends he could be kindly and uncomplicated.[18] In photographs as in life, both aspects — a softness and an irascibility — were detectable. It was a face "so mobile," Elias Canetti wrote, "that it couldn't be pinpointed, penetrating and exotic, like the face of an animal, but with a new, different face, an unfamiliar one."[19] His voice was shrill and penetrating — "unnaturally vibrating," Canetti put it, "like a decelerated crowing."[20] It proved a perfect instrument not only for his many public readings but also for communicating with Loos, who was already having difficulty hearing those given to speaking softly.

In Kraus, even more than Altenberg, Loos found a kindred soul and intelligence. Kraus's insistence on viewing aesthetic problems through the lens of cultural and social meaning had a decisive influence on his thinking. The two shared a belief that such questions had moral import. For Kraus, it was language itself that embodied moral truth. He repeatedly disparaged the press for corrupting the German language, which, he charged, used artful and opaque prose to manipulate the public and serve the interests of the court and clergy. Through close analysis of selected newspaper stories, he sought to expose deeper factual and moral truths. Loos applied the same standards to architecture and design. The virtues of the new aesthetic — simplicity, modesty, and unobtrusive-

FIG. 18 Karl Kraus, 1908, photo by D'Ora Benda. Bildarchiv der österreichischen Nationalbibliothek, Vienna.

ness — were, he believed, not mere matters of appearance or functionality: they were bound up with ethical considerations and social justice.

For the young Loos, Kraus and Altenberg became his twin Virgils, guiding him through the heights and depths of the city's literary culture and nightlife. Over the years they developed a fervent friendship. Kraus christened it the *besserer Dreibund* — the superior triple alliance — a reference to Austria's ill-chosen pact with Russia and Germany.[21] For the next decade they saw one another nearly every night (Kraus usually slept during the day, dined at a coffeehouse, and wrote through the night), sitting together for hours on end, working or exchanging views on art and politics.

It says much about Loos's preoccupations that his closest friends were writers, not architects. After leaving Mayreder's office he worked alone, rarely socializing with other architects. The measured distance he kept from the architectural world was a consequence of his self-imposed status as an outsider, but it was a result, too, of his heightened critical stance.

At first, Loos sought to convey his message of cultural progress through writing. A year after his return from the United States he began contributing articles to the weekly newspapers *Die Wage* and *Die Zeit*. The most important texts for his developing ideas, however, he wrote for the empire's leading liberal daily newspaper, the *Neue Freie Presse*. Between mid-May and November 1898 he published twenty-one articles in the paper, mostly reviews of the various displays at the exhibition marking Emperor Franz Joseph's fiftieth year on the throne.

Loos's verdict on the Austrian contributions to the exhibition was direct and unsparing. He charged that the majority of the country's applied artists were still consumed with the outmoded ideas of late historicism and lagged badly behind their contemporaries in America and England. Those few who embraced modernism—the Secessionists—understood that the old historic revivalism was outmoded and misguided, but their answer to the problem was the imposition of an invented aesthetic. Loos attacked this position on two fronts. He rejected the idea that a new modernist aesthetic would come about only when artists, architects, and designers made a full break with the past. And he assailed Hoffmann and the other Secessionists' search for a novel idiom: "For me," he wrote, "tradition is everything, the free unfolding of the imagination is secondary."[22]

Instead of a headlong search for a new style, Loos called for a return to older modes of production—and to craft traditions and common sense. He wanted not to develop a new form of applied arts, but to remove art from the crafts: "Here [in Austria] people still believe that before a person can be trusted to design a chair, he must know the five classical orders inside and out. I think, above all, that he should know something about sitting."[23]

The articles brought Loos his first public notice and a few jobs, among them a commission to remodel the interiors of the Café Museum (fig. 19). His design, which relied on straightforward bentwood furnishings and minimal treatment of the walls, floors, and ceilings, prompted the critic Ludwig Hevesi to refer to it mockingly as Café Nihilismus (Café Nihilism). Loos's response—one that he would repeat during the controversy over the Michaelerplatz building—was that he was merely following Viennese tradition. He had not attempted to fashion something new, he said, but to reimagine a typical Viennese café circa 1830, which relied on Biedermeier notions of plainness and reserve.

After the Imperial Jubilee, Loos continued to write sporadically. In 1900 he produced two articles for the daily *Neues Wiener Tagblatt,* and, as late as 1902, in an autobiographical essay, he described himself as a "writer on art."[24] By this time, though, he was already at work on the interiors of a number of apartments, most of them for friends and acquaintances. Among his commissions were several shops, including one for the exclusive tailor Ernst Ebenstein, on Kohlmarkt, and another for Goldman & Salatsch.

Loos's connection to Goldman & Salatsch extended back to 1896, when, as he would later recall, he began having his clothes made there.[25] In 1898 he designed the façade and interiors of the firm's shop on the Graben.

Loos claimed that the commission had come to him because he had persuaded the owners to allow him to undertake the work to settle his bill, which, by his own account, was "always much larger" than he could pay.[26] Yet it is more likely that he won the commission for a very different reason: he demonstrated to the clients an understanding of the English style. Goldman & Salatsch were tailors "in the English mode," offering gentlemen's fashions in keeping with the best salons on London's Savile Row. English tailoring was widely admired at the time for its quality, and outfitter shops selling "English clothing" operated in all of the continent's major cities.[27] Vienna had a number of such establishments, including Ebenstein and Kniže (in later years, another of Loos's clients). He may well have received the Goldman & Salatsch commission because Michael Goldman had seen his interiors for Ebenstein, one of his principal competitors. Perhaps, though, there was another reason: Loos had written about men's fashion in his reviews of the Imperial Jubilee and spoken publicly on the topic; in each instance, he had singled out Goldman & Salatsch for praise.[28]

The spaces for the new interior were tiny. The entire shop was only about eight hundred square feet (seventy-five square meters)—undoubtedly why

FIG. 19 Adolf Loos, interior of Café Museum, Vienna, c. 1899. Graphische Sammlung Albertina, Vienna, ALA 2495.

Goldman and Aufricht wanted to move to larger quarters in 1909.[29] Downstairs, framed by show windows, was a single room housing a sales area for *Wäsche* — underwear, socks, and other accessories (fig. 20). Upstairs were several additional rooms: a combined reception area and office, a fitting room, a dressing room, a toilet, and a small workspace (figs. 21, 22).

Despite being highly compressed, the spaces were replete with ideas. Loos's design, the critic Ludwig Abels wrote at the time, "demonstrates an unmistakable striving for English elegance."[30] But Abels was also quick to recognize

FIG. 20 Adolf Loos, Goldman & Salatsch Men's Clothing Salon, Graben 20, Vienna, 1898. Sales room for underwear and accessories. *Das Interieur* 2 (1901).

FIG. 21 Goldman & Salatsch salon, changing room. *Das Interieur* 2 (1901).

FIG. 22 Goldman & Salatsch salon, sitting area in the reception room. *Das Interieur* 2 (1901).

Loos's attempt to reproduce this look without direct borrowings: the "main elements" of the rooms, "smooth, reflective surfaces, concise forms, bare metal," all referenced English craftsmanship, yet they were, in fact, original and distinctive.[31]

The most dramatic of the spaces, the downstairs sales area, relied on the rhythmic patterning of modular display cases fabricated from Guyanese snakewood (a dark brown and red wood, with streaks of black, resembling the pattern of snake skins), and the glass, lamps, and mirrors on the upper walls, edged with polished brass mullions. The contrast between the richly colored cabinetry and the light reflective elements conveyed a sense of refinement and luminosity, a look that would soon become Loos's trademark.

The upstairs rooms, though more subdued, continued the theme of an elegance founded on plainness, economy, and rationality. One of the recurrent themes was Loos's use of geometries—in the dressing room, expressed in its doors and paneling, and in the office, through the modular construction of the furniture.

The most original features of the design were Loos's renunciation of Jugendstil motifs and his growing absorption with the possibilities of radical simplification. Instead of embellishment as a strategy for forging a modern aesthetic, he pursued a willful and considered reduction. In one of his essays for the *Neue Freie Presse* that summer, he paraphrased Leon Battista Alberti's definition of beauty: "An object is beautiful if it is so perfect that one cannot add or remove anything without in some way diminishing it."[32] In the shop's interiors he applied this idea with great rigor, fashioning rooms and individual pieces that were reticent but also manifestly elegant.

These first interiors that Loos designed for Goldman & Salatsch were of signal importance for his mature work. With them he began to work out the means to apply the ideas he was developing in his writings: how to translate his belief in the pointlessness of inventing a new style into a practicable design strategy. The shop's rooms show how far Loos had already moved from the mainstream of Viennese modern design—a position that would only become more pronounced over the next decade. He is engaged in a struggle, Schaukal wrote, "against the arrogance of the 'decorative element.' He prizes the historical, esteems the organic ornament of bygone days. In our time, the age of machines, he sees that ornament has died of exhaustion. He does not mourn. On the contrary: he rejoices."[33]

3

EXPLOSIONS OF LIGHT

Loos continued to work sporadically for Goldman & Salatsch after he completed the shop on the Graben. In 1901, and again in 1903, he made additions and alterations to his original installation, and in 1904, he began work on an apartment for Aufricht and his wife that adjoined the store on the second floor.[1]

Goldman and Aufricht, in turn, supported Loos's efforts to propagate his ideas, taking out front-page advertisements in both issues of his short-lived magazine *Das Andere* (fig. 23). Loos published the first issue of *Das Andere* as a supplement to Altenberg's cultural review, *Kunst*. The little journal—to which Loos appended the peculiar but nonetheless accurate subtitle, *Ein Blatt zur Einführung abendländischer Kultur in Österreich* (A Periodical for the Introduction of Western Culture to Austria)—expanded on the themes he had developed at the turn of the century, calling for a revision of Austrian architecture and

FIG. 23 Advertisement for Goldman & Salatsch. Cover of Loos's magazine *Das Andere* 1, no. 1 (1903). Author's collection.

design along "Anglo-Saxon" lines. His aim, he explained, was "to make my professional life easier. I design interiors. I can only engage in this activity for those who embrace Western culture. I was so happy to live in America for three years and to discover Western forms of culture. And, convinced as I am of their superiority, I would consider it a sign of weak character to descend, subjectively speaking, to the Austrian level."[2]

The appearance of the second and final issue of *Das Andere,* in October 1903, marked the start of a break in Loos's publishing efforts that would last nearly four years. One reason he stopped writing was that he was now busier than ever with design work. Between 1903 and 1906 he undertook an extensive enlargement and alteration of the Villa Karma, a large country house outside Montreux, Switzerland, and during this time he labored on the interiors for more than two dozen apartments and several shops.

The shape of Loos's personal life, too, saw changes. In 1902 he married Lina Obertimpfler, daughter of the owner of the Café Casa Piccola, another haunt of Altenberg and his circle (fig. 24).

FIG. 24 Lina Loos, c. 1904. Photo by Atelier Carl Pietzner. Bildarchiv der österreichischen Nationalbibliothek, Vienna.

Lina later told the story that Loos had tested her by showing her two cigarette cases, one, his own, a simple, smooth box made of birch wood, and the second, a highly ornamented silver case by a "noted design professor," and asked her which she preferred. She selected Loos's. He believed that this was a sign of her deep understanding of his ideas, and he promptly asked her to marry him.[3]

The marriage proved to be a stormy one: Loos discovered that Lina was having an affair with Heinz Lang, the nineteen-year-old son of one of the city's leading women's rights advocates. Under pressure from Loos, she agreed to end the affair; Lang, inconsolable, committed suicide.[4] In the aftermath, the couple separated, and in 1905 they officially divorced.

Loos's problems, however, did not stop there. In the midst of his marital crisis, he learned that Dr. Theodor Beer, his client for the Villa Karma and his principal source of income, had been charged with child molestation. Loos, convinced of Beer's innocence, agreed to serve as a character witness at the trial. Beer was found guilty and sentenced to a short prison term. Beer's wife, Laura, committed suicide.

Loos's relationship with Altenberg was also badly strained. Altenberg had been smitten with Lina before the couple's marriage, and he remained jealous even after their separation. He blamed Loos for the demise of *Kunst,* which had folded a short time after Loos suspended publication of *Das Andere.* (He believed that Loos had tried to take control of his journal and, after the attempt failed, persuaded the financial backers to withdraw.)[5] The two men reconciled for a time but soon came into conflict again over a young English dancer.

Loos and Altenberg met her in 1905 at a cabaret, the Casino de Paris. She was performing there with a group called the Four Magnets, one of the first Cakewalk acts to reach Vienna. Only nineteen, Bessie Bruce was the daughter of a single working-class mother in East London (fig. 25). Her pale skin, rosy lips, and soft eyes lent her face a sweetness and fresh beauty. "She had the delicate complexion," Oskar Kokoschka wrote, "of those Lancashire girls who work all day at their looms and never see the sun."[6] Altenberg was infatuated with her from the first moment, and he courted her forcefully and unceasingly. Despite — probably because of — his attentions, she began having a torrid relationship with Loos. Altenberg was irate. Loos wrote to Lina: "He has threatened to shoot me, and is running around with a revolver. I have not seen him, but everyone is afraid. They say he is completely insane."[7]

Loos and Bessie persevered, forming an attachment that would last until the end of World War I. In Bessie, Loos found very nearly Lina's opposite. Lina had a keen mind — she later made a career as a writer — was independent, and was given to sudden mood changes; Bessie, by contrast, was compliant, had a sunny disposition, and bore no intellectual pretensions. She and Loos were unable to marry because the church in Catholic Austria would not recognize his and Lina's civil divorce, but they lived together, and all their friends accepted them as husband and wife.

The divorce, Beer's trial and his wife's suicide, and his break with Altenberg left Loos shattered and depressed, but he soldiered on. In 1904, while going through the breakup with Lina, he began work on a design for a bank, the Allgemeine Verkehrsbank, on the Mariahilfer Straße, one of the city's main shopping streets. The client, Leopold Langer, had asked him to redesign the ground and mezzanine floors in a building from the 1860s. Loos instead proposed to modernize the entire structure by removing its historicist detailing and replacing it with a smooth plastered surface (fig. 26).[8]

FIG. 25 Bessie Bruce, 1905, with an inscription by Peter Altenberg. Wien Museum.

FIG. 26 Adolf Loos, project for a commercial and residential building for the k.k. Priv. Allgemeine Verkehrsbank, Mariahilfer Straße, Vienna, 1904. Photomontage. Graphische Sammlung Albertina, Vienna. ALA 2003.

FIG. 27 Adolf Loos, façade for the Sigmund Steiner Decorative Feather Store, Kärntner Straße 33, 1906–7. Bildarchiv Foto Marburg.

The startling design reconfirmed, for the first time at large scale, Loos's commitment to a radical simplicity. The Verkehrsbank was an unmistakable premonition of his later idiom: a stringent exercise in the possibilities of formal elimination, its cubic mass relieved only by a regular pattern of fenestration, overscaled lettering, and a large double-headed eagle — the bank's logo. In obvious respects, the design, especially the treatment of the upper façades and its basic, matter-of-fact roof (shown in the photomontage only in pencil outline), forecast the Goldman & Salatsch Building on the Michaelerplatz. Yet there were telling differences. It lacked the elaborate stone veneer of the Michaelerplatz building: because of its location in an ordinary commercial shopping district, Loos opted for a less upscale palette of materials. And his neoclassicism, so insistent in the later Michaelerplatz building, was subdued. He relied instead on a flattened, arcadelike arrangement along the ground floor, with the windows framed by thin columns. The project fell through — Langer apparently thought it too unconventional — but it offered a powerful and confident statement of Loos's aesthetic, and he doubtless recalled some of its features while working on the design for the Goldman & Salatsch commission.

Two of Loos's realized works of this period also point directly toward the Michaelerplatz building. The first was the façade for Sigmund Steiner, a shop in the inner city selling decorative feathers and artificial flowers for women's hats and hair. Loos had provided a new exterior for the other of Steiner's stores on the Mariahilfer Straße a few years before; in 1906 the owners asked him to redesign their Kärtner Straße store inside and out.

He repeated many elements of the Goldman & Salatsch salon, expending costly woods, brass, and glass to contrive a simultaneous image of richness and austerity. The exterior of the shop introduced what would become a regular feature of his commercial façades: a refined sheathing of marble, the panels cut and matched to take full advantage of their sumptuous, intertwining grain patterns (fig. 27). Through deluxe materiality Loos had found a means to introduce bespoke adornment without resorting to applied ornament.

His breakthrough was not lost on at least one observer. Ludwig Hevesi, who only a few years before had been content to satirize Loos's efforts in the Café Museum, now wrote the first comprehensive review of his work. In the interior of the Steiner shop he found "everything rectangular, sharply linear, nowhere a trace of ornament. . . . An interior of geometric elegance and meticulous, perfectly tuned cleanliness, as if the whole were a steel safe."[9] He thought Loos's other designs were equally impressive: "I have now seen many of the apartments Loos has furnished, both moderate and expensive ones, for inhabitants with very different intellectual and physical needs. He has extended both his simplicity and his [concept of] luxury, doing justice to the most manifold requirements."[10]

The review also provided the first serious critical response to Loos's ideas.[11] Hevesi described Loos's approach and quoted him on the problem of orna- ment: "In order to invent an ornamental pattern, someone would have to have a very average mind; a higher intelligence does not produce ornament now, he has better things to do."[12]

Not long afterward, Loos commenced work on the Kärntner Bar (figs. 28, 29). The diminutive space drew from his now standard repertoire of materials: marble, onyx, exotic woods, polished metal fittings, and mirrors. "The whole," Altenberg (once more reconciled with Loos) observed in a review, is "of unprec- edented richness and, at the same time, not overdone, but, rather, with the appearance of serenity like the most precious treasures of nature itself!"[13]

The interior was replete with new ideas: visual expansion through mirrors; the alliance of classicism and the new language of functionalism; an exer- cise into what might be conveyed in a very limited space. It underscored, as never before in his work, the needlessness of ornament, a point he drove home by demonstrating, in seemingly unbounded ways, the varied possibilities of material opulence.

In late 1907, after a long period of silence, Loos began to write again. In December, in reaction to a comment Hevesi had made about showing his

FIG. 28 Adolf Loos, Kärntner Bar, Kärntner Durchgang, Vienna, 1908. *Moderne Wiener Geschäftsportale* (Vienna, c. 1914), plate 16.

FIG. 29 Kärntner Bar, interior, c. 1930. Photo by Martin Gerlach. Graphische Sammlung Albertina, Vienna, ALA 3281.

designs to the public, he organized a two-day tour of more than a dozen of his apartments and produced an accompanying guide.[14] Over the following two years he composed more than a half dozen new essays, including some of his most well-known texts, "Die Überflüssigen" (The Superfluous Ones) and "Kultur" (Culture).

Throughout this time, Loos sought to spread his ideas to the city's youth. Almost daily he sat in the Café Museum, near the Technical University and the Academy of Fine Arts, holding forth before groups of architecture students from both schools about his perceived shortcomings of the Secessionists and Austrian design education. His impact on them was pronounced — and, in the view of some, pernicious — so much so that Carl König, who taught at the Technical University, once posted a notice forbidding his students from attending Loos's impromptu lectures.[15]

An article on Loos that Robert Scheu published in *Die Fackel* in late June 1909 (aside from the portrait by Hevesi, one of only two other feature articles on Loos that appeared before he began work on the Michaelerplatz building) conveys the power of his talks: "There he sits, serene and calm, drawing connections. . . . The moment he begins to utter a word, everyone instinctively falls silent. . . . What he says are explosions of light."[16]

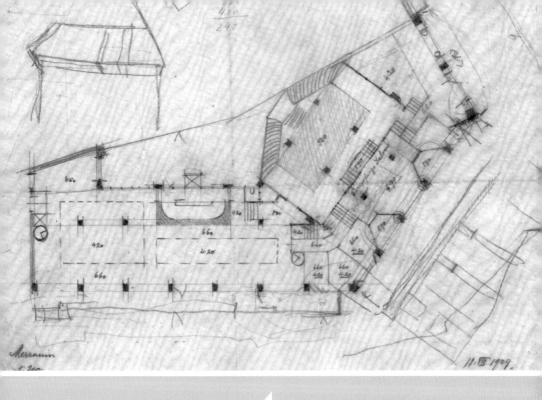

4

THE FIRST DESIGNS

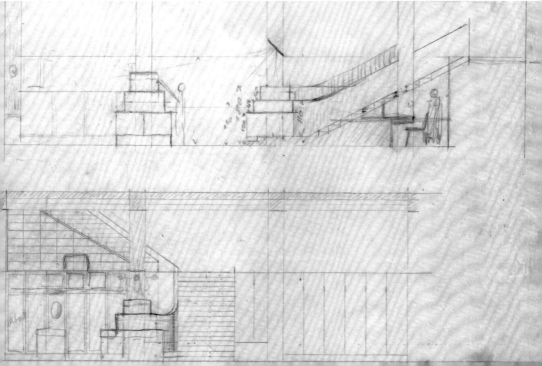

FIG. 30 Oskar Kokoschka, drawing of Adolf Loos, 1910. Kokoschka, *Menschenköpfe* (Berlin: Der Sturm, 1916), plate 1.

Precisely when Loos received the commission to design Goldman & Salatsch's new building on the Michaelerplatz is unknown (fig. 30). His statement that the firm's owners had turned to him after the competition failed to yield a satisfactory project seems to fit the surviving records. If the competition was indeed held in early June, as the dating on Stephann's drawings appears to indicate, that means that Goldman and Aufricht must have presented him the commission by late July or early August. His earliest dated drawing is from the second week of August.

But several assertions Loos later made call into question his description of the events leading up to the time he received the contract. For one, Loos claimed that he had declined to take part in the competition because of his standing policy against architectural competitions.[1]

In fact, he entered several competitions during this period. The year before, he had taken part in the competition to design the new War Ministry Building.

(His entry was excluded during the second round of judging because he failed to meet the requirements for the stipulated number of façade studies, a cost estimate, and other documents.)[2] And Loos entered the competition for the new Technisches Museum with his cousin, Victor Loos. The competition was announced at the end of May 1909, with the deadline set for June 5 — exactly at the moment the Michaelerplatz competition presumably was taking place. The project the two men prepared, a long low building with pared-down, almost reticent, classical detailing ("intentionally unpretentious," in Hevesi's words), had been painstakingly worked out, suggesting that they must have spent a substantial amount of time on it.[3]

Did Loos decide not to submit a proposal to Goldman and Aufricht in order to devote his time to the Technisches Museum project, a potentially more important prize? Or did he already know that the Michaelerplatz competition was a pretense and that he would be awarded the commission? Whichever the case, he did not turn down the invitation to participate because of a self-imposed prohibition from taking part in architectural competitions.

Loos also failed to mention that he was already working for Leopold Goldman on another project, his own house at Hardtgasse 27–29 in the nineteenth district. Goldman had purchased the property in late March. When he engaged Loos to design the house is not recorded, but the earliest plans were submitted to the city building office in mid-July 1909, so he must have been at work on them for some time.[4] (The U-shaped, four-story house was completed in 1911, around the same time as the Goldman & Salatsch Building.)

It is telling that Loos never mentioned in any of his writings — at the time or later — that he had designed Goldman's house. It was not identified as one of his works until Burkhardt Rukschcio undertook his research on Loos in the 1970s.[5] Whether this connection was key to Goldman and Aufricht's decision to ask Loos to design their new building is not clear, but the fact that he was already working for Goldman must have played a part.

All that we know about the contract for the design of the Michaelerplatz building comes from Loos himself:

I told the clients, therefore: I will work only if I have a clear mandate. Let us make a contract. And I wrote the following:

1. *We assign the building on the corner of Kohlmarkt and Herrengasse to the architect Adolf Loos.*
2. *In the event that we find someone who can produce a better ground plan than Adolf Loos, he will withdraw from this commission.*
3. *The final decision concerning the disposition of the ground plan is ours. We have no say in the design of the façade.*[6]

One might question why Goldman and Aufricht, both experienced businessmen, would have signed such an agreement. In particular, why, if they were concerned enough about the appearance of their building to organize a competition, would they have agreed to hand over to Loos all responsibility for the exterior?

A plausible explanation is that the two men had been satisfied with Loos's previous designs. Perhaps they simply had faith in his ability to design the new building. Yet, if this was indeed the case, it raises questions once more about their intentions for the competition.

Part of the truth might be found in Heinrich Kulka's account of the genesis of the Michaelerplatz building. In his 1931 book *Adolf Loos: Das Werk des Architekten,* Kulka offers an alternative story of how Loos came to receive the commission.[7] He was in a position to know details that had not been made public. He had studied with Loos around the end of World War I and began working for him in the mid-1920s, overseeing most of his later projects. During the last years of Loos's life, Kulka spent a great deal of time with him, and he talked to him at length about his earlier work. Loos, Kulka wrote, "had made his participation . . . dependent upon the condition that only the ground plans would be judged, not the façades, because one could talk about practical matters, such as the planning and arrangement of spaces, but façades were too often subject to prevailing taste."[8] This suggests a different sequence of events than Loos described — that he may have entered the competition only after stipulating the conditions of his participation. Most scholars have dismissed Kulka's story because it conflicts with Loos's version of the events. The fact that Loos apparently never prepared a full competition project — no such drawings have survived — seems to undermine Kulka's assertions. But his portrayal may hint at what actually happened.[9]

It now seems fairly certain that Stephann, Augenfeld, Epstein, and the other unnamed architects who submitted entries to the competition did so around the beginning of June. It appears, though, that Goldman and Aufricht did not judge them immediately because they were immersed in a family crisis. Michael Goldman was seriously ill. In June he wrote his will, and he died on July 16 from what was described as an "ulcer attack."[10]

Loos, meanwhile, had continued his work on the Hardtgasse house. During this time he may have also designed Michael's gravestone in Vienna's Central Cemetery. The minimal composition is consistent with his ideas, and, given that he was already working for the Goldman family, it is likely that the design is his (fig. 31).[11]

It was perhaps not until after Michael's death and funeral that Goldman and Aufricht, disappointed with the competition entries, showed the drawings to Loos. They must have asked him to undertake the design for them, as Loos later reported. It is possible, though, that they approached him initially only for his opinion. He may have suggested to them that he could produce a design superior to any of the submissions (but without considering the façades) and that, were the two men satisfied, he should receive the commission for the building — a version of the events that is close to what Kulka describes.

One of the drawings in the Loos archive, a plan of the building's ground floor, seems to confirm this (fig. 32). The undated rendering shows what was almost certainly Loos's first effort to configure the lower portion of the shop and adjacent spaces. In contrast to his subsequent plans, which are more tentative, it is meticulously rendered, suggesting that he presented it to Goldman and Aufricht as his belated entry to the competition. The drawing was undoubtedly made after the other competition drawings: it follows several of the submitted designs closely, repeating, for example, Epstein's and Stephann's placement and form of the staircase and elevator leading to the upstairs apartments. In Loos's executed design, he adopted a very different solution for this part of the building. The configuration of the building's front also deviates from his final design. In this early version, the principal façade is wider, and there are no freestanding columns, which Loos would introduce only later in the design process.

FIG. 31 Adolf Loos [?], grave marker for Michael Goldman, 1910, Central Cemetery, Vienna. Photo by Wolfgang Thaler.

In critiquing the other entries for Goldman and Aufricht, Loos must have underscored the advantages of his design, as well as his belief that Stephann, Augenfeld, and the others had largely neglected the second-story *piano nobile*. He later wrote:

It was notable [in the plans of the other architects] that they disregarded the principal floor, which was to house the main spaces of the store. . . . I speak of the level above the ground floor. In former times, when buildings were erected in Vienna, the second-floor piano nobile *was the prime space. If the owner of a property in the eighteenth century had commissioned one of the great architects of the day to make the story above the ground floor into the main level, he would have accomplished this task readily. Only a minor builder would have bristled at the idea.*[12]

Loos understood well the spatial and practical requirements of an elite tailoring firm like Goldman & Salatsch; he exploited this knowledge to convince the clients that he could design a superior building. What he offered them was a vision of a grand and efficient sequence of rooms ideally suited to their tastes and requirements. Convinced that Loos could provide them with an appropriate building, they presented him with the commission.

This must have been some time in July or early August. Another preliminary plan of the second-story mezzanine, which likely dates to the first week of August, shows that he had already started to refine his initial concept (fig. 33). In addition to working out in detail the positioning of the stairs and various spaces, he considered, for the first time (in the lower right corner of the sketch), the possible finishes for the ceilings and walls, and the placement of furnishings.

Goldman took the lead in dealing with Loos and overseeing the work. Aufricht, who had been the store's accountant before marrying Bertha, Michael's oldest daughter, was very much the junior partner, and, as in the running of the store, he assumed a subordinate role in the planning and fitting out of the new store.

Born in 1875, Goldman was five years younger than his architect, but he was already an experienced and self-assured businessman — composed, determined, and ambitious. Of slightly more than medium height, he stood out with his sharp features, resolute jaw, intense eyes, and confident manner (fig. 34). As befit one of the city's elite tailors, he was always immaculately dressed, sporting the latest men's fashions, precisely calibrated to be neither too trendy nor too traditional.

His father had groomed him from childhood to take over the family business. He attended a *Realschule* in Leopoldstadt and completed his final *Matura* examinations in 1892. After a year at a private business school and another year completing his compulsory military service, his father sent him to England to

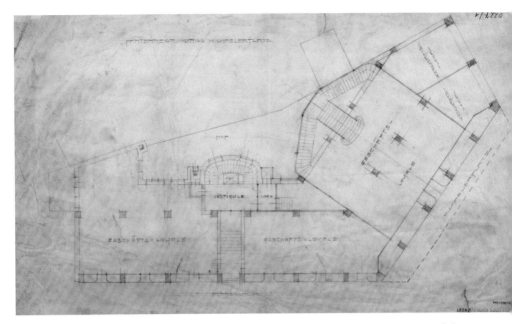

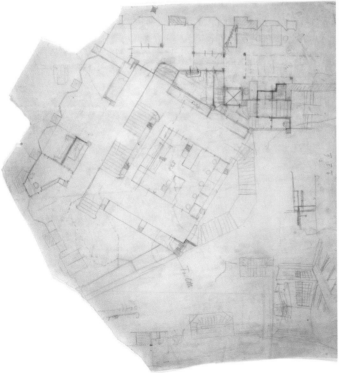

FIG. 32 Adolf Loos, preliminary plan for the ground floor of the Goldman & Salatsch Building, July 1909 (?). Pencil and colored pencil on paper, 11 $\frac{1}{2}$ × 19 $\frac{3}{4}$ in. (29.2 × 50.1 cm). Graphische Sammlung Albertina, Vienna, ALA 227.

FIG. 33 Loos, preliminary plan for the mezzanine floor of the Goldman & Salatsch Building, early August 1909 (?). Pencil on paper, 23 $\frac{5}{8}$ × 25 in. (60 × 63.6 cm). Graphische Sammlung Albertina, Vienna, ALA 351.

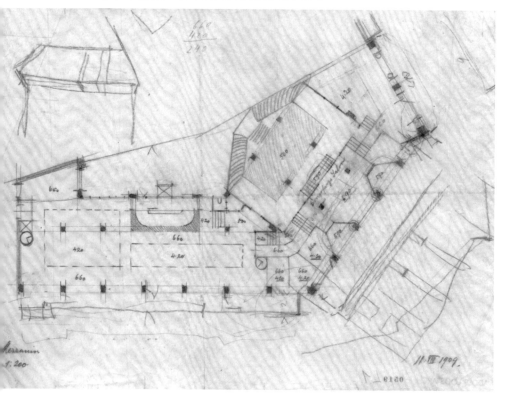

learn the tailoring business as an apprentice.[13] When he returned to Vienna he began working at Goldman & Salatsch, gradually assuming more responsibility. From the start he proved to be an innovator, experimenting with new clothing ideas and techniques. He succeeded in winning the status of "preferred provider" for the newly formed Austrian Automobile Club, and he secured a number of patents (most of which he designed with his brother Robert, an engineer), including a special drinking cup and carrying bottle for use while driving.[14]

Loos must have worked closely with Goldman. He later credited him with helping to determine the store's layout: "Through his collaboration," he wrote, "his brilliant flashes of inspiration, his business acumen, all of which crystallized into real innovations, the plan came into existence."[15] But the specific nature of Goldman's contributions remains unclear. Goldman & Salatsch's emphasis on catering to members of the aristocracy and bourgeois elite meant that the new store had to be both private and elegant. Goldman doubtless pushed Loos to consider solutions that presented an image of exclusivity and refinement. He was also very much aware of the realities of running the business; here, too, he must have offered ideas and suggestions.

A second, fragmentary sketch Loos made at this time shows only a portion of the second floor. It reveals that he had already made several decisions that would affect the building as a whole. In the center top of the drawing is evidence that he was considering flipping the smaller staircase to the apartments inward so that it no longer extended out into the narrow rear courtyard. Moving the stairwell into the main body of the building, he explained, permitted him to fashion a single, more ample courtyard than the original competition projects had specified: "What was even more curious [in the designs of the other entrants] was the number of courtyards they used. The building code, quite correctly, specifies that a certain proportion of the building site be given over to courtyard space. One knows that a large courtyard provides a great deal of light, a small one very little. Almost all of those who submitted projects had three or four courtyards."[16]

Around this time Loos also began to reconsider the outer building envelope. In his first plan he had set the exterior walls flush with the edge of the concrete frame. He was evidently dissatisfied with this solution because he soon began investigating the possibility of adding bay windows between the piers, an idea that he would retain, in modified form, in his final design. As his early drawings demonstrate, Loos had resolved, almost from the outset, to place the building a little more than six feet behind the original city-sanctioned building line. His decision, he said, had been driven by his belief that the property line extended too far out into the Michaelerplatz, "to the great disadvantage of the square."[17]

The old Dreilauferhaus had indeed jutted well into the square, impeding the transition between the Herrengasse and Kohlmarkt. City officials had initially specified a building line almost identical to the one Loos advocated, but they subsequently extended it outward, thereby enlarging the building site. It was this larger footprint that all of the original entrants had used for their projects. Loos insisted that configuring the building in this fashion not only obstructed the flow of traffic through the square but would have made the building's front façade almost nine feet narrower, with the unfortunate consequence that the "main façade, with its thin profile, would appear disproportionately tall and overwhelm the adjacent church."[18] With this in mind, he approached the head of the city building office and requested a variance to reduce the size of the site. Loos later revealed that he had an additional motive for this unconventional move: to cast the front façade in such a way that it would not detract from the Hofburg.

His intention to devise a building that would be an appropriate and dignified addition to the square also explains a number of the changes he made in another early plan. The drawing — the first bearing a date, August 11, 1909 — also shows

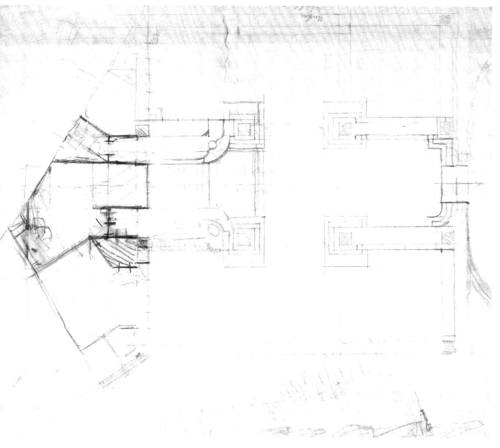

FIG. 36 Loos, plan of the sales area on the ground floor of the Goldman & Salatsch Building, n.d. Pencil on paper, 16 1/4 × 14 7/8 in. (41.4 × 37.7 cm). Graphische Sammlung Albertina, Vienna, ALA 242.

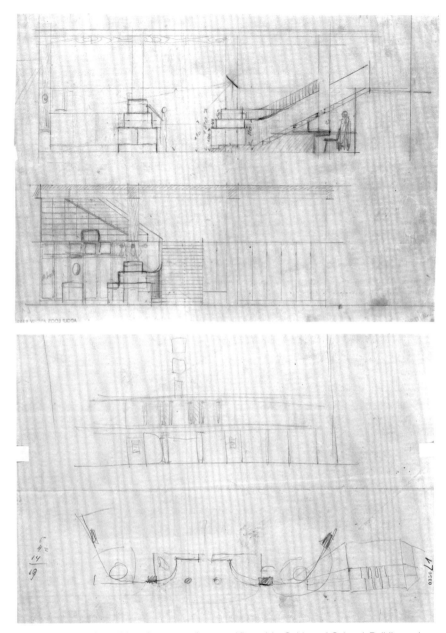

FIG. 37 Loos, elevations of the sales area on the ground floor of the Goldman & Salatsch Building, n.d. Pencil on paper, 10 ¹/₈ × 14 ¹/₄ in. (25.8 × 36 cm). Graphische Sammlung Albertina, Vienna, ALA 395.

FIG. 38 Loos, elevations of the façades and plan of the entry, Goldman & Salatsch Building, n.d. Pencil on blueprint, 12 ¹/₂ × 18 ¹/₂ in. (31.9 × 46.9 cm). Graphische Sammlung Albertina, Vienna, ALA 350 (detail).

the second, mezzanine level of the building (fig. 35). Aside from working out a number of details, such as positioning the elevator in a shaft extending out into the courtyard (an idea he apparently took from examples he had seen during his American travels), he began to work out some of the central features of the lower façade.[19] He considered, for the first time, the use of classical columns in the entry portal and the canted corners on each side.

But Loos's focus was on the building's interior. Two other surviving sketches from this period disclose that he was already considering in detail the arrangement of the vitrines and display cases on the ground floor (figs. 36, 37). On the other hand, there is only a single extant drawing from this early design phase that considers the overall appearance of the façades.

The perspective sketch shows that, from the outset, he had settled on a tripartite division consisting of the lower two floors housing the Goldman & Salatsch shop and several ground-floor rental spaces for stores; a middle portion of several floors of apartments; and, though not shown, an attic story (fig. 38). The disposition of larger and smaller columns on the first and second levels, respectively, was also apparently in Loos's mind from the beginning, though a small plan of the entry reveals that he had initially considered a distyle, or two-columned, arrangement before deciding on four columns.

Loos undertook this initial design work on his own. Around the end of August, however, it seems that Goldman and Aufricht asked Epstein to aid with the execution of the building. It was a logical and prudent decision. In terms of building at large scale, Loos was still a neophyte; Epstein, though eleven years younger, was already an experienced builder. He had constructed a number of commercial and apartment structures, and Goldman had already engaged him to work with Loos on the design and construction of his Hardtgasse house. Epstein would come to have a prominent role in the controversy over the building, but at first he seems to have acted primarily as adviser on technical issues.

Over the next six months they would work together on the final design — well out of the public eye.

5

THE DISCOVERY OF VIENNA

Loos continued to work on the building through the latter part of August.[1] In early September, he and Bessie traveled to the town of Gloggnitz, in the foothills of the Alps south of Vienna, for a short vacation. Accompanying them was the young artist Oskar Kokoschka.[2]

Loos had taken notice of Kokoschka only a few months before. While strolling through the Internationale Kunstschau exhibition in the late spring, he had seen the small room that had been set aside for Kokoschka's work. Loos was especially taken with a painted clay bust, a writhing, anguished self-portrait, which he purchased.[3] In its febrile honesty he detected a fresh and potent vision: Kokoschka's attempt to shed the influences of the Secessionists in favor of a new, exaggerated primitivism struck Loos as something new and promising.

Loos learned that Kokoschka would present the premiere of his play *Mörder, Hoffnung der Frauen* (Murderer, Hope of Women) at the Kunstschau's open-air theater in early July, and he persuaded Kraus to accompany him.

The performance, as Kokoschka later recounted, devolved into a near riot: "A flimsy barrier separated the stage from the rows of seats, which were full to the bursting point. The garden was too small to hold the throng of society, intellectuals, and the merely curious. . . . The audience maintained a chorus of catcalls throughout the play, [and] eventually, as the foot-stamping, scuffling, and chair-

FIG. 39 Oskar Kokoschka, portrait of Adolf Loos, 1909. Oil on canvas, 29 1/8 × 35 7/8 in. (74 × 91 cm). Nationalgalerie, Staatliche Museen zu Berlin/Art Resource, New York.

brandishing increased in pitch," a group of Bosnian soldiers "stormed in and a free-for-all followed between them and the audience." The police arrived to bring order. Loos and Kraus, who knew the chief of police, intervened to prevent Kokoschka from being arrested. Afterward, they took him to the Kunstschau bar and bought him a whiskey to steady his nerves.[4]

The furor over the event prompted the minister of education to write a letter to Alfred Roller, director of the Kunstgewerbeschule, where Kokoschka was a student, stating that he "could no longer answer to the press for the presence of such a disruptive element." Kokoschka was forced to withdraw from the school.[5]

Loos immediately began an energetic campaign to aid the young artist. In spite of being chronically short of money, he purchased as many of Kokoschka's paintings and drawings as he could and asked Kokoschka to make portraits of Bessie and him (fig. 39).[6] He also began to help Kokoschka find clients and commissions, introducing him to many of his friends and acquaintances, among them Goldman, who asked Kokoschka to paint a portrait of his infant son, Fred.[7]

To ease the working-class student's way into society, Loos took Kokoschka to Ebenstein and had him properly outfitted with a gentleman's wardrobe (fig. 40). Kraus also showed an interest in him: he recognized Kokoschka's talent and his innate capacity for seeing through the pretense of Viennese life, and he admitted

FIG. 40 Oskar Kokoschka, c. 1909. Universität für angewandte Kunst, Vienna.

him to the select few invited to join his table in the evenings. Immature and awkward, painfully aware of his lack of literary understanding, Kokoschka bore up to Kraus's incessant questioning with quiet stoicism, which only strengthened Loos's admiration.[8]

Loos's patronage of Kokoschka was merely a part of his larger quest for cultural reform. By 1909 he had become an active supporter of an array of radical modernist causes. He expended much time and energy in support of Arnold Schönberg and his disciples, Alban Berg, Anton von Webern, and Alexander von Zemlinsky (who had collectively earned considerable enmity from the Viennese critics and much of the public), as well as a number of other young writers and intellectuals, including the playwright Frank Wedekind. Loos viewed them all as allies in his struggle for a purified culture. Schönberg remarked once, "It seems almost as if for Loos I am just a modern matter."[9]

In Loos's eyes, Kokoschka, Schönberg, and the others had opened an assault on aestheticism and pretention. He was convinced that their attempt to confront the realities of modern life gave them a shared mission, and he supported them in every way he could. As the battle over the Looshaus raged, his cultural campaign would continue unabated.

Shortly after the couple's return to Vienna in late September, Loos faced a new problem: Bessie was suffering from tuberculosis, and her health was deteriorating. She had long exhibited symptoms of the disease, which she had contracted before she met Loos. Meeting him, in fact, Kokoschka wrote years afterward, had saved her life: "She was already ill and would certainly have soon died if she had not left the stage."[10] After consulting with her doctors, Loos decided to take her to a sanatorium in Leysin, on the eastern end of Lake Geneva in Switzerland, for treatment.[11]

Loos had discovered the village five years before while working on the Villa Karma. He thought it the ideal place for her to begin her recovery. The 110-room sanatorium, situated high above the village at nearly 4,800 feet, was noted for its sunny location and view of the distant peaks of the Dents du Midi and Mont Blanc. Treatments stressed exposure to fresh air — patients spent as much as ten hours a day on the south-facing balconies — modest exercise, and vigorous rubbing of the skin.

Loos secured Bessie a place and helped her settle in. But his stay was brief. He was soon forced to depart to attend to his new project.[12]

After returning to Vienna he threw himself into work on the design. Gradually the building began to take shape. Over the next two months he continued to develop its interior spaces and façades. He had already made several decisions about its final form. He was determined that the new building reflect both its location and its intended purpose as a commercial structure. Both of these decisions, he recognized, necessitated a novel approach. The building's "proximity to the palace and position across from the church," he would later explain, demanded a different solution from the standard large glass show windows common in Viennese stores: "It must be a commercial building, but a distinguished one."[13] It was especially important, he insisted, that it communicate the nature of the store housed within. "I said to the clients: you are tailors, whose prices are between those of Rothberger [a mass retailer] and Frank [an exclusive custom tailor]. That has to be expressed on the exterior. While Rothberger has large plate glass windows facing the street, one can see nothing of Frank's shop from the outside. You must be between them."[14] Loos was also certain that the articulation of the façade should show that the Goldman & Salatsch store was "not a simple retail store, but an elegant shop" (nicht ein Warenhaus, sondern ein vornehmes Geschäft).[15]

The term he used, *Warenhaus,* referred to large retailers, usually of clothing or furniture. There were many such establishments in Vienna — mass merchants akin to modern department stores but usually offering a more limited range of goods.[16] By the turn of the century, the buildings housing them had a standard look. The Rothberger store, on Stephansplatz facing the cathedral, constructed in two phases in the 1880s and 1890s, was typical (fig. 41).[17] The upper portions of the building repeated the language of late historicism — in this instance,

FIG 41 Ferdinand Fellner and Hermann Helmer, Warenhaus Rothberger, Vienna, 1884–85 and 1893–95. Paul Kortz, ed., *Wien am Anfang des XX. Jahrhunderts* vol. 2 (Vienna: Österreichischer Ingenieur- und Architekten-Verein, 1905), 363.

FIG. 42 Otto Wagner, Warenhaus Neumann, Kärntner Straße 19, Vienna, 1893–96. Bildarchiv Foto Marburg.

the Northern Renaissance revival — but the lower three floors were given over to great expanses of glass, intended to display the wares for sale. The arrangement of the lower glazed surfaces, analogous to a modern curtain wall, necessitated the use of a structural frame — iron, steel, or concrete — since the lower walls were not load bearing.

Many of the city's leading architects designed related buildings. Otto Wagner's Warenhaus Neumann on the Kärtner Straße, completed in 1896, offered one of the most accomplished and progressive examples (fig. 42). Wagner preserved the idea of a bifurcated façade, employing a modified Renaissance ornamental idiom for its uppermost level, but he glazed the other four stories. The result was assertively modern: from the street, the structure appeared to be made up of a nearly uninterrupted glass wall. Other architects pushed this strategy even further. Ferdinand Fellner and Hermann Helmer's Warenhaus Gerngroß, for instance, which opened in 1904, relied on a widening of the bays and the introduction of even larger sheets of glass (fig. 43). The building's cornice alone carried over the traditional notion of the wall as enclosure.

Loos, too, had experimented with expansive surfaces of glass in his design for the Steiner Store in 1906. Very early in the design process for the Michaelerplatz building, though, he had become convinced that the new Goldman & Salatsch store required some form of screening for the show windows, allowing the display of goods but presenting a more dignified face to the square and to the

FIG. 43 Ferdinand Fellner and Hermann Helmer, Warenhaus Gerngroß, Mariahilfer Straße 44 – 46, Vienna, 1902 – 4. Bildarchiv Foto Marburg.

Hofburg. He wanted, above all, to avoid the crass commercialism of *Warenhäuser* like Jakob Wohlschläger's Erstes Wiener Warenmuster- und Kollektivkaufhaus on the Mariahilfer Straße, then also under development (fig. 44).

Loos, thus, was faced with several problems. He needed to find a means to give the new building a dignified outer shell that expressed its purpose and that lent privacy to the interiors. But the building also had to be modern — not a contrived modernism, but an honest expression of the new age. And that modernism, in keeping with his belief that the new architecture had to be a response to the long evolution of Viennese culture, had to be rooted in local tradition.

When Loos later sought to explain his decisions for the design, he resorted to a metaphor befitting an elite tailor shop: the building, he wrote, had to be like a modern suit — comfortable, practical, and appropriate.

When I was finally presented a commission for a building, I said to myself, "In its external appearance, a building can at most have changed as much as a tail coat. That is, not very much." And I saw how our ancestors built, and I saw how, from century to century, from year to year, they had liberated themselves from ornament. I had to go back to the point when the chain had been broken. One thing I knew for certain: in order to continue the line of this development, I had to become significantly simpler. I had to replace gold buttons with black ones. The building had to be inconspicuous.[18]

Loos had found one model for his design years before. In the second issue of *Das Andere* he had published a photograph of the façade of an old Biedermeier-era storefront on Wildpretmarkt in the inner city (fig. 45). The establishment, he explained in the accompanying text, belonged to a family named Exinger, who had opened a butcher shop for wild game in the 1810s and for more than ninety years had left the façade intact, only repainting it from time to time with its original green and white color scheme. Loos lamented that the building in which the shop was housed was slated for demolition in a few weeks' time, and he contended that, given its significance, the proper thing to do would be to save it and place it in the city's museum.[19]

He founded his argument not on the façade's historic value or its remarkably pristine condition, but on its usefulness as a prototype for modern design. In the simple, dignified lines of its façade, its vestigial classicism, its forthright expression of middle-class values, he believed he had found an alternative to Art Nouveau and late historicism.

Loos was hardly alone in turning to the aesthetic of the Biedermeier era for inspiration: in the decade before World War I, Hoffmann, Peter Behrens, Bruno Paul, Heinrich Tessenow, and Ludwig Mies van der Rohe all saw in it the spark of an emergent and novel language for modern architecture and design.[20]

FIG. 44 Jakob Wohlschläger, Erstes Wiener Warenmuster- und Kollektivkaufhaus, Mariahilfer Straße 120, Vienna, 1910 – 11. Bildarchiv Foto Marburg.

FIG. 45 Johann Exinger Wildgame shop, Wildpretmarkt, c. 1810. Anonymous photograph, 1903. *Das Andere* 1, no. 2 (October 15, 1903), 2.

The renewed interest in the Biedermeier in Vienna had begun just after the turn of the century.[21] It had been prompted in part by a display of Biedermeier furniture in the 1901 winter exhibition at the Österreichisches Museum für Kunst und Industrie. All of the pieces were replicas from the living room of a marvelously preserved early nineteenth-century country house in Atzgersdorf, then a village on the city's outskirts. The simplicity and directness of the ensemble struck most viewers as quaint. Hevesi, in a review of the exhibition, wrote that they were "enchanting" — an avowal of a different era "before factory-made furniture came in supposed Gothic or pretend Renaissance."[22] He did not think they could serve as direct models for the new aesthetic: it would be "foolish" to readopt the Biedermeier style; it was now "dead." Still, he suggested, Biedermeier principles — "functionality, genuineness of its materials, appropriateness to its time, and the highest-quality handicraft one could imagine" — remained vital.[23]

Loos's own conversion to the possibilities of a reimagined Biedermeier form-language had come even earlier, at the time of the 1898 Imperial Jubilee. It grew out of his conviction that the Vormärz (literally, "before March," referring to the period before the revolution of 1848) was the last time in which a harmonious, genuine, and original culture had existed in Central Europe. The time of Schubert, Beethoven, and Goethe — a period of intellectual and artistic promise and fulfillment, of cultural accord and probity — he believed, stood in direct opposition to the falsity and sham pretensions of the 1880s and 1890s. Like many other young modernists, he saw the revival styles of the second half of the nineteenth century as an aberration, a break from history and tradition. In turning to the first half of the nineteenth century for inspiration, he thought it might be possible to reestablish the connection with an earlier, authentic past.

Implicit within these ideas, too, was a social message: Biedermeier, in contrast to the Baroque, which spoke of the dominance of the aristocracy and clergy, was the aesthetic creation of the ascendant bourgeoisie, whose embrace of simplicity, hard work, and truthfulness was reflected in their surroundings and objects of daily use. But as important for Loos was the possibility of finding a route to the present without abandoning history.[24] Not only did the architecture and design of the Vormärz afford a strategy for a novel aesthetic vision, but it suggested that modernism could be part of a longer, evolutionary path; the new design need not necessarily entail a radical break with the past.

What that might mean in specific terms remained for him open. What form exactly should his new building take?

Loos, it seems, found another model, an even more immediate one, in another surviving Biedermeier building, the old pharmacy of August Moll, also known as the Apotheke zum weissen Storch (Pharmacy at the White Swan), on Tuchlauben in the inner city (fig. 46). Although modest in scale, it had several features that

Loos would adapt for his much larger work: the four columns (two expressed as pilasters) framing the entry, the compressed second level, and the prominent cornice separating the lower floors from the upper ones.

There is no direct evidence that Loos drew from it, but it is a virtual diagram of his design. He must have passed by it very often, and it is hard to imagine that it did not influence his ideas about the form of his new work. (Loos's design for the portal of the Hugo & Alfred Spitz jewelry store on the Kärtner Straße in 1918 would have the same configuration [fig. 47].)

Loos's recourse to the Biedermeier aesthetic issued from his belief that it provided a means to reestablish a bond with the city's history. Two years before, in "The Discovery of Vienna," an essay he published in the newspaper *Fremden-Blatt,* he had lavished praise on several of Vienna's historic monuments, calling St. Stephen's Cathedral the "most beautiful building in Vienna" and citing the old War Ministry Building, scheduled for demolition, as its "most beautiful dying building."[25]

FIG. 46 Apotheke A. Moll (Apotheke zum weissen Storch), Tuchlauben 9, Vienna, late eighteenth century. Photo by author.

FIG. 47 Adolf Loos, portal for the Hugo & Alfred Spitz jewelry store, Kärntner Straße 39, 1918. Graphische Sammlung Albertina, Vienna, ALA 097.

What is most arresting in the piece, however, is Loos's description of what he thought was the city's best new building: a simple commercial and residential edifice at Kärntner Straße 27 (fig. 48). It was the work of a man named Johann Walland. Walland was an engineer employed by one of the city's leading construction firms.[26] The building was his first design (he would eventually produce several others), and, because of its resolute sobriety, it had attracted almost no attention.

But Loos saw in the building all of the marks of an authentic modern statement. He was struck not only by its honest construction but also by Walland's unaffected façades, which relied on a modest and uncontaminated neoclassicism:

When a building in the central city is torn down, do not people tremble at the thought of the monstrosity that will occupy its site? I trembled, too, when the building at the corner of Kärntnerstraße and Himmelpfortgasse was pulled down last year. But what joy: a building appeared that fits perfectly with the spirit of the Kärntnerstraße, which seems like a continuation of the old style of Vienna's inner city, modest, calm, and refined. This building will not appear in the art magazines, it is not considered "artistic" enough. Nor is it what people call modern, i.e., vulgar. But the builder of the building is as impervious to criticism of "old fashion" hurled at him by modern architects as the man who dresses correctly is to the same gibe from the lips of a provincial tailor's apprentice.[27]

FIG. 48 Johann Walland, commercial and residential building at the corner of Kärntner Straße and Himmelpfortgasse, Vienna, 1906 – 7. Adolf Loos, *Sämtliche Schriften* (Vienna: Herold, 1962), after 263.

In Walland's forthright massing and his avoidance of unnecessary ornament, Loos thought he had found the qualities of a "true" modernism.[28]

The new building on the Kärntner Straße relied on large windows on the lower two floors set flush with the outer envelope. But for the Goldman & Salatsch building, Loos required a solution that would permit him simultaneously to present and cloak the store's entry sequence. He decided to invert the display windows within the porch, screening off the area with four large Tuscan columns. (He added similar, smaller columns to frame the English-inspired bay windows along the mezzanine level.)

The form of the columns Loos adapted from the portico of the adjacent Michaelerkirche. In mirroring a prominent feature of the church, he sought to pay homage to the square's history and lend a dignified face to the new store. With them, he also intended to draw a direct line to the time "around 1800." Such simple columns were standard features of Viennese townhouses in the late Josephine age; they were a signature of middle-class propriety and self-esteem, and, also, a symbol of the city's unbroken link to Roman times.

The columns became an emblem of Loos's cultural mission. Set into the porch, they would speak, he hoped, with a clarion voice about his desire to honor Vienna's past and reclaim its present.

6

IN PRAISE OF THE PRESENT

"When I reflect on the past centuries," Loos wrote in his essay "Lob der Gegen-wart" (In Praise of the Present) in 1908, "and ask myself in which age would I have most liked to have lived, I answer: in the present one. Oh, I know there were many times when it was a joy to be alive. Many eras offered this or that advantage. And perhaps people in every other age have been happier than they are now. But in no other time were people so beautifully, so well, and so practically dressed as today."[1] In "dressing" his new building on Michaelerplatz, Loos wanted to fashion an outer cloak that could meet modern needs. But which modern cloak precisely? If the contrived ornament of the Secessionists was unsuitable, he still had many other possibilities from which to choose.

By the late summer of 1909, Vienna's inner districts were dotted with new buildings, many of them offering adroit responses to the problem of building in the new age. A decade before, in the third district, Max Fabiani, then Wagner's assistant at the Academy of Fine Arts, had contributed one of the most radical and innovative responses to the challenge of making a new architecture: the Portois & Fix Building on the Ungargasse (fig. 49). Spare and matter of fact, its simple mass and modular fenestration broken only by the geometrical pattern-ing (in the form of majolica tiles) distributed across its façade, it presented a novel expression, one that, despite its application of ornament, turned its back on the past. A year later, only a block from the site of the future Goldman & Salatsch Building, at Kohlmarkt 9, Fabiani had offered another interpretation of a modern architecture, this time by melding new and old (fig. 50). The lower two stories of his Artaria Building (a publisher of maps and fine prints) relied on a

FIG. 49 Max Fabiani, Portois & Fix Building, Ungargasse 59–61, 1899–1900. *Die Architektkur des XX. Jahrhunderts* (Berlin: Ernst Wasmuth, 1914), plate 104.

FIG. 50 Max Fabiani, Artaria Building, Kohlmarkt 9, 1900–1902. *Kunst und Kunsthandwerk* 7 (1904): 336.

muscular and purified classicism. On the walls of the upper stories, however, he peeled away all ornament, confining it to the cantilevered cornice.

Loos seems to have drawn much from Fabiani's experiments. The English-inspired bay windows and unadorned surfaces of the Artaria Building appear especially to have attracted his interest. He must have also taken inspiration from Fabiani's bifurcated façade: the idea of pairing a reduced classicism on the lower portion with completely "reticent" upper stories would become one of the key features of his Michaelerplatz design.

But Loos also certainly borrowed from other sources. Jože Plečnik's Zacherlhaus, completed in 1905 at the corner of Brandstätte and Wildpretmarkt (where the Exinger shop had stood), issued a forceful statement about raising functional form to the level of monumentality (fig. 51). Plečnik, who had studied with Wagner at the turn of the century, carried over his teacher's penchant for flattening the surfaces of his buildings with smooth, continuous stone cladding. Like Wagner and Fabiani, he fused the classical and modern, fixing them into a seamless whole. Loos could not have been unimpressed with Plečnik's use of thin sheets of stone and his dexterous handling of the irregular site. He seems to have been taken, too, with Plečnik's nearly square divided windows, which he would repeat for the Michaelerplatz building's upper stories.

FIG. 51 Jože Plečnik, Zacherlhaus, Brandstätte 6, Wildpretmarkt 2–4, 1903–5. Bildarchiv Foto Marburg.

More important, the Zacherlhaus bore witness to the changing nature of modern construction in the city. It was among the earliest examples of the new reinforced concrete frame systems then revolutionizing the building industry. Developed in France in the 1870s by François Hennebique, the technique had soon spread to England, Germany, and the United States. Austria had lagged behind. It was only at century's end, when the architect-engineer Carlo von Boog employed a concrete frame for the psychiatric hospital in the village of Mauer-Öhling, that the new technology was introduced there. And as late as 1909, only three companies, Ast & Company, Gustav Adolf Wayss (the builder of Walland's block on the Kärntner Straße), and Pittel & Brausewetter (who would become the contractor for the Michaelerplatz building), constructed nearly all of the new concrete frame buildings in Vienna.[2]

Behind the thin, gray-brown sheets of granite that sheath the Zacherlhaus lies a tight grid of ferroconcrete piers and beams, which make up the building's structural skeleton. The cost savings of the new technology had in part driven Plečnik's decision to rely on a frame. But he also opted for the new technology because it would allow the client, a large maker of insecticides, to reconfigure the interior spaces by altering or removing the nonstructural interior walls.

This lesson was not lost on Loos. His earliest plans for the Michaelerplatz building show that he had decided from the outset to rely on a concrete frame. Indeed, the fact that the other entrants in the competition had all elected to use traditional load-bearing walls had been, he thought, among their chief failings.[3]

The issue for Loos was not merely that such masonry walls were out-moded, but that they also did not allow for the most efficient use of space: "The plans [of the other architects] all took into account only the regular horizontal layering of the floors whereas, in my opinion, the architect should think in terms of space, in the form of the cube. Thus, I already had an advantage in the economic use of space. A toilet does not have to be as high as a formal hall. If one gives each room only the height that it requires, he can build much more economically."[4]

Here, in Loos's argument about space, is the first mention of what would become the most radically innovative feature of the new building, his concept of a *Raumplan*—a system of interlocking volumes of varied heights on different levels. Loos had recognized—before almost any of his contemporaries—that the use of a reinforced concrete frame not only would allow a reduction in the size of the interior walls, but also would provide the necessary flexibility to form rooms on multiple levels. Simply by pushing the cross beams up or down, rooms could be shifted in relation to each other and given different heights; removing supports or piers within the three-dimensional grid, in fact, permitted the interior space to be configured in almost limitless ways. Plečnik and others had realized that space within a frame could be expanded or delimited horizontally; Loos (and a few others at the time) understood that it could be manipulated vertically as well.

It was a stunning breakthrough—one that would shape architecture ever after. Yet it is unclear how far Loos had thought through the consequences of his new design idea in the early summer of 1909. The first ground-floor plan he prepared of the building (no early sections have survived) offers no hint at the complex arrangement of spaces that he would introduce on the mezzanine level.

This poses yet another question, perhaps the most important one concerning the building's design. There was no precedent for this sort of spatial play in Loos's works. The handful of architectural commissions and projects that he had completed before undertaking the Michaelerplatz building were all more or less conventional exercises in spatial planning, dependent on standard volumes positioned on undifferentiated horizontal levels. The single exception is an undated sketch of an atrium house (fig. 52).

Loos evidently produced the drawing in 1909, in all likelihood around the same time he was working on his design for Goldman & Salatsch.[5] It shows four stories of what appears to be a taller building with a tower. The reserved classical detailing on the façade and tower block recalls his design for the War Ministry project. But the interior seems to be related to the Michaelerplatz design. The accompanying section discloses evidence of a Raumplan. It is most conspicuous in the transition from the office to the kitchen above, which are connected by a spiral staircase. The room adjacent to the office is arranged as a traditional piano nobile, with a high ceiling. The kitchen and office, by contrast, are compressed—a pointed example of Loos's desire to build economically. Whether this design preceded his work on the Michaelerplatz building or came later is impossible to determine, but it reveals that he was already beginning to consider how the Raumplan might be applied to different situations.

Loos left no explanation for why he took this extraordinary step. Perhaps he had been thinking about it for some time, or perhaps it was a response to the particular needs of the tailor shop. Perhaps the impetus for it had come from Goldman, who had a distinct vision about the layout of the new store.

In his architectonic designs, Loos displayed a peculiar disjuncture: he often pursued new ideas, but only rarely was he a true experimenter. The exception is the way he handled space. From the time of the Michaelerplatz commission until his death, he investigated and reinvestigated strategies of spatial manipulation, testing varied means to foster pleasing, affective, and functional volumes. The trajectory of his later works—mostly villas—was toward ever-greater spatial complexity and control. His late houses, the Moller and the Müller villas, for example, are attempts to enhance—to vitalize—the rituals of daily life. Loos's application of the Raumplan to the Goldman & Salatsch shop, however, seems to have sprung from other concerns. From the start he appears to have concentrated on heightening the feeling of exclusivity and privacy. The shifts and disconnections he would introduce into the second-story mezzanine all seem calculated to segment the space into functional zones, ensuring that the clients' needs and the requirements of making clothing were well served. Goldman's experience in these matters and his input must have been essential for Loos.

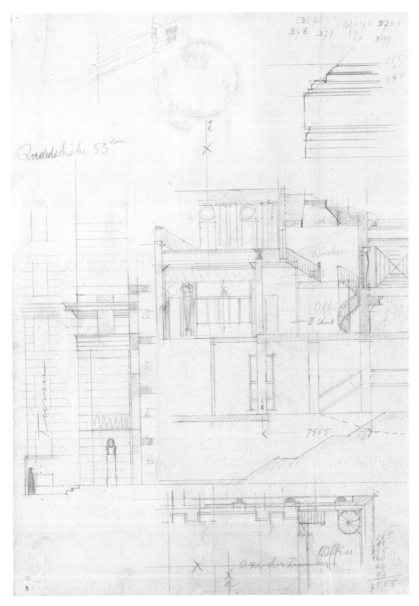

FIG. 52 Adolf Loos, drawing of an atrium house with tower, c. 1909. Pencil on paper, 15 ⅜ × 11 ⅛ in. (39.1 × 28.3 cm). Graphische Sammlung Albertina, Vienna, ALA 528.

No full plans from this period have come down to us, but it is clear from some of the drawings Loos made in the late summer that he had a well-developed conception of the interiors — especially the complex spatial play on the mezzanine. The sketch he made of this space on August 11 shows that he had already begun to work out the different heights (they are shown in the drawing, in centimeters) of each space, stair, and landing (see fig. 35). How he worked out the sequencing and placement of the different areas is impossible to determine, but these ideas were clearly in his mind very early in the design process.

The grouping and articulation of the spaces Loos would adopt for the shop suggest that he sought a means to overcome the standard interior arrangement of the Viennese Warenhäuser. The newest Warenhäuser, such as Fellner and Helmer's Gerngroß store, offered an impression of openness and transparency (fig. 53). The Gerngroß interior functioned exactly as its owners had directed — as a series of stacked platforms for displaying and selling goods. The sweeping twin stairways, great glass-roofed court, and open loggias all performed as devices for the enticement of its customers.

Loos's determination to overcome the Warenhaus modus — to counter the vulgarity of such popular merchandising — drove his conception of the interiors, just as it did that of the exterior. In his pursuit of a new refinement for the store he returned to his earlier works, to the original Goldman & Salatsch shop and the salon for Ebenstein. The problem was that both of those spaces were very small; the question that must have concerned Loos was how to adapt their elements to a much larger space — without falling prey to the tasteless ostentation of the Warenhäuser.

He would do so in great measure through rigorous segmentation, through dividing and subdividing the various sales and fitting areas. In the main downstairs space he was able to achieve this by introducing counters, vitrines, and two cashier stands. These ideas, as his early sketches show, had been in his mind from the beginning.

For the upstairs areas, which were to house the reception, changing, and fitting spaces, Loos resorted to other devices. Through the application of the Raumplan, he partitioned this zone, granting each area a distinctive identity. The shifting levels — many of the spaces are reached by going up or down short staircases — established a series of displaced thresholds, bounded by railings or low walls. The stair from the ground floor to the upper sales areas, which splits into two routes, serves as a screen; it was, for Loos, another means of ensuring privacy. All of these became tools of segregation. The effect was one not only of a certain intimacy — an idea at complete remove from the Warenhaus type — but, also, of a notable complexity. If the open floors of the Gerngroß store were based on continuous movement and sight lines, the spaces in the new Goldman & Salatsch store — on especially the mezzanine levels — were about

FIG. 53 Ferdinand Fellner and Hermann Helmer, Warenhaus Gerngroß, Mariahilfer Straße 44–46, Vienna, 1902–4. View showing the grand stair. Bildarchiv Foto Marburg.

FIG. 54 Robert Örley, Sanatorium Luithlen, Auersperg Straße 9, Vienna, 1907 – 8. Bildarchiv der österreichischen Nationalbibliothek, Vienna.

containment. And though there is an unmistakable coherence and order to these spaces, they are neither easily legible nor typical responses to modern building. The concrete frame in the hands of most of Loos's contemporaries became a means to prevail over traditional enclosed spaces through openness; for him, it was a mechanism to curtail and bind volumes.

Because we know so little about Loos's design process in the fall of 1909, it is difficult even to speculate about how his idea of the building evolved. But one thing is evident: what drove his thinking had to do largely with meeting the requirements of the salon. The form of the remainder of the building appears to have crystallized only gradually. In terms of spatial planning, the upper floors, intended for apartments, were wholly conventional, scarcely deviating from the plans for other new residential buildings in the city. There is no attempt at a Raumplan or at other modern spacemaking there. Most of the rooms are regular, orthogonal boxes, and — in keeping with standard practice for the apartments of the Viennese *Großbürgertum* — they are arranged *enfilade* (in a straight line). Loos's only concession to newer planning ideas was the expansion, in some instances, of these passages between the principal spaces.

It also appears that Loos's focus on the store carried over to the design of the building's façades. Only gradually, it seems, did his ideas about the exterior finish on the upper stories evolve. If he had determined almost from the start to shroud the lower stories in marble, the detailing for the building's upper portion — as his later pronouncements make plain — was a secondary issue for him.

Loos was already certain, though, when he began work on the commission in late July or early August, that he would split the façade; the upper stories would be articulated simply since they were to be residential, and, therefore, in his mind required no "artistic" elaboration. But what that would entail precisely would be determined only later.

In thinking about the upper façades, Loos was assuredly influenced by another new Viennese building, Robert Örley's Sanatorium Luithlen, on the Auersperg Straße in the eighth district (fig. 54).

Örley was one of the few architects in the city with whom Loos maintained a close friendship. Only a few years younger than Loos — he was born in Vienna in 1876 — he was the son of a local cabinetmaker. To prepare him to take over his father's large business, he learned the trade, and, while still an apprentice, he entered the Kunstgewerbeschule to study drawing. After graduating, he undertook a year long trip to Italy, then traveled to France, Germany, England, and the Netherlands. Along the way he decided to become an architect. When he described the plans for a new house his father had commissioned as "miserable," the elder Örley challenged him to produce better ones. With the aid of friends who were students at the Technical University, he completed the design. Later, he continued his training and earned a certification as a master builder.[6]

Örley's first independent commission, an apartment building on the Lazarettgasse completed in 1901, drew the admiration of Hoffmann, Plečnik, and many of the other younger Secessionists. But by then, Örley, who had offered a spirited defense of Loos's Café Museum, had earned a reputation for his independence. The episode forged a strong bond between him and Loos. They discovered they shared a deep appreciation for each other's work and for the importance of handicraft. They also shared a belief in developing their buildings "from the inside out."[7]

Örley's first works drew from the language of the Jugendstil, but, by 1905, he had begun to steer a new course, like Loos, between proto-rationalism and a revival of classicism. His design for the Sanatorium Luithlen, a private hospital for the treatment of skin and venereal diseases, exemplified his turn toward a new functionalism: among the building's innovative features were two large glass-framed operating rooms positioned along the roofline to take full advantage of the natural light.

Loos must have been equally impressed by the building's exteriors. Örley treated the inner façades, which enclosed a large courtyard, matter-of-factly, avoiding any elaboration. It was an undeniable augury of the upper façade of the Michaelerplatz building. Loos must have taken lessons, too, from the sanatorium's street-side façades. In Örley's scrupulous division between the ground floor and upper stories and his recourse to simple stringcourses are harbingers of the two solutions — the plain one and the one with horizontal banding — that Loos would put forward while working out the final disposition of the Goldman & Salatsch Building.

Completed just a year before Loos embarked on his own attempt to capture a new modern expression, Örley's design confirmed his belief in simplicity as the source of a new vernacular — a language that he would use boldly in his hymn of praise to the present.

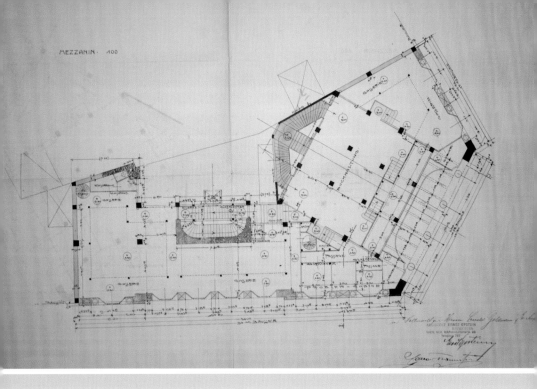

7

ORNAMENT AND CRIME

By the end of 1909, Loos and Epstein had completed a preliminary version of the project. Sometime before December, Loos constructed a model of the building. He showed it to several of his friends, including Schaukal and Örley, and, also, to Goldman and Aufricht.[1] From descriptions — the model no longer exists — it seems to have displayed the upper stories with little or no applied ornament. Örley wrote afterward that he thought the building "promised to be something good." He noted, though: "In the beginning, there will be a great deal of criticism."[2] Schaukal was fascinated with the "naked" upper stories (which he said he much preferred to the more elaborate lower section), but he, too, sensed that they would be controversial. He warned Loos that he thought he would face a bitter fight with public opinion.[3]

Loos was undeterred. He was determined to pursue his assault on ornament, come what may. In September he had begun to make arrangements to present a public lecture on the topic in Berlin.[4]

His contact there was the composer, art dealer, and publisher Herwarth Walden. Born Georg Lewin, in 1878, Walden had studied composition and piano in Berlin and Florence. In the early years of the century he wrote modern *Lieder,* but he is now remembered as the founder of the Expressionist magazine *Der Sturm,* which he launched in 1910.[5] Loos had met him only a short time before. In April 1909, Walden had taken over the directorship of the biweekly magazine *Das Theater,* and, in June of that year, during a trip to Vienna, he approached Kraus about writing for it. It was then that Kraus introduced him to Loos (fig. 55).[6] Both men recognized in Walden a kindred spirit, and they began corresponding with him.

Walden arranged for Loos to present his lecture, which he titled "Critique of Applied Art," at the gallery of the prominent modern art dealer Paul Cassirer on November 11. No manuscript or notes for it have survived, but reports in the Berlin newspapers offer a glimpse of what he said — and how it was received.

Loos had never given a public talk before, and he arrived in Berlin unprepared. (In a note to Walden a short time before, he reported that he was planning to travel the day of the lecture and would stop over in Dresden for a few hours to work on the talk.)[7] It seems that rather than writing out a full manuscript he merely jotted down a few notes. Consistent with his beliefs, Loos attacked the traditional applied artists and their use of ornament for objects of daily use.[8] But his presentation was neither particularly coherent nor well presented. Inexperienced and ill prepared, he rambled on. Loos would become a brilliant speaker, but in 1909 he still had much to learn.

The lecture was also poorly attended. There had been little publicity, and Loos was still unknown in Berlin. Most of the people there — probably no more than two dozen in all — were friends of Walden's or Cassirer's. They were generally receptive to his message, but Loos had hoped to arouse a controversy, and

FIG. 55 Adolf Loos with Karl Kraus (center) and Herwarth Walden (right), late October 1909 (?). Karl Kraus Collection, Special Collections and Archives, University of Massachusetts at Amherst.

he was deeply disappointed with the response.[9] Almost immediately he began forming plans to present a more strident assault on ornament in a public talk in Vienna in January.

In late December Loos traveled to Leysin to visit Bessie for the Christmas holiday. He left for Switzerland on December 23 but returned to Vienna around New Year's Day. A few days later he went back to Leysin, this time accompanied by Kokoschka. He thought that Kokoschka, who had never been abroad, would benefit from the chance to travel, and that he could look after Bessie and provide her company. To aid Kokoschka's budding career, Loos also made contact with a number of prominent Swiss he knew, asking them to sit for portraits.

Kokoschka later recalled that Loos did not have the money to pay Bessie's bill at the sanatorium. He brought along a number of valuable Oriental carpets, which he sold; he used the proceeds to settle the account.[10] After a week in Leysin he left Kokoschka in nearby Les Avants and went back to Vienna.

Over the next week he must have labored intensively on his talk, which he presented on January 21. This time he wrote out a full script, intending to read it. In the end, though, he seems to have adlibbed much of it.

The sponsor for the event was the Akademischer Verband für Literatur und Musik (Academic Association for Literature and Music), a student group that regularly held evenings of modern music and readings of new literary works. To rouse interest, Loos chose an incendiary title: "Ornament and Crime." It would be the opening salvo in his public anti-ornament crusade, which he would follow with an even more visible strike, his new building on Michaelerplatz.

So much has been written about "Ornament and Crime" since that day that its origins and meanings have been obscured. Most later accounts place the date of its composition in 1908 (the result of a misdating when the essay was first published in German two decades later). But all of the evidence suggests that Loos did not begin work on it until after his talk in Berlin, and he probably completed it only a short time before he presented it.[11]

In most respects, "Ornament and Crime" extended the line of argument from "Critique of Applied Art." But its central ideas extended back nearly a decade, repeating assertions and even exact phrases from his earlier writings. Loos had polished its themes over the years in his impromptu coffeehouse lectures. (Scheu, Kraus, and Schaukal had all cited its key pronouncements in their portraits of Loos in the preceding months and years, only leading to further confusion about when he had written it.[12])

Its argument can be readily summarized: like embryos, humans in their development pass through a series of stages on their way to full adulthood. Cultures replicate this evolution, moving from more primitive states to more advanced ones. The standards of acceptable behavior also evolved over time. Thus, what is moral or appropriate in a primitive culture is often considered criminal or degenerate behavior in a more advanced one, just as what is acceptable in the behavior of children is not appropriate for adults. The unfettered use of ornament may be fitting for an aboriginal Papuan, but, over time, such decoration loses its relevance. A modern, urban culture no longer needs ornament, and it is incapable of generating new ornament that is both genuine and meaningful. Ornament may still be suitable for peasants living in the Austrian empire's outlying villages, but not for a modern Viennese. For this reason, Loos argued, the efforts of the Secessionists to create modern ornament were not only culturally misguided but also socially injurious because those who actually made it, craftspeople, were not adequately compensated for their work, and the rapid change in fashion further wasted workers' labor. If someone wished to ornament an object for his or her pleasure, or to revel in ornament from the past, that was one thing, but ornament could "no longer be produced by someone living on the cultural level of today."[13]

But few would have remembered the talk if that is all Loos had said. He realized, after his Berlin lecture, that he needed more forceful images to fix his ideas in the minds of his listeners. From the title to its references to primitive Papauans tattooing themselves and eating their enemies — everything was conceived to shock and incite reply. His linkage of criminality to modern designers (in the original text, he mentioned not only Olbrich and the Munich designer Otto Eckmann, but also Hoffmann) was provocative — and intentionally so. He had meticulously honed a polemic to excite and inflame.

The audience that first heard the lecture that January day did not react as Loos had hoped, however. Only a single report of the event has come to light, in the Viennese newspaper *Fremden-Blatt,* and the unsigned review offers several surprises. The reporter noted that the lecture lasted "barely a half hour," and he castigated Loos for being a less-than-scintillating speaker: "Adolf Loos," he wrote, slightly tongue-in-cheek, "is not a speaker in the usual sense; his lecture was lacking somewhat on ornament, on rhetorical accompaniment."[14] The reporter also observed that Loos received "loud applause" at the end, and that afterward, there was an "often very animated discussion," but one that "for the most part did not extend much beyond superfluous banter."[15]

Once more Loos had failed to stir up real controversy. Given his audience, this was hardly surprising. Undoubtedly many who were there were his friends and acquaintances. And another sizable group likely in attendance were architecture students from the Technical University and the Academy of Fine Arts, a large number of whom had already encountered Loos in the coffeehouses. Most were sympathetic to modernism and familiar with his anti-ornament views.[16]

Loos's close pairing of ornament and crime was an attempt to spread a combustible mixture of ideas. But too often absent from discussions of the piece is that he was using satire to make his point. The Viennese Expressionist poet Albert Ehrenstein, a member of the circle around Kraus and Loos, wrote of one of Loos's later talks: "[He] presented his serious thoughts in an extremely amusing form. The anecdotes, which he used to illustrate the lack of culture on the part of the Viennese, were like precise target shooting."[17] This was lost on many later commentators. The English architecture critic Reyner Banham, for example, would dismiss "Ornament and Crime" as "*Schlagobers-Philosophie* that whisks up into an exciting dish on the café table, and then collapses as you look at it, like a cooling soufflé."[18]

There is indeed much in the later published text that is now dated and airily insubstantial. It is saturated with the ideas of late nineteenth-century thinkers, from the Italian criminologist Cesare Lombroso, who had asserted that there was a distinct connection between tattoos and criminality, since only criminals and primitive peoples tattooed themselves; Ernst Haeckel, who had famously maintained that there was a relationship between the "history of the embryo (ontogeny)" and the "history of race (phylogeny)"; and Max Nordau, who assailed the early modernists in the same terms as Lombroso had the wayward and the backward "atavists" he encountered in his clinical practice.[19] Loos's main point nonetheless emerges clearly and powerfully: ornament in most instances no longer had either meaning or purpose in modern times; to continue to employ traditional ornament violated the spirit of the new age.

But Loos was not, as later commentators would often insist, calling for the wholesale eradication of ornament. He wanted only to banish ornament that was no longer appropriate or that no longer had meaning. Ornament had no place in objects of daily use because in Loos's view it was associated solely with art, not with ordinary, functional articles. He did not exclude the possibility that ornament might still have a role in monumental building, whose purpose was much different from such articles of daily use. He summarized this essential point in the only line italicized in the later published version of the talk: "*Evolution der kultur ist gleichbedeutend mit dem entfernen des ornamentes aus dem gebrauchsgegenstände*" (The evolution of culture is synonymous with the removal of ornament from objects of daily use).[20] This would be a guiding premise in Loos's design for the Michaelerplatz building, and it would ultimately spawn much of the criticism and misunderstanding about his work.

When Loos presented "Ornament and Crime" in early January 1910, however, he was not issuing a manifesto about his new building — at least not directly. He was responding instead to the ongoing debate in the German-language architectural press about the use and appropriateness of ornament — a discussion that had preoccupied him for some time.

The period between 1907 and the beginning of 1910 saw the publication of a number of articles about modern ornament.[21] The question had been stirred up in part by the ornamental excesses of the Jugendstil, but it was also an outcome of the mounting discussion in Germany and Austria about the functionalist architecture and design that was then just beginning to emerge in both countries. The immediate trigger for the debate seems to have been the appearance of an essay by the German critic Joseph August Lux in *Innen-Dekoration* in 1907. Lux, who also wrote studies of Olbrich and Wagner, asserted that the "renewal of ornament" by the reform architects and designers at the turn of the century was the "first creative accomplishment of modern art."[22] His and similar pronouncements from several other writers touched off a series of responses from critics of the Jugendstil, most of them arguing that the recourse to ornament had been not the salvation of design but a serious misstep.

The following April, Schaukal published a scathing attack on those calling for the development of modern ornament. His article, in the German monthly *Deutsche Kunst und Dekoration,* "Gegen das Ornament" (Against Ornament), begins with a paragraph that could have come directly from Loos's pen: " If a thinking person today, who is vexed, even saddened, by the commercialized culture of the present, asks himself why it is that the world, at least in terms of that which is man-made, has become so very ugly and disconcerting, it will occur to him, if he has sharp eyes and a sense of the joy of beauty, what the answer is: the evil foe is ornament."[23] Schaukal condemned ornament as "superfluous" and "purposeless." He characterized the work of the Secessionists as a symptom of the "ornamental disease" (Ornamentkrankheit), and he lauded Loos as the only architect who had a clear vision of the future — one without ornament.[24]

The German critic Wilhem Michel responded in *Innen-Dekoration* in July 1909, presenting a spirited defense of traditional architectural ornament but agreeing with Schaukal that the Secessionists' tendency to divorce ornament from the logic of materials and structure — in Michel's words, the "kulturlose Emanzipierung des Ornaments" (uncultured emancipation of ornament) — had resulted in a mounting loss of faith in ornamental design. He suggested, however, that this development might have had a positive impact: "In all likelihood, the historic verdict of the future will be that the Jugendstil did achieve something positive: at least it possessed the will to forge something creatively new. It was destructive and it generated new possibilities — though the latter was only an indirect byproduct."[25]

Loos had followed the debate closely; he may have been the most voluble of those assailing the continued reliance on ornament, but he was far from alone.[26]

Loos spent the last week of January and the first part of February working out the final details for the new building. Sometime in late February or early March he and Epstein submitted the drawings to the city building office for approval. All bear the signatures of "Architekt Ernst Epstein" and Goldman and Aufricht. A few also include the stamps of Eduard Frauenfeld, the contractor, and Pittel & Brausewetter, who were responsible for the structural engineering of the project. Loos's name is notably absent.[27] Lacking a university degree, he could not legally use the title of architect. (Only after World War I would he be granted the right.)

There are several preliminary sets of drawings for the building. The earliest, the so-called Vorprojekt, or preliminary project, was probably finished in January or February. These drawings differ from the final version in a number of details. The upper mezzanine gallery is not yet fully developed; the stairs from the ground floor of the main shop to the mezzanine level are positioned on either side of the room, not in the center, as they would later be; and the two corners of the front façade lack their sharply profiled edges.[28]

A short time later, Loos and Epstein prepared another set of plans, this time with a fully developed "Mezzanin-Galerie," or entresol, positioned on the second floor of the shop, and with sharply profiled corners along the main façade. It was this version they submitted and that the city council approved on March 11, 1910 (figs. 56, 57).[29] The council's only proviso at the time, following a request from councilman Hans Schneider, was that the roof be no higher than four meters, "in keeping with the surroundings."[30]

The swift approval of the design no doubt had much to do with the fact that the façade drawings deviated markedly from what would be the executed design (fig. 58). The windows in the four upper stories are shown with traditional — if understated — surrounds, and there are inset panels on the uppermost story and pediments surmounting the windows just above the mezzanine level. The amalgam of the columns and marble veneer on the lower portion, together with the classically derived detailing on the upper stories, served to normalize the building, diminishing noticeably its hard-edged look. The upper façade details almost certainly came from Epstein: not only are they consistent with his earlier work (including a preliminary drawing for the façades he apparently made in late 1909 or early 1910), but the drawings are in his hand.

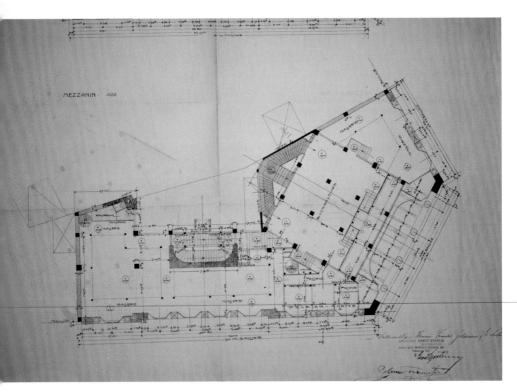

FIG. 56 Adolf Loos, submitted plans for the Goldman & Salatsch Building showing the ground floor, March 11, 1910. Plan- und Schriftenkammer der Magistratsamt (MA 37), Vienna.

This raises yet another question about the design process and about Loos's intentions. If Örley's and Schaukal's descriptions of the model are accurate, and Loos had intended from the beginning to eliminate ornament from the building's upper stories, why submit these drawings?

The most likely explanation for the modifications is that Loos, fearing a negative response, offered a more acceptable version to the authorities to win quick

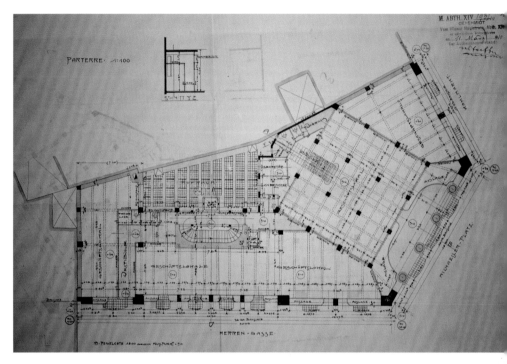

FIG. 57 Loos, submitted plans for the Goldman & Salatsch Building showing the mezzanine level, March 11, 1910. Plan- und Schriftenkammer der Magistratsamt (MA 37), Vienna.

FIG. 58 Loos, submitted plans for the Goldman & Salatsch Building showing the façades, March 11, 1910. Pencil on paper, 17 ³/₈ × 32 ⁷/₈ in. (44 × 83.5 cm). Graphische Sammlung Albertina, Vienna, ALA 250.

approval. He likely planned to substitute a more radical design later, when the building was under construction. This is precisely what happened. Yet it is equally possible that Loos, as he later claimed, had not yet reached a final decision about the treatment of the upper façades and wanted to install the marble veneer first to gauge its effect. He and the clients may have simply asked Epstein to prepare a passable design to hasten the permitting process.

Another reason Loos may have turned over the task to Epstein was that he was absorbed with other matters. Throughout this time Loos was immersed in his campaign to promote his friends and protégés. At the beginning of 1911 he helped to arrange a musical evening for the Schönberg circle. The concert took place on January 14 in the Ehrbar Saal. Among the pieces performed was Schönberg's Gurrelieder, with a six-part piano accompaniment arranged by Webern. The event turned out to be a triumph for Schönberg — his first real success in Vienna. In late February, Loos arranged for Walden to give a concert of his Lieder at his apartment in the Gisela Straße, and he and Kraus were busy collecting subscriptions and donations to aid the launch of Walden's magazine, Der Sturm, in March.[31]

Loos was also facing personal problems. Altenberg was once more suffering from a nervous breakdown, threatening suicide. And Loos was still having trouble finding the money to keep Bessie at the sanatorium; early in the year he was forced to move her to a less expensive pension in the village of Les Avants, above Montreux.[32]

To publicize the release of Der Sturm and his own work, Loos agreed to return to Berlin and speak again, this time to present "Ornament and Crime."[33] Hoping for a better response, he sent Walden one hundred crowns to advertise the lecture and asked him to arrange for publicity in the newspapers.[34]

He gave the talk on March 3. Again it was held in Cassirer's gallery (fig. 59). Despite Loos's efforts, once more it was a disappointment. The event was largely ignored in the mainstream press; only the Berliner Tageblatt ran a short announcement the day of the lecture.[35] An unsigned write-up in the same newspaper the following day noted that it had been sparsely attended: "The twenty people in the audience yesterday gave him a warm round of applause."[36]

But to Loos's surprise (and, evidently, perverse delight), a second, unsigned review appeared a week and a half later in the Berlin satirical magazine Der Ulk. It made light of his ideas, painting him as a fanatic who wanted to have "fifty of Berlin's most prominent citizens" — its leading industrialists and pattern makers — tortured and jailed for their alleged criminal application of ornament.[37] Loos penned an acid response, a one-line rebuttal that appeared in the April 7, 1910, edition of Der Sturm: "Dear Ulk: And I tell you, there will come a day when incarceration in a jail cell decorated by court wallpaperer [Eduard] Schulz or Professor Van de Velde will be considered a more severe sentence."[38]

The *Ulk* satire turned out to be much-wanted publicity, but by the time the piece appeared, Loos had already left Vienna.[39] Shortly after his return from Berlin he made plans to travel to North Africa, Italy, and Greece to acquire marble for the new building.[40]

He first went to Morocco, then to Algeria. In Ain Smara, near the ancient city of Constantine in the mountains of central Algeria, he found a source for high-quality marble and purchased several blocks. (He would end up using the stone in his later interior for the Café Capua.)[41] By early April he was in Greece.[42] He traveled to the island of Evia and bought a large quantity of blue-green Cipollino marble for the building's exterior cladding and four columns, then he went to Skyros, where he acquired the marble for the lower portion of the staircase leading to the upper-floor apartments. Along the way he visited the ruins of the old city in Corinth.[43] By month's end he had reached Italy. In Cararra he selected

FIG. 59 Advertisement for Loos's second Berlin presentation of "Ornament and Crime" published in *Der Sturm,* March 3, 1910, 8.

marble for the main floor of the tailor shop and for the upper staircase. After brief stops in Bellagio, on Lake Como, and Pallanza, on Lake Maggiore, where he met Bessie, he arrived back in Vienna.[44]

Immediately upon his return Loos launched into work for another commission, a villa for his old friend Hugo Steiner and his wife, Lilly. Loos had met the couple before the turn of the century through Kraus. Kraus and Hugo Steiner had been friends and classmates at Gymnasium, and they had continued to see each other in the intervening years. Loos also developed a close friendship with the Steiner family. Steiner's mother, Katharina, was the owner of the Steiner feather shop for which Loos had designed stores in 1904 and 1906, and Hugo and Lilly had commissioned one of his first designs, their apartment on Gumpendorfer Straße, in 1900.[45] When the couple acquired a lot in the suburb of Hietzing, on the city's western edge, they asked Loos to design a single-family villa for them.

Loos faced a daunting problem. Building codes for the area permitted only single-story structures with a mansard roof; the Steiners wanted a much larger house on their small lot. He solved the problem by devising what was essentially a four-story building, one level of which was mostly below grade and the upper two concealed by a large, curving standing-seam metal roof (fig. 60).

Inside, Loos employed his now standard vocabulary of modern English-inspired furnishings and replicas, sheathing many of the spaces with extensive wainscoting and beamed ceilings. He made broad openings between the main public rooms, but the house had none of the sophisticated spatial planning of the Goldman & Salatsch salon; his introduction of the Raumplan to his villas would come only later.

Loos submitted the plans for the Steiner House to the building authorities in mid-April. More pressingly, he was concerned with preparing a new set of façade drawings for the Michaelerplatz building. Construction had commenced

FIG. 60 Adolf Loos, house for Hugo and Lilly Steiner, St. Veitgasse 10, Vienna, 1910. Photo by Wolfgang Thaler.

OPPOSITE
FIG. 61 Drawing of the reinforcement for the front concrete frame of the Goldman & Salatsch Building, 1:250, 1910. Courtesy Hermann Czech, Vienna.

while he was away, and the contractor was making quick progress. One of the remaining issues had to do with the structure of the building's front portion. Loos had specified that the four marble columns that formed the entry not be load bearing. This meant that the entire structure above had to be carried by a single concrete beam supported by the two piers at the corners. The beam needed to extend across the full length of the opening — slightly more than forty-six feet (fourteen meters). The space between the tops of the columns and the new floor was extremely narrow, a little more than fifteen and half inches (forty centimeters), too slender for a standard reinforced concrete support. The engineers at Pittel & Brausewetter came up with a novel solution to the problem by hanging the iron reinforcing from the frame above, thus suspending the lintel over the entry (fig. 61).[46]

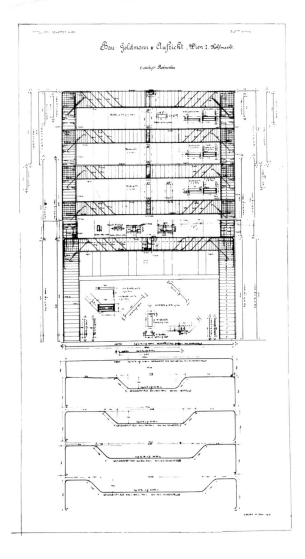

Work on the frame proceeded quickly. By the end of June it was nearly complete. The decision to suspend the lintel had resulted in a thin, attenuated profile. It was a conspicuously modern effect, but one that Loos would soon conceal with the columns (fig. 62).

With the completion of the building's basic structure, decisions about the final disposition of the interiors and façades — and approval for them — were due. Loos petitioned the authorities for two sets of changes. The first came in early July, for minor alterations to the organization of the ground and mezzanine levels of the store and to the stairs leading to the apartments. The more important changes had to do with the composition of the façades. In late July, Loos and Epstein submitted a new set of exterior drawings. The renderings, dated July 25, 1910, showed the building not only with the new lower roof profile, as Schneider had requested, but also with all of the ornamental details removed from the upper four floors (fig. 63). The effect was striking, revealing the full impact of its radically simplified exteriors.

But in a curious twist, Loos submitted a second set of drawings bearing the identical date. They showed the façades with evenly spaced horizontal "meander" bands — composed of alternating dark and light squares in a "wave" pattern — extending across the full length of the surface (fig. 64).[47] In an interview in

FIG. 62 Goldman & Salatsch Building under construction, summer 1910. *Österreichischer Betonverein. Bericht über die IV. ordentliche Hauptversammlung Wien, am 15. April 1912* (Vienna, 1912).

FIG. 63 Adolf Loos (with Ernst Epstein), revised façade designs for the Goldman & Salatsch Building, approved July 25, 1910. Black line print on paper, 15 ¾ × 32 ½ in. (39.9 × 82.5 cm). Graphische Sammlung Albertina, Vienna, ALA 356.

FIG. 64 Loos (with Epstein), revised façade designs for the Goldman & Salatsch Building, submitted July 25, 1910. Plan- und Schriftenkammer der Magistratsamt (MA 37), Vienna.

September, after the controversy broke, he said that he was still undecided about the material to be used for the banding: "Whether they are porcelain or terra-cotta, cement or artificial stone, or some other material, whether these stripes have a profile or are set into the wall," he could not yet say. It would depend entirely "on the impact of the marble veneer."[48]

Here once more, we can only guess at Loos's intentions. It may be that he was indeed undecided about the final disposition of the upper façades. He used similar horizontal banding in several other designs, including his projects for a hotel on the Friedrich Straße, in 1908, the War Ministry building of the following year, and, most famously, his later unrealized house for Josephine Baker in Paris. It would not have been out of character for him to employ such a visual device.[49] Perhaps, in the midst of building his first important building, he really was of two minds, wavering between quite different solutions.

But Loos may have already resolved to leave the upper façades blank and submitted the second set of renderings as a way of satisfying the authorities. Two bits of evidence speak for the latter interpretation. The first is the testimony of Schaukal and Örley about the appearance of the model, which hints that he had made his decision by the end of 1909. Even more telling is that the first set of drawings he submitted in late July displayed the façades almost exactly as they would be realized. In any event, the municipal authorities sanctioned the design, and construction on the building continued unabated.

The stage was now set for the bitter fight that would commence that fall.

8

A MONSTROSITY

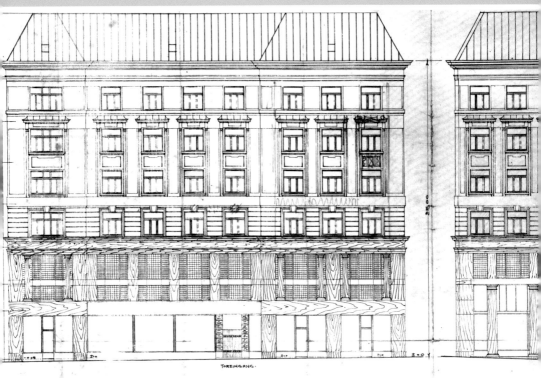

TOREINGANG.

Work on the new building continued through the summer of 1910. By mid-September the upper façades had received a taut plaster finish and the scaffolding had been removed. Glaringly absent were the horizontal meander bands or any other form of elaboration. And that was not all. The window openings, of sharply varying sizes, seemed strangely discordant, and many of those on the lower floors did not align with the ones above.

Almost immediately, the newspapers took notice. A short piece in the daily *Neuigkeits-Welt-Blatt* on September 17 reported that the strange new building had begun to attract attention. Passersby were referring to it as the "grain elevator" (*Kornspeicher*): "Because of its immense plainness, it stands out to pedestrians even from afar. It is constructed of completely smooth concrete walls, with square windows lacking moldings either above or below."[1]

But the unnamed reporter noted that changes were afoot: "The builder has received an order not to leave the façades quite so unadorned, and, in fact, those portions of the building from which the scaffolding has already been removed have once more been sheathed in scaffolding, and a façade is being applied that will undoubtedly correspond more closely to public taste."[2] Whether the municipal building office had interceded by the time the article appeared is uncertain. But by month's end, as several papers announced, the authorities had suspended the building permit.[3] The reason for the action, the *Fremden-Blatt* reported on September 30, was that the "execution of the façade did not correspond with the plans that had been submitted" — presumably referring to Loos's second approved façade design with the meander banding.[4]

The unusual action on the part of the authorities "caused a stir in architectural circles," the *Wiener Allgemeine Zeitung* reported. The problem, however, according to the paper, stemmed not from Loos but from the negligence of city officials, who had continued to condone "tasteless" and overblown works, with "cupolas, high roofs, towers, and balconies," while issuing a general prohibition against "façades that rely on naturally simple ordering."[5]

Loos, who was identified as the building's architect in all of the articles, defended his decision to leave the façades blank. He wanted to wait, he told one reporter, until the Cipollino marble was installed on the lower stories. Marble of this sort "has not been used in such a monumental way since the time of the Romans. Whether the façades will appear more serene or opulent will depend on the marble."[6]

The same day, in a lengthy piece in the morning edition of the conservative *Reichspost,* Loos offered further explanation. The design, he told readers, had been the result of his attempt to fashion a building that was appropriate to Viennese tradition and to its specific setting on Michaelerplatz. He founded his argument, as he would throughout the controversy, on local tradition. What befit one city, he wrote, was not suitable for another: "The brick buildings of Danzig would lose all of their attractiveness if they were transplanted to Vienna. . . . Danzig is a

city of exposed brick buildings, Vienna is a city of lime plaster [*Kalkputzstadt*]."
The flat, unadorned plaster surfaces, he insisted, were in keeping with "good
old Viennese plasterwork." In recent times, in the hands of less sensitive architects, such plasterwork "had been maltreated and prostituted . . . used to imitate
stone." To do so, Loos argued, was fundamentally dishonest: "A lime plaster finish
is a skin. Stone is constructive. Despite their similar properties, there is a great
difference in their artistic application." His building, immediately adjacent to the
imperial palace, required honesty and tastefulness. "If one wants to know if an
object is good or bad, one simply has to ask: would it be suitable for the palace?"[7]

Loos's task, he wrote, had been to design a "modern store" across from the
palace. To present an appropriate face to the square, he had elected to use
marble for the colonnade and cladding for the lower two levels, which housed
the Goldman & Salatsch store and other shops; the other four stories required
only a plaster surfacing, consistent with standard Viennese practice. "What
might be necessary for decoration, should be applied by hand, as the Baroque
masters had done." Every decision about the façade would be founded on his
desire to produce a work "in harmony with the imperial palace, the square, and
the city."[8]

The previous day Loos had met with municipal authorities in an effort to resolve
the matter. They visited the building site and, after some deliberation, decided to
reinstate the building permit. As Loos had requested, they would wait until the marble cladding on the lower stories had been installed before rendering judgment.[9]

FIG. 65. "The Grain Elevator Across from the Hofburg." *Illustrirtes Wiener Extrablatt,*
October 26, 1910.

That would have ended the matter had public outcry not begun to mount. A flurry of newspaper articles prompted increasing attention — and outrage. The *Wiener Allgemeine Zeitung* reported on September 29 that "in the course of the day, hundreds of curious onlookers stood around" gawking at the building.[10]

Vienna was no stranger to architectural controversy. Within memory of older Viennese was the contentious reception of the Vienna Opera, the first of the major public buildings erected along the Ringstrasse. Even before its completion, the massive neo-Renaissance building, the work of August Sicard von Sicardsburg and Eduard van der Nüll — the city's most accomplished architects at midcentury — had incited the wrath both of the critics and public, who thought its lucid massing and lean ornamental program were markedly inferior to the newly completed Heinrichshof opposite. And the chorus of criticism only swelled when, after construction began, the level of the Ringstrasse was raised a full meter, leaving the new building in what looked like a shallow hole. The new structure was likened to a "sunken chest," and wags began referring to it as the Königgrätz of architecture, an allusion to the disastrous battle of 1866 in which the Prussians had overwhelmed the poorly prepared Austrian forces. Even Emperor Franz Joseph publicly criticized the design. Despondent, van der Nüll — who had already been suffering from depression — hanged himself, and barely ten weeks later Sicardsburg died. Neither man lived to witness the building's completion.

Joseph Maria Olbrich's Secession Building, erected on nearby Karlsplatz, was similarly greeted with derision when it was completed in 1898. Locals referred to its open gilded dome as the Golden Cabbage, a reference to the nearby market, or "the Mahdi's tomb," because of its vaguely Eastern cast. But the discord over the Opera and Secession nearly paled in comparison to the contentious struggle over the proposed Vienna city museum on Karlsplatz, which was still raging when the Michaelerplatz controversy began.[11] In 1900 the municipal authorities had announced a competition for the building, set for completion in 1908, in time for the jubilee marking the emperor's sixtieth year on the throne. Wagner won, but his ebullient Jugendstil design drew the ire of conservatives, who thought it manifestly out of place next to Fischer von Erlach's Baroque Karlskirche. Wagner prepared a series of variant projects over the next eight years. Finally, in late 1909, he erected on the site a partial full-scale mock-up of his latest design.

What Wagner thought would tip opinion in his favor brought only further censure: the historic monuments commission declared that the building would be "injurious" to the image of the celebrated church and "irreparably destroy one of the most valued views of it."[12] (The debate would continue for several more years, and it was only in the 1950s that the museum, based on a design by Oswald Haerdtl, Josef Hoffmann's former assistant, was realized.)

There was ample precedent, then, for the fight over the Michaelerplatz. None-theless, Loos, in a short article in another newspaper, the *Illustrirtes Wiener Extrablatt,* announced — more than a little disingenuously — that he had been startled by the attention:

Both the clients and I were surprised that the conflict between us and the city building office had reached the press. We thought we could resolve the dispute quietly. We were, and are now, of the opinion that, of course, we did require the consent of the council, but that it was not within the purview of this body to determine the sequence of work. Our approved plan shows a façade with the ground floor and mezzanine clad in Greek marble, the other four floors in plaster. The decoration of this plaster façade is made up of horizontal meander stripes, spaced equally from the cornice to the mezzanine.[13]

He repeated that he was uncertain what the impact of the marble cladding would be: "Therefore, I suggested to the building authorities that we should wait until we can see the effect of the marble, and only then would I make a request for the remainder of the façade."[14]

If Loos's intentions all along were to leave the façades blank, it was a daring gambit. Yet he seems to have been convinced that the sumptuous marble veneer would deflect much of the criticism. He was unwilling, though, to let the matter rest there. A few days later, on October 3, he published a lengthy satire in another newspaper, *Der Morgen.* He was grateful, he wrote, that the authorities had interceded, for their response had amounted to an advertisement: "My first building! Finally, a building!" Even more gratifying, he told his readers, the actions of the authorities had confirmed that he really was an artist: "I have been censured, censured by the police, just like Frank Wedekind and Arnold Schönberg."[15]

Lacking other commissions, he continued, he had been forced to rely on designing interiors

until one day a poor unfortunate had come to me and ordered plans for a build-ing. It was my tailor. This brave man — actually, two brave men — had delivered new suits to me year after year, and, patiently, every year, on the first of January, sent me a bill, which, I cannot deny, never got any smaller. . . . I warned the two brave men about me. In vain. They wanted to make my bill smaller — no, pardon me — not to give the building over to an officially certified architect. I said to them: Do you, men who have had sterling reputations up to now, want to have the authorities hanging around your necks? They did. And it happened, just as I said it would happen.[16]

If Loos thought the piece would stem the outcry, he was badly mistaken. Over the next several weeks, the newspapers, which had been content at first merely to report on the matter, became more and more critical, responding, it seems, to widespread negative public sentiment. Much of the negative response came, as one might imagine, from the city's many tabloids, which were all too eager to fan the flames of dispute in order to sell more papers. The most damaging criticism, though, came from the liberal newspapers, especially the *Neue Freie Presse,* which would remain a thorn in Loos's side for the next two years.

The newspaper's opposition was partly a reflection of its conservative stance in matters of art and design. The majority of its readership came from the older liberal-bourgeois elite, many of whom found the new modernism — especially functionalism — repugnant. The paper's opposition to Loos was also an attempt to settle scores with Kraus, who had repeatedly singled out the newspaper for its political and moral hypocrisy. Attacking his close friend was a way to get even.

But the chorus of outcry came from across the spectrum (with the exception of the Socialist newspapers). An editorial in the *Publizistische Blätter* on October 3 claimed that the authorities had been right to register their veto on "moral and aesthetic grounds. The throngs of the curious who have surrounded the building amount to a popular vote, sanctioning the decision of the building police to intercede."[17] And the *Illustrirtes Wiener Extrablatt* ran a photograph of the building, still partially enveloped in scaffolding, under the title: "The Grain Elevator on the Michaelerplatz" (fig. 65).[18] Newspapers in Berlin and Munich also took notice of the mounting controversy. The *Berlin Lokal-Anzeiger* commented (not quite accurately): "On the plans, he pretended that he intended to use ornament, but with the execution [of the façades] the building authorities caught him *in flagrante,* with disconcertingly bare marble walls."[19]

Matters went from bad to worse when the Vienna city council took up the question of the building at its meeting on October 21. One of the representatives, Karl Rykl, attacked Loos and his design, charging that the officials at the building office had failed to provide due diligence to protect the face of the city:

It is only with disdain and derision that such a tasteless building — one without a shred of feeling for architecture and design — can be erected across from Fischer von Erlach's masterpiece. Against such "away-with-architecture-and-ornament architects" [Los-von-Architektur-und-Ornamentik-Architekten — a pun on Loos's name], one must adopt a stand and register the strongest possible objections. We must undertake action against an architect such as this, whose intention, as is the case here, is to disfigure one of the city's most beautiful squares.[20]

But Rykl was not content merely to disparage the design. He demanded that the occupancy permit for what he called this "monstrosity of a building" (Scheusal von einem Wohnhaus) be delayed until the "entire façade can be brought into harmony with its surroundings."[21]

Rykl's attack no doubt was a sincere attempt to preserve the character of the Michaelerplatz. But, as Loos would soon discover, he had an ulterior motive: he was a sculptor and manufacturer of cast stone products, and the area he represented, the lower-middle-class seventh district, was heavily populated with traditional artisans. He had a vested interest in resisting the new architecture: he understood very well that a modernism à la Loos, which rejected traditional architectural ornament, posed a real threat to his livelihood and that of many of his constituents.

There were also larger political forces at work. Rykl was a member of the Christian Socialist party, which dominated the city government in Vienna. Founded by the populist Karl Lueger in 1893, the Austrian Christian Socialists drew on the urban lower middle class and the rural population for support. The party was staunchly Catholic (a number of its leading members were priests) and determinedly conservative. After victories in the 1895 and 1896 municipal elections, Lueger became mayor and embarked on an ambitious program of municipal socialism.[22]

Like most of the party leadership, he was anti-Semitic — at least in public. To challenge the Jewish-owned banks he established a municipal mortgage bank, and over the course of his fifteen-year administration he pursued various other "anti-capitalist" initiatives, seizing control of the street railways and electrical works and founding a city-owned gas company. Yet even Lueger's critics acknowledged his contributions to the city's development. He reformed the bureaucracy, built much of the new infrastructure, and led the charge to save the Vienna Woods. He was also a resolute supporter of Wagner and the other Secessionists.

But by the autumn of 1909 the aged Lueger, in constant pain and nearly blind from diabetes, was losing his clutch on power. Even before his death, in March 1910, the party was in disarray; the younger and more radical party members, whom he had long reined in and directed for his own causes, were restive.[23] His vice-mayor, Josef Neumayer, a member of the party's old guard who would succeed him, was nearly deaf, and he delegated much of the day-to-day decision-making to others.

The bulging power void led to a precipitous decline in the Christian Socialists' fortunes. The party began to experience setbacks at the ballot box as the Socialists gained growing acceptance from the working class. Rykl and the other rank-and-file Christian Socialists on the council sought new avenues to appeal to voters. In the controversy over the Michaelerplatz building they found the possibility of a cause célèbre, which they hoped might bring them back into favor with voters, especially with their conservative and lower-middle-class base. The building was an easy and logical target: it flew in the face of convention and petit-bourgeois Viennese taste.

But not all of the Christian Socialists agreed with Rykl's assault on Loos. The debate highlighted a split within the party's ranks: many in the leadership (including Neumayer and Albert Gessmann, another of the old party hands) who were better educated and more culturally sophisticated were untroubled by the design and saw no reason to interfere. But they were also wary of publicly endorsing a work that so many of their supporters found repugnant.

The whole matter also touched an exquisitely sensitive nerve in the Viennese body politic. It was not lost on anyone — whether politician or casual observer — that the new building was intended to house a large Jewish-owned clothing firm. The city's legions of small shopkeepers bitterly resented the competition from the new department stores, most of which were Jewish businesses. The emergence of these stores after 1860 had, in fact, fueled renewed anti-Jewish feelings in the city. From the start the Christian Socialists had worked to protect the *Gewerbestand* — the country's sizable artisanal class — from large-scale factories and retailers (the great majority of which were Jewish owned), promoting legislation to lessen competition from industrial concerns and regulate the trades.[24]

There was no mention of Goldman's or Aufricht's Jewish heritage in the press during the months of controversy about the Looshaus (and, it is worth noting, a number of Loos's harshest critics were Jewish). Still, anti-Semitism undoubtedly occupied a place in the debate. As a custom tailoring firm, Goldman & Salatsch was spared the opprobrium the mass retailers faced. Nevertheless, there was a prevailing hostility toward Jews among the city's lower middle class. And because so many of the clients of Vienna's modern architects and designers were Jewish, there was a widespread belief that the new style was linked with Jewish culture; many regarded it as alien and incompatible with the city's traditions. Rykl's attack thus issued from both political and economic reality and cultural conviction.

Loos, though, found a temporary reprieve. At the October 21 meeting, Neumayer, who by then had replaced Lueger as mayor, sided with Loos and his clients. He accepted Loos's argument that the current façade was provisional and proposed that he be given until the end of January 1911 to submit an acceptable design. At that point, Neumayer insisted, the plans would have to be followed exactly. It was the responsibility of the building office, he said, to ensure that the façade would not "disfigure the cityscape."[25]

The resolution, which the council adopted, did little to appease the most vocal detractors. In an article in the October 27 issue of *Die Zeit,* Josef Strzygowski, a conservative professor of art history at the University of Vienna, assailed the recent commercial buildings in the inner city, singling out Loos's design as an egregious example of the recent trend toward radical simplicity — one, he charged, that was very much at odds with the capital's historic architecture.[26] Adalbert Franz Seligmann, a painter and the art critic for the *Neue Freie Presse,* also cited Loos's design as one of the most inappropriate of the recent spate of modernist buildings in the inner city, pointing in particular to the discordance between its upper and lower sections.[27] And an unsigned editorial in the October issue of the *Wiener Bauindustrie-Zeitung* leveled similar charges at Loos, taking strong exception to his "humorous defense" of the building in *Der Morgen.*[28]

Even more troubling for Loos, another of the Christian Socialist representatives, Hans Schneider, took up the attack when the council met again in mid-November. Schneider was a conservative architect, well known and well connected in court circles. Early in his career he had worked on the restoration of the Lower Belvedere Palace, the Hoftheater, and the Hofburg itself, and a short time before his election to the council the Archduke Franz Ferdinand had named him director of the Central Commission for the Preservation of Historic Monuments. He was also, gratingly for Loos, the winner of the 1909 competition for the new Technical Museum. (Wagner, in fact, had won the competition, but eventually, after much political wrangling, Schneider was awarded the commission.) Schneider's design, a Neo-Baroque confection, insipid and undistinguished even by the standards of the official *Stilarchitektur,* touched off a vociferous debate between the "traditionalists" and the "reformers," becoming itself the target of a great deal of public denigration (fig. 66).[29]

FIG. 66. Hans Schneider, Technical Museum, Mariahilfer Straße 212, Vienna, 1909–13. Technisches Museum, Vienna.

The criticism had only emboldened Schneider and further incited his dislike of the modernists. In a speech before the council he unleashed a torrent of criticism, describing Loos's design as amateurish and ill considered. Taking up from Rykl, he set upon the building's bare upper stories with special vehemence, demanding that they be redesigned with new detailing. To illustrate his ideas he made quick pencil sketches on the second set of plans Loos had submitted in July, suggesting a traditional façade with moldings, inset panels, and rustication (fig. 67). He requested that Epstein, who was present at the meeting, make a full set of revisions based on his corrections. At Schneider's urging the council voted to deny Goldman and Aufricht an occupancy permit and levied a penalty of 18,000 crowns on them for having failed to carry out the project as it had been proposed.

Epstein complied with Schneider's request and prepared a new façade design, with traditional window surrounds and other details. The council approved it at its meeting on December 7 (fig. 68). Included in the resolution was a proviso that the new façades be completed by the end of June 1911 and that the owners put down a deposit of 40,000 crowns, which they would forfeit if they failed to comply with the order to submit an acceptable design.[30]

Whether Epstein undertook the redesign with the clients' approval or acted on his own is unclear. Goldman and Aufricht were now threatened with consid-

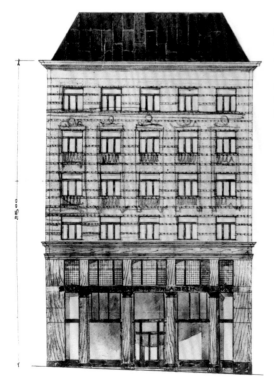

FIG. 67. Loos (with Epstein), revised façade designs for the Goldman & Salatsch Building, submitted July 25, 1910, showing the pencil corrections made by Hans Schneider. Plan- und Schriftenkammer der Magistratsamt (MA 37), Vienna.

FIG. 68. Ernst Epstein, revised façade designs for the Goldman & Salatsch Building incorporating the suggestions made by Hans Schneider, approved December 27, 1910. Black line print on paper, 17 × 32 ³/₈ in. (43.2 × 82.1 cm). Graphische Sammlung Albertina, Vienna, ALA 229.

erable delays and expense in completing their building. It is unlikely that Loos encouraged Epstein — unless he viewed the action as another stalling tactic. Epstein, on the other hand, had his own motivation to comply: he was a prolific builder, and at the time he was at work on several other commissions. He had no wish to incur the wrath of the authorities.[31]

But there were some on the council who objected to the idea that government officials could force an owner to carry out a mandated design. At the next meeting, on December 15, another representative, Ludwig Zatzka, moved to allow the owners to implement the July 25 design (though it is not clear which of the two he had in mind), which the building office had already sanctioned.

Zatzka, too, had ulterior motives. He was a wealthy building contractor who had often run afoul of the authorities. He had faced charges of improperly using his influence to determine the allocation of official contracts and facilitating real estate deals in which he had a financial interest. He doubtless wanted to prevent further meddling on the part of the council. But few were sympathetic, and even those who were found Zatzka's intentions suspicious. His motion was voted down, resulting in another victory for Rykl and Schneider.[32]

By year's end, the situation for Loos and his design began to appear bleak. In late November or early December he had the upper façade painted a light gray, toning down somewhat the starkness of the natural white plaster. He said that he had planned the move from the start to provide a more neutral background against which to judge the marble veneer; the delay in doing so had been a result of waiting for the stucco to dry completely.[33]

The new color had no discernible impact on the chorus of voices now clamoring for changes. On December 7, another of the tabloids, the *Neue Zeitung,* published an "artist's interpretation" of how the new building would appear when completed (deliberately simplified, it seems, to amplify the shock effect) under the headline, "The Dung Crate on the Michaelerplatz" (fig. 69). The associated copy read: "Dear reader! If you wish to see a dung heap in the midst of the city, then proceed to the Michaelerplatz, where you will behold the highest form of perversity, in the form of a modern palace. . . . Is there no one in the city

FIG. 69. "Die Mistkiste" (The Dung Crate) on Michaelerplatz. *Die Neue Zeitung,* December 7, 1910.

FIG. 70. Caricature "Los von der Architektur." *Illustrirtes Wiener Extrablatt,* January 1, 1911.

„Los von der Architektur."
(Aus der Silvesterzeitschrift des Oesterreichischen Ingenieur- und Architektenvereines.)

— Kunstbrütend ging der Modernste durch die Straßen. Plötzlich blieb er erstarrt stehen; er hatte gefunden, was er solange vergeblich gesucht:
(Bitte wenden!)

building office that can nip such plans in the bud? Does such a deformity have to come into the world before someone notices that a beautiful square will be . . . irretrievably destroyed? We demand most energetically that the building office put an end to such works, before the whole city is shot to hell."[34]

Other newspapers joined in. The *Illustrirtes Wiener Extrablatt* published a cartoon under the caption "Los von der Architektur" (Away with Architecture — again, a pun on Loos's name) showing a "modernist" — presumably Loos — staring at an open sewer grate, implying not very subtly that it was the source of his inspiration for the façade (fig. 70).[35] And *Der Morgen* ran a cartoon showing the great Fischer von Erlach standing before the building proclaiming: "What a shame that I was not aware of this style, otherwise I wouldn't have despoiled the square with all of my stupid ornament" (fig. 71).

In good Viennese fashion, the list of epithets for the building also grew impressively: in addition to the "grain elevator" and the "dung crate" (Mistkiste), which appear to have been the most popular, local wags referred to it as the "house without eyebrows" (Haus ohne Augenbrauen), the "factory building" (Fabriksgebäude), the "prison" (Gefangenhaus), the "matchbox" (Feuerzeug), the "chopped-up crate" (gehobelte Kiste), and the "dresser-drawer building" (Schubladenkastenbau).[36]

Even more stinging was an attack that appeared in the *Neue Freie Presse*. Its author was Hugo Wittmann, a well-known cultural critic and regular contributor of feuilletons to the paper. Wittmann was not an anti-modernist per se, but he was sharply critical of the building's design and of Loos's comments about it. He conceded that Loos had solved ably the problems of engaging the irregularly shaped plot and forging usable space — "something the modern architects understand very well." Still, he pronounced the building an abject failure: "Rarely has an architectural work evoked such complete displeasure." The problem, he thought, resided in Loos's odd merging of historical and modern elements: "On the ground and mezzanine floors, frivolous marble, immense monolithic columns, all precious materials, and, above, bare walls without even the shadow of ornament, punctured with completely undecorated windows, a sad scantines." Had it been in another quarter of the city, he wrote, the building would not have stood out, but in the end, it belonged "on Broadway in New York or in a commercial zone in Beijing or Yokohama, not in Vienna, and, especially, not on the Michaelerplatz." The building was a "stab in the heart" of old Vienna; it was a "declaration of war."[37]

But what most disturbed Wittmann was Loos's heavy-handed attempt to make a polemical statement: "Unfortunately, it was not enough for him merely to deliver a tolerable speculative building to the clients, he wanted to use the opportunity to preach loudly to the Viennese about his new architectonic wonder drug. His building is supposed to be a programmatic statement, a revelation. The simple, the practical, one should say an almost military severity, must be our point of reference if a new building will be a true reflection of our time."[38] The fundamental flaws of the building, Wittmann added, were the result not of a lack of money ("the overabundance of marble on the lower stories is ample evidence that Loos did not want for funds") but of a lack of taste and judgment, which he thought was endemic among the city's younger architects. It was fitting and proper for them to experiment in the outer districts, but to build in the inner city required them to respect tradition.[39]

Loos immediately prepared a rebuttal, which appeared in the paper two days later. What he found especially troubling, he wrote, was Wittmann's accusation that he had committed a "crime against the old city." He had, in fact, taken pains

FIG. 71. Rudolf Herrmann, cartoon showing Fischer von Erlach's reaction to Loos's proposed design. *Der Morgen,* early 1911.

to design the building precisely so that it would fit harmoniously into the square. The adjacent Michaelerkirche had inspired its austere neoclassical style, and the form of the windows had arisen from his desire to maximize light and air — "a justified demand of our age." He had selected real marble because he found "any form of imitation repugnant." And he kept the upper stucco façade as simple as possible because that was how the Viennese bourgeoisie had always built: "Only the aristocrats had employed pronounced architectural elements, and not in plaster, but in stone." He had, he explained, tried to draw a sharp division between the store and the residential portions of his building, and to do so in a way that followed the spirit of the old Viennese masters. He also promised that the new marble façade, "which will be completed next summer, will be more beautiful and opulent than that of all of the buildings constructed in the inner city in recent decades."[40]

Goldman now also came to Loos's defense, for the first time speaking out publicly. In an article in *Die Zeit* he responded to Wittmann's charge that the building did not fit into the square. He chose a peculiar standpoint, however, addressing not Wittmann's assault on the façade but his assertion that the building was "across from the Hofburg." The front of the building, Goldman argued, was actually part of the extension of the Herrengasse; it did not actually confront the palace directly, implying that it was not as out of place as Wittmann had suggested.[41]

A more vigorous defense came from Richard Schaukal. "It seems to me," he wrote in an elegantly crafted essay in the culture magazine *Der Merker,* that the onslaught against "Loos and his building is symptomatic of the problems of our senseless age." Loos had simply sought to erect a new building. It was an "everyday event" for which no explanation was necessary. The critics had missed his true intentions. Vienna was replete with "injurious buildings" — overblown, poorly designed, banal: "Loos had wanted to erect a sensible building in the midst our city, which has already been hopelessly despoiled by a false, ostentatious, and soulless architecture." He wanted to build in the only way that was appropriate in the modern age, employing a language that was direct and practical: "The modern idea of a city is . . . consciously styleless [*stillos*]." Schaukal expressed reservations about the building's lower marble "cloak," which he deemed "perhaps too elaborate," but he thought Loos's "idea was good," and he would wait to see the final product before issuing judgment.[42]

Most of the critics remained unconvinced. Karl Marilaun, in an essay in the *Reichspost* a few days afterward, issued another negative assessment. But he was more measured than most of Loos's detractors: "I do not want to say here that one has to like the building on the Michaelerplatz thoroughly (I, too, do not personally care for it), but instead of stopping and making fun of it we should stroll by and at least once regard it with a critical eye remembering what all the buildings erected in Vienna in the past ten years actually look like."[43]

9

ON ARCHITECTURE

In late November, in spite of the council's official opposition to Loos's design, the building office issued a permit for the ground-floor retail spaces adjacent to the main store. On December 1, Loos attended a party celebrating the opening of the first of these shops, the Österreichische Hausindustrie, a store selling handcrafted articles. Among the guests were a number of government officials and members of the royal court, many of them clients of Goldman & Salatsch.[1]

A few days afterward Loos departed for Berlin, where he was again to present a talk.

The sponsor this time was Walden's Verein für Kunst, but the idea had come from Loos, who continued to look for allies in his fight and hoped to find support outside Vienna.[2] Loos's two previous lectures in Berlin had drawn scant attention. But the mounting controversy in Vienna had begun to attract notice, even in the German capital, and the hall, the Hagensaal on the Wilhelm Straße, the largest venue he had yet spoken in, was filled nearly to capacity.

The lecture, which he titled "Über Architektur" (On Architecture), took place on December 8 (fig. 72). Much of it was a restatement of the ideas in "Ornament and Crime." Loos even repeated some of the exact phrases: he made reference to the primitive Papuan, tattoos as symbols of degeneration, and his beliefs about stylistic obsolescence.[3] But "On Architecture" presented a greatly expanded version of his cultural argument, applying his critique to building in the modern age. He engaged for the first time, directly and at length, the problems of modern architecture.

At its core was Loos's attempt to draw a distinction between art — monumental architecture — and ordinary building. His argument was straightforward: modern life had led to a cultural decline; architects, like other city dwellers, were "rootless," no longer in touch with tradition or instinct. Beginning in the second half of the nineteenth century they started to look to the past and to other traditions because they had no understanding of their own culture. But they had "misunderstood earlier epochs," he said. "Since only those objects survived which, thanks to their purposeless ornamentation, were of little practical use and there-

VEREIN FÜR KUNST

Donnerstag, den 8. Dezember, abends 8 Uhr
Architektenhaus (Hagensaal) Wilhelmstr. 92/93

ADOLF LOOS

Vortrag: ÜBER ARCHITEKTUR.
Karten à Mk. 3 u. 2 an der Abendkasse.

FIG. 72 Advertisement for Loos's lecture "On Architecture" in Berlin. *Der Sturm*, December 8, 1910.

fore did not wear out, only objects with ornamentation have come down to us, and people came to assume that in earlier times there were only ornamented things."[4]

Those who still practiced the crafts, Loos claimed—the peasants living in the countryside, for example—had been unaffected by the headlong search for past sources; they had continued to fashion objects and buildings that were truthful and appropriate. Architects, by contrast, "took everything from books." But the publication of so many works on architecture had "poisoned our urban culture" and "prevented us from remembering who and what we are." Rather than building to suit a purpose, architects became obsessed with imagery: "Through the actions of architects, the noble art of building has been reduced to graphic art."[5] The growing reliance on drawing had led to confusion between what was good and bad architecture. The same was true of photography: "A true building makes no impression when it is depicted in two dimensions. It is my greatest pride that the interiors I have created are wholly lacking in effect in photographs."[6]

Loos also sought to establish a clear distinction between art and building. Buildings, he exclaimed, unlike works of art, were fundamentally about fulfilling a purpose: "A work of art is brought into the world without a need for it. A building meets a need. A work of art has no responsibility to anyone, a building to everyone. The aim of a work of art is to make us feel uncomfortable. A building serves for our comfort. A work of art is revolutionary, a building conservative. A work of art is concerned with the future and directs us along new paths. A building is concerned with the present."[7]

Because architecture and art served entirely different purposes, Loos told his audience, "Only a very small part of architecture belongs to the realm of art: grave markers and monuments. Everything else, which has some purpose, is excluded from the province of art."[8] Since most building has nothing to do with art, the role of the architect is to erect works that serve the requirements of ordinary people. Forthright and legible designs that communicate their meaning clearly constitute the only legitimate approach to the problems of building: "If we come across a mound in the woods that is six feet long and three feet wide, we become somber and recognize: someone is buried here. *That is architecture.*"[9]

Though the later published version of the talk contained only a single reference to the Michaelerplatz building, Loos spoke at length about his intentions for the design.[10] Many in the audience embraced his message: the threshold of tolerance for modernism in Berlin had already far outstripped that in Vienna. Walter Gropius, like many young Berliners, found encouragement in his words. "Adolf Loos is a prophet. In an age of sleepwalking in the most vapid eclecticism" he formulated a "distinct vision that defined precisely what he now calls functional form."[11]

Loos received a very different response when he presented "Ornament and Crime" in Munich a little more than a week later. The lecture took place on December 17 in the grand ballroom of the Hotel Vier Jahreszeiten on Maximillians Straße.[12]

The sponsor for the talk was the Neues Verein, a group of mostly younger artists, writers, and designers. On the surface, the makeup of the audience might have suggested a sympathetic crowd. Loos knew better. Munich had been the center of the Jugendstil in Germany at the turn of the century, and it was still a hotbed for new ornamental design in 1910. Hoping to issue a direct challenge to his opponents, he was more shrill than usual, challenging those in the audience to defend their reliance on what he insisted were outmoded aesthetic ideals. An anonymous reporter for the *Münchner Neueste Nachrichten* wrote the day afterward that had he "declared war on ornament." For him "it is a has-been, dead, a vestige of a long-dead culture."

The reaction was swift and vociferous. Though much of the audience, the reporter noted, had been "fascinated by Loos's presentation" and charmed by his "amusing defense" of his ideas, some vigorously "assailed Loos's statements."[13] He had expected criticism, but the response surprised him. Later he would write that the "lecture was the cause of riots among the applied artists in Munich."[14] That was surely an exaggeration. There is little doubt, however, that the bellicose reaction took him aback, and he returned to Vienna chastened and a little shaken.

But on Christmas Day came an unexpected gift: grudging praise from no one less than Otto Wagner. In an interview in the *Neues Wiener Journal* Wagner remarked that the building was "not without its problems." He added, however: "In the veins of its designer there is more artistic blood than in those of the architects of many palaces, which have been left in peace because they had nothing to say."[15]

10

AN ARCHITECT AT WAR

In late December 1910, Loos left Vienna once more, this time to spend Christmas with Bessie in Leysin.[1] During his absence, Kraus, who had been away for much of the fall giving readings of his works in Germany, Bohemia, and Moravia, published an essay on the controversy.[2] A month before, he had confided in a letter to Walden that the whole Michaelerplatz affair was, in his words, "demonstrating the consequences of his friendship with Loos." The fight, he told Walden, would go on for some time, because Loos was "determined to hold out until summer if bureaucratic pressure to ornament [the building] came crashing down on him."[3]

Kraus wrote in the essay, which appeared in *Die Fackel* just after Christmas, that he thought the struggle over the building was foremost an ideological one. He was convinced that the animosity toward Loos stemmed from the fact that his friend had offended the sensibilities of the Viennese: "He had built them an idea," a gesture of real progress. But the forces of reaction had awakened: "Mediocrity," Kraus exclaimed with characteristic acerbity, "is rebelling against functionality" (Die Mittelmäßigkeit revoltiert gegen die Zweckmäßigkeit). In place of their revered ornament Loos had substituted a "tabula rasa," an idea the Viennese simply could not abide.[4]

Kraus could not resist the opportunity to take a swipe at Loos's leading critics. He called Seligmann a "failed painter" who had been forced to take up journalism, and he described Wittmann as a writer unable to overcome his own "need for ornament" — comments that would hardly endear either man to Loos's cause.[5]

Loos found an unexpected ally in the novelist and critic Felix Speidel. Speidel was neither a member of the Kraus circle nor an obvious modernist supporter. But in an essay in the *Neues Wiener Tagblatt* he wrote that he had been moved by Loos's impassioned defense about following tradition. What Loos had achieved, he found after inspecting the building carefully, was not a rekindling of the past but a genuinely novel architectural expression: "Art was trapped in a dead end. . . . Then, a new architect dove deeply into modern life. [Loos] erected what has never existed before, a real store building, and he invented a new style for it. He built in response to the requirements of the age, functionally yet monumentally; he is like the Greeks at work."[6]

Still, some critics — even those who championed modernism — questioned whether Loos's design truly fulfilled the needs of the new age. In early February, an article appeared in the *Wiener Bauindustrie Zeitung* "on the Michaelerplatz question." Its author was the Viennese architect Stefan Fayans. Fayans was a frequent contributor to *Moderne Bauformen,* one of the leading pro-modernist journals in Germany.[7] But he voiced doubt about whether Loos's design had made any valid contribution to the cause: "Good intentions alone are not enough to find the proper solution to the problems of the present," he wrote. Loos's building lacked a "fresh tectonic expression"; the design was not only static, but it fell well short of presenting a "clarified formal beauty."[8]

Fayans had worked for a time in Berlin for Alfred Messel, one of the first architects to explore how to join the new concrete frame technology with a modern aesthetic language; his critique reflected his own views about the need to express structure. He was unquestionably right to assert that Loos's design concealed its underlying constructive fabric — a charge that a number of critics would level. But Fayans did not stop there. He castigated Loos for confusing deliberate simplicity with a valid modernist gesture. "The Puritanism of the upper stories," he wrote, "is frankly shocking." By contrast, Loos's application of expensive marble to the lower stories "contained a dangerous tendency toward materialism." He added that the building's "tortuous, childishly simple window forms" and oddly tacked-on roof only served to highlight these "extremes."[9]

Loos returned from Switzerland on January 3, 1911. He departed again a few days later, meeting up with Bessie, whom he now accompanied on a recuperative trip.

Her year long stay at the sanatorium had done little to improve her health. Her spirits remained high, however, even though, as she often complained to Loos, she was bored with her confinement. Kokoschka's attempts to "keep an eye on her" the previous winter had come to little avail: "How can you hold back a pleasure-loving young thing like Bessie? When the doctors had gone to bed, she used to climb out the window and go off dancing with the other patients — those anyway who still had enough life left in them."[10] The trip offered both a chance to escape.

They traveled first west and south by rail, stopping in Nice, and then sailed via Corsica to Lisbon. There they boarded a British steamer bound for Madeira. Loos was jubilant. He was thrilled to be far from Vienna and its oppressive atmosphere. "Can you imagine," he wrote to Kraus, "a world without any Viennese. No Viennese, no Viennese, absolutely no Viennese! Being on an English ship is simply splendid."[11]

After spending time in Madeira and making stops in Annaba and Skilda, in Algeria, he and Bessie reached their final goal: the desert oasis of Biskra.[12] Situated south of the Aurès Mountains, some 150 miles from the coast, Biskra was a favored winter resort for well-heeled Europeans. Loos had discovered the town while searching for stone the previous year. He thought that the warm, dry climate and the town's famed thermal baths would aid Bessie's ailing lungs. The setting was idyllic. Nestled in a large oasis, the town was surrounded by thousands of date palms and fruit trees. A group of ancient sun-baked brick houses formed old Biskra, and caravans of Bedouins astride camels still passed down the main road. André Gide, who visited at the turn of the century, set some of the key sections of his 1902 novel L'immoraliste there, and the Hungarian composer Béla Bartók would spend time in the town collecting the folk music of the area.

Loos and Bessie found lodging in the Hotel de Sahara, on one of the principal streets of the new town, which boasted "modern comfort" and electric lighting. They explored the surrounding countryside, taking in the sights and reveling in the exotic scenery. But Loos's stay was brief. He needed to return to Vienna to oversee the installation of the marble veneer. He left Bessie at a sanatorium and undertook the journey back to Austria alone.

In his absence, Rykl had prepared a detailed report, which he passed on to the minister for public works, the mayor's office, and the governor of Lower Austria (the province in which Vienna was located), documenting the steady decline of the "Bildhauergewerbe"—the artisanal sculptors. He hoped to pressure the government to reverse the "complete stagnation" of the industry brought on by the trend toward modern, unornamented buildings.[13]

By then, the municipal authorities had already taken the first steps to "correct" Loos's design. At the end of December the building office formally sanctioned the new Schneider-Epstein plan after the council had turned down Loos's petition to reinstate the first, approved façade. The decision met the late January deadline that Neumayer had set to have a final design approved.[14]

When Loos returned he faced a precipitous uphill battle.

During his absence Kraus had sought to rally support. In the late February issue of *Die Fackel* he published an essay by one of their friends, the writer Otto Stoessl. The issue also contained a cloying poem by a young architecture student, Paul Engelmann (Ludwig Wittgenstein's future collaborator on the villa he built for his sister, Margarethe Stonborough, on the Kundmanngasse), extolling the building's merits.[15]

Loos, though happy for the praise, preferred to lodge his faith with the new marble cladding, which he believed would tip opinion—and the broader fight—in his favor. He was sure that once the public saw the building's sumptuous stone veneer, most people would come over to his side. He bided his time, convinced that he could reverse the council's decision.

Over the next several months there was a lull of sorts in the controversy. The period from mid-February to early May marked an uneasy truce. A few articles —for and against Loos—and several cartoons (including a marvelous send-up showing the Hofburg made up in Loosian dress) appeared in the press. But the newspapers and critics now seemed willing to await the completion of the building before weighing in again.[16]

Work on the lower façade, which had continued through January and February, gained pace when the weather began to warm in March; by mid-April the marble work had been completed. On April 26, the *Illustrirtes Wiener Extrablatt* published a photograph of the Looshaus (the name by then was becoming common), showing the recently installed Cipollino cladding (fig. 73).

For the first time, the building appeared in nearly complete guise.

In the meantime Loos continued to speak out publicly, arguing for his design and his broader ideas about modernism. In mid-March he repeated "Ornament and Crime" in Prague.

The lecture took place at the German Technical University, which housed one of the city's three architecture schools. Unlike his first two Berlin talks, it was well publicized. On the day of the lecture the *Prager Tagblatt* profiled Loos in a feature article, describing him as "one of the most interesting figures" among the Viennese architects and a representative of the "radicalism of functionalism," a principle that he "demonstrated in his new building on the Michaelerplatz."[17]

Loos spoke in German, but a number of the younger Czech architects attended, as did the writer Franz Kafka.[18] The audience, to judge from a review the next day, was taken with the lecture and with Loos. At the end of the piece, the unnamed reporter wrote that the talk had "captivated the listeners, which mostly included architectural professionals, to such a degree that although many had strong private reservations, there was thunderous applause afterward."[19]

The following day, in Vienna, Loos presented another lecture, "Vom Stehen, Gehen, Sitzen, Liegen, Schlafen, Essen und Trinken" (On Standing, Walking, Sitting,

FIG. 73 Looshaus with the newly installed marble veneer. *Illustrirtes Wiener Extrablatt,* April 26, 1911.

Lying, Sleeping, Eating, and Drinking), at the Technical University.[20] Among the least well known of Loos's texts from this period, it draws on the main themes of "Ornament and Crime," in particular his assault on "applied art" and his affirmation of the value of craft production.[21] Missing, though, were Loos's usual images: the primitive Papuan, tattoos, the references to criminality. In their place he substituted a forthright argument about the ways in which objects of daily use should serve their basic functions.[22] He took the opportunity to speak at length about his ideas for the Michaelerplatz building and defend his design, and the audience — made up mostly of students from the school's architecture department — was supportive; even his detractors were generally respectful.

Loos spoke again publicly in Vienna on April 4, presenting a slide lecture he titled "My Struggles" (Meine Kämpfe). The event took place at the Volksbildungsverein, an adult education center.[23] The audience, this time made up mostly of working-class Viennese, was decidedly less friendly. As Loos sought to explain his ideas on ornament he was repeatedly interrupted with catcalls. He persevered, showing a series of images of the works of other architects and designers — including Olbrich and Hoffmann — explaining what he would have done differently. Loos also addressed the Michaelerplatz controversy directly, chiding the authorities for their decision to "paste" a new façade on the building in the coming summer.[24] If the building turned out to be a disaster, he insisted, the fault would rest firmly with them.

He ended his talk to jeers and derision. Many simply found his design and ideas unacceptable, and there was little he could say or do to convince them otherwise.

But that was not the worst of it. Throughout that summer and fall, people sometimes hurled insults at him on the street, and, after a photograph of the Steiner House (which had been completed at the end of 1910) appeared in *Der Architekt,* it was damaged repeatedly by stones thrown by passersby.[25]

Loos carried on as best he could, but problems in his personal life added to his woes. Throughout this time he remained immersed in the lives of his friends and protégés. Kokoschka, who had been in Berlin working for Walden, returned unexpectedly in the spring and began preparing, with Loos's assistance, for a show of his paintings at the Hagenbund. Once more the critics savaged the exhibition. Loos scarcely needed any more negative attention, but he stood by Kokoschka and continued his efforts to help him find patrons and commissions.

Loos was concerned, too, for Altenberg. His alcoholism had continued to worsen. But his addiction only masked deeper psychological problems. After a stay in a detoxification clinic failed to help his condition, several of Altenberg's friends arranged for him to enter a sanatorium in Inzersdorf, south of Vienna. Loos opposed the measure, convinced that it would only exacerbate his friend's problems.[26] The press caught wind of his treatment for mental issues, confirming what many had long thought—that Altenberg really was crazy. The lurid newspaper reports only served to depress him further, especially the fact that so many people found his illness amusing. Kraus tried to help. He asked Walden to publish some of Altenberg's articles in *Der Sturm,* and he wrote a defense of his friend in *Die Fackel.* But Altenberg, suffering from deep paranoia and sleeplessness, complained incessantly that Loos and Kraus had not visited him. In a barrage of letters and postcards he appealed to them for aid and money. When they failed to meet his demands, he accused them of adding to his mental and physical agonies.[27]

Kraus was undergoing his own spiritual crisis. After long deliberation he had resolved to convert to Catholicism. His decision was prompted in part by a mounting belief that modern urban life was eroding values and sweeping away what remained of tradition. He thought that a return to old-fashioned values might rescue spirituality from the corrosive effects of contemporary materialism.

Kraus was not alone in his quest for stability: throughout Europe in the years just after the turn of the century, many intellectuals sought solace in a renewal of Catholicism, seeing in the revival of the church a means to shore up the old order. But the issue for Kraus was particularly complicated. He had long had an uneasy relationship with his own Jewish identity and with the role of Jews in Austrian society. He had also been very vocal in his criticism of Jews who converted to Christianity, especially those who converted for social and economic advantage.

Kraus's decision came at a time when he was waging a battle against the church over its repressive attitudes toward sexuality. Repeatedly in *Die Fackel* he had assailed the church leadership and Christian attitudes, and, in 1908, he had published a book, *Sittlichkeit und Kriminalität* (Morality and Criminality), a compilation of his attacks on the church and the Austrian legal system's moralistic stance toward sex, which Kraus thought only masked deeply hypocritical actions on the part of the clergy and society at large.[28]

After much soul searching, Kraus decided to keep his baptism into the church a strict secret; he feared that revealing it would only spur his critics. Loos, as ever, was supportive. On April 8, 1911, at a secret ceremony in the Karlskirche, he stood as godfather at Kraus's baptism into the Catholic Church. Loos presented him with a large silver crucifix. Kraus, deeply grateful, hung it over his bed, where it remained until he left the church in 1923.[29]

11

THE SECOND COMPETITION

Shortly after the baptism, Loos departed for Algeria to escort Bessie back to Vienna. They stayed in Biskra for two more weeks, undertaking a side trip on April 19 to visit the ruins of the Roman city of Timgad.[1] A few days later they left for Tunis, where they boarded a ship for Sicily. After a stop in Palermo they made their way back to Austria (fig. 74).[2]

Loos was hardly prepared for the maelstrom that greeted him. What was certainly the bitterest blow for him in the long struggle came at the beginning of May. While on the return journey he learned that, in his absence and to nearly everyone's surprise, Goldman and Aufricht had announced a competition to redesign the Michaelerplatz building's upper façades.

The two men had published a notice in the *Wiener Bauindustrie Zeitung* specifying the rules and restrictions. It called for an "artistic solution." Only architects residing in Vienna were eligible. The new design, they wrote, should encompass only the upper four stories; the arrangement and placement of the windows could in no way be altered. But they left open the possibility of adding a different cornice and changing the appearance of the mansard roof. The announcement also laid out the possibilities for decorating the bare walls, which could include the "application of frescos, sgraffito, or glass mosaics." It was especially important, they noted, "that the architectonic effect of the façade merge with its surroundings."[3]

The deadline for entries was set for June 15. Four prizes would be awarded: the first prize would come with 2,000 crowns; second prize, 1,500; third prize, 1,000; and fourth prize, 500. The Austrian Association of Engineers and Architects would oversee the competition. The names of the judges were also listed: Ludwig Baumann, Hermann Helmer, Carl König, Eduard Veith, and a "representative of the building's owners."[4]

Almost everything about the announcement was irregular. It was highly unusual to have a competition to design only a portion of a building, and it was unheard of for such a competition to be carried out for a new structure. In all likelihood, Goldman and Aufricht took the step to avoid losing any more money. They were under enormous financial pressure to complete the building and avoid forfeiting their large deposit. Why they finally took the step in May remains a mystery. One possibility is that, in Loos's absence, they had decided — naïvely — that he would be in agreement with the idea of a competition to complete the façades.[5] It may have been, though, they simply exploited the fact that he was away — hoping to score a fait accompli. Once the results were announced, there would have been little that Loos could have done to prevent the new design from being executed.

This time Goldman and Aufricht decided to approach the Austrian Association of Engineers and Architects to administer the competition. Perhaps learning their

FIG. 74 Loos and Bessie in Italy, 1911. Graphische Sammlung Albertina, Vienna, ALA 2071.

lesson from the first competition, the men did so in a bid to head off public criticism; by asking the association to oversee the process and enlisting such a prominent panel of judges they could ensure that the authorities would assent to the building's completion.

Even more remarkable is that the association would have agreed to oversee the competition. There was no precedent for such an action, especially because the architect responsible for the project — Loos — had not given his consent (though it may be that Goldman and Aufricht misinformed the association's directors on this issue). In any event, the move was so out of the ordinary that the only explanation is that many of those in the leadership must have taken offense at Loos's design and wanted to see it "corrected."

The press reacted immediately. An article in the *Wiener Mittags-Zeitung* the same day commented:

Of the many stages that the Loos-Haus has passed through, this is certainly the most ridiculous. It was already laughable enough when the city authorities decreed that a new façade should be glued onto the exterior. The building's owners, who have a great deal of money at stake, are, of course, free to attempt to protect themselves from material loss in any way possible. But what is astonishing and worth commenting upon is that an architects' organization would consent to taking part in meddling with another architect's work, whether they are in accord with the design or not.[6]

The unsigned article also questioned the motives behind the selection of the jury: "It is with obvious malice that this same organization elected to choose for judges architects who stand about as far as possible from the artistic convictions of the building's designer."[7]

The jury was indeed heavily weighted against Loos. All four of the named jurors were members of the old guard. Baumann already had a long career behind him as an architect of Neo-Baroque and Secessionist buildings. He was well connected in imperial government circles — one reason he had won the commissions to design the Austrian pavilions for the 1900 Paris and the 1904 St. Louis world's fairs. He had recently completed the new War Ministry Building, a grandiloquent Neo-Baroque structure that turned out to be the last of the imposing monumental government edifices erected on the Ringstrasse.[8] Helmer was one of the most successful architects in Vienna, but also a staunch conservative. With his partner Ferdinand Fellner he had erected theaters and opera houses across Central Europe, all of them in either the Neo-Renaissance or Neo-Baroque styles. König, doyen of the Technical University, was one of the most respected practicing representatives of the old historicism; in the 1880s he had taken the lead in the development of the Neo-Baroque.[9] And Veith was an artist and teacher of architectural drawing at the Technical University with traditionalist tastes. Loos could scarcely have imagined a less receptive group for his ideas.

At some point the association also asked Otto Wagner to serve on the jury.[10] Why his name was not included in the initial list is unclear. Perhaps it was an oversight; perhaps he was added subsequently. His inclusion may have been an attempt to provide some balance. Wagner was, at least by virtue of his progressive outlook, more likely to be favorably disposed to Loos's design, in spite of his public criticisms.

Who Goldman and Aufricht intended to serve as the "representative of the building's owners" is not documented. It is possible that they had Loos in mind. If this was the case, it would have been a cruel position for him: he would have been forced to take part in a process to undermine his intentions for the building. And given the tenor of the jury — even with Wagner's support, which was by no means a given — he would have been heavily outvoted.

Loos caught wind of the planned competition when he read about it by chance in one of the Vienna newspapers while on the train from Rome.[11] He left Bessie in Florence and caught an express to Vienna, arriving in time to attend a meeting of the prize committee, chaired by Helmer, on the afternoon of May 13.[12]

The exact course of events at the meeting is clouded. The newspaper reports are incomplete and, on some of the details, contradictory. What all of the accounts agree on is that Loos explained to the assembled jurors that he was vehemently opposed to the idea of the competition and that he intended to complete the building according to his own design.

Wagner responded first, declaring that "no artist had the right to infringe upon another's work." The building, he said, "though not free of errors, because Loos had not previously had the opportunity to build at large scale," still had much to recommend it, and he described at length what he thought were its "significant artistic merits."[13]

At this point, Wagner announced his decision to withdraw from the jury, and he encouraged the others to do so as well. He insisted further that the association no longer have any role in the competition. Helmer, persuaded by Wagner's plea, also resigned, as did, apparently, Baumann and Veith. Only König dissented. The jurors then issued a statement declaring that the decision to hold a competition had been based on the erroneous information that Loos had supported the idea, and they called on all architects to boycott it: "It is incompatible with the association's views of art, which reject any move to deface the work of a living architect with exterior additions."[14]

The jury's decision was a victory for Loos, his first since Neumayer had intervened with the authorities the previous year. Whether intentional or not, the announcement of the association's refusal to take part in the competition also helped to win over some of the press and public.[15] Even Archduke Franz Ferdinand, the emperor's nephew and heir to the throne, known for his outspoken conservatism in matters of architectural taste (earlier the same year he had called Jože Plečnik's spare design for the all-concrete Church of the Holy Spirit in Vienna a "mishmash Russian bath," "stables," and a "temple to Venus"), rendered a positive verdict, telling a reporter that he "liked the new building very much."[16]

What remains unexplained is why Goldman and Aufricht had decided to organize a competition in the first place. Loos's subsequent good relationship with them suggests that it may have really been a misunderstanding. If the move sprang from a rift between Loos and his clients, there is no evidence of it.

But without a façade design, they still had not satisfied the council's dictate, and the deadline was fast approaching. It was up to Loos to find a way to solve the impasse.

As the summer of 1911 dawned, two of the most advanced buildings in Europe were nearing completion in Vienna. The new Goldman & Salatsch Building on Michaelerplatz was now almost finished. The exterior was missing only its lamps, bronze medallions, and lettering, and work was progressing on fitting out the new gentlemen's tailor shop on the lower floors. The building had already become a familiar sight on the square. Yet it remained for many an unwanted presence. When Loos's former employer, Karl Mayreder, published a souvenir book of photographs of the city by Martin Gerlach, he selected an image of the square framed in such a way that only a sliver of the building was visible — as if to negate its existence (fig. 75).

At Neustiftgasse 40, in the seventh district, work on Wagner's new apartment house was also in its final stages (fig. 76). Construction had commenced the previous summer, several months after work on the Goldman & Salatsch Building had begun. As the scaffolding was removed, it revealed a startling and novel design. It was the most fully realized — and, in all respects, radical — statement of Wagner's growing preoccupation with forging a *Nutzstil* — a functional idiom that could meet the requirements of modern urban life.

Wagner had first applied his utilitarian language to a series of commercial structures in the early years of the century; now he turned it to residential architecture. His new style was a distillation of the Renaissance revivalism of his early years — a rigorously pared-down classicism in modernist guise. Still present

FIG. 75 Michaelerplatz, looking down Kohlmarkt, with the Goldman & Salatsch Building just visible on the left, summer 1911. Photo by Martin Gerlach. Karl Mayreder, *Wien und Umgebung* (Vienna: Gerlach & Wiedling, n.d.).

were the basic conventions of traditional architecture: a reminder of a rusticated base in its black glass banding, a prominent cornice with bracketing, and customary and regular proportions and massing. Cut into the surface were modular windows, uniform in size and sill-less, which rendered the façade blank and unexpressive. The building's rectilinearity heralded what was to become the familiar look of the new century — pure geometry, almost artlessly presented, its monumentality dependent on scale and repetition. It was an even more adamant statement of the new functionalism than was Loos's building.

But Wagner's apartment house drew almost no mention in the press. Even the professional journals gave it little heed. Tucked away in an ordinary residential area, it was inconspicuous and unheralded. Only much later would it take on importance as an early — and precocious — exercise in modern building.

In the wake of the architects' association meeting in May, the newspapers and public alike began to show a more favorable attitude toward Loos and his design. There was now genuine sympathy for him in some quarters, a sense that the authorities had treated him unfairly. Many believed that the move to devise a competition had been a transgression of his rights as an artist. A short editorial in the *Wiener Allgemeine Zeitung* in July sounded a conciliatory and supportive tone. Noting that the original deadline for an approved façade was approaching, it called for an "end to the whole story." The building should be left as it was, its

FIG. 76 Otto Wagner, apartment building, Neustiftgasse 40, Vienna, 1909–11. *Der Architekt,* 1910.

editors wrote: "We quite like it. It is a simple and beautiful building" and "belongs completely in the traditional line of the old Viennese houses: just compare it with the adjacent buildings on both sides, the church, the bank, and others."[1]

Loos's detractors remained unconvinced. A week later, Seligmann, writing in the *Neue Freie Presse,* attacked the building with renewed vigor: "One hears now that the indecent nakedness of the upper façade will be masked with surface motifs." That would "do little or nothing," he thought, because the problem lay "not only with the baldness of the upper portion" but also "with the . . . almost square windows, evenly distributed across the surface, and the narrowness of the spaces between them (which ornamentation would only make more obvious)." Seligmann conceded that the building offered an unabashed modern statement and that, despite its large size and lack of ornament, it "left the impression of a comfortable and livable building." Nonetheless, he wrote, he found it "genuinely dilettantish."[2]

On May 15, two days after the architects' association meeting, Kraus gave a reading of works by various *Fackel* authors. The event was in part a benefit for Altenberg, still in the sanatorium. Among the works he presented was Engelmann's sonnet about the Michaelerplatz building.[3]

Kraus's and Loos's thoughts, however, were focused elsewhere. On May 18 came word that Gustav Mahler, lingering near death for several weeks, had died. Mahler had recently returned from New York, where, weary of the Viennese musical establishment's incessant intrigues and backstabbing, he had served as director of the New York Philharmonic and conductor of the Metropolitan Opera. But he found the creative atmosphere in New York even more stifling than in Vienna. In February, severely weakened from a heart ailment, he had come home and entered a sanatorium. The newspapers chronicled his decline over the following weeks.

Loos and Kraus had never been close to Mahler. Counted among his supporters were a sizable number of their enemies, including most of the Secessionists. But both men, along with the rest of the city's vanguard, had long viewed Mahler as the leader of the effort to establish a new aesthetic culture. Each of his dramatic performances had been tantamount to a rallying cry against the establishment. Most had seen Mahler's departure for America, in December 1907, as a bitter defeat issued by the forces of reaction. A large contingent of his supporters had gathered at the Westbahnhof to see him off. As the train pulled out of the station, Klimt uttered aloud what all those assembled must have been thinking: "Vorbei" — it's over.[4] The young music critic Paul Stefan later wrote simply that the "commonplace had triumphed."[5]

In the immediate wake of Mahler's death, Kraus railed against the newspapers, which had prepared stories of his passing even before he had breathed his last — as if they had been all too eager to bury him.[6] Loos, like many of the city's progressives, viewed Mahler's death, at the age of fifty, as a direct consequence of his unremitting persecution by the old guard; it seemed to underscore his belief that modernism continued to face intractable opposition in Vienna. Not lost on him were the parallels between Mahler's sad fate and his own experience. It was, he believed, merely another sign of the continuing power of the establishment to impede progress and crush those who resisted.

Loos was not the only modernist to feel the sting of criticism that summer. Hoffmann's pavilion for the International Exhibition in Rome, an exercise in stark neoclassical forms, and the large gallery of Klimt's paintings within, as Stefan recounted, had garnered praise from outside, but at home there had been persistent rumors that the Romans and foreign visitors had ridiculed it.[7] It was merely more evidence of what Stefan called the "grave in Vienna" — the conservative forces that thwarted reform at every turn and sought to "bury" all innovation.

Mahler's funeral was held on May 21 at the tiny cemetery in the suburb of Grinzing. Hundreds of mourners assembled at the graveside, standing beneath umbrellas in a steady rain. The whole Viennese modernist world turned out. In addition to most of the city's leading musicians and actors, the entire large circles surrounding Schönberg and Klimt — both longtime Mahler supporters — attended. Loos, Kraus, and Altenberg made the trek to Grinzing to pay their respects.[8]

Loos's own struggle continued through the late spring and early summer. In spite of the more positive tone in the press, his standoff with the authorities showed no signs of easing. He remained dead set on completing the building without making significant changes, and there was no indication from the city council or the building office that a compromise was possible.

The deadline, set for July 30, 1911, was fast approaching. Goldman and Aufricht, feeling acute financial pressure to complete the project, applied for an occupancy permit to allow them to rent out the remaining spaces and complete the fitting out of the shop. In response, the authorities appointed a commission — which included representatives from both the council and the building office — to look into the matter and issue a report.[9] They met on July 11 and upheld the council's decision that the façade would have to be altered. They did, however, grant Goldman and Aufricht a three-month temporary occupancy permit, with the proviso that the two owners make another 40,000-crown deposit (in addition to the 40,000 crowns they had put down the previous December).[10] They now had until August 15 to complete an "approved façade."[11]

The growing pressure weighed on Loos. He began to reconsider the problem. He was certain that he did not want to incorporate the horizontal banding he had first proposed. And any other conventional ornamental devices, such as window surrounds or moldings, were out of the question. For a time he thought about painting the frames of the windows on the upper floors a brilliant red (Stoessl made mention of the idea in his article in *Die Fackel* in March), but he soon rejected it.[12] He recognized that the authorities were unlikely to sanction the building as it was; he would have to make changes. The question of how to alter the façade in a way that would make it acceptable to the authorities dogged him for weeks.

A solution finally came to him in mid-July: he could place bronze window boxes below each window on the upper story. The boxes could be planted seasonally — with flowers in the summer and evergreen boughs during the winter months. The effect would relieve the pronounced plainness of the upper façades, animating their stark off-white surfaces. Just as important for Loos, the use of window boxes would in no way violate his beliefs. The boxes in his mind were functional additions; they were not mere decoration. The use of bronze — pure and unconcealed or modified — would satisfy his conviction that materials should be presented as they were; their inherent qualities alone would yield an ornamental effect. The bronze boxes would also match other features of the façade — the bronze window and door mullions on the lower floors, the soffit in the entry, and the appliqués and lettering.

FIG. 77 Photograph of the Goldman & Salatsch Building with Loos's drawing showing the placement of the new window boxes, mid-summer 1911. Photo courtesy Hermann Czech, Vienna.

Loos first tested the idea with a quick sketch on a photograph of the building, drawing in boxes under the windows on the front (fig. 77). Soon afterward he prepared a watercolor — now lost — of his new design, which he circulated to the press.

The response was overwhelmingly favorable. The editors of the *Reichspost* wrote that the idea was an "inspired solution." It would not only address the concerns of the authorities and critics, they suggested, but create an "artistic liaison between the grand bronze-framed entry and the copper roof."[13] A reporter for the *Fremden-Blatt* echoed the assessment: "Anyone who had complained about the smoothness and unadorned façade has to be delighted" with Loos's proposal, and "those who had already been pleased with his basic ideas and the building would not be disturbed by the changes."[14] Even the *Neue Freie Presse* rendered a positive verdict.[15]

Loos submitted the drawing to the building authorities. Heinrich Goldemund, the head of the office, now interceded directly for the first time.

An architect and a planner, Goldemund had had a major part in Lueger's attempts to remake Vienna into a modern metropolis.[16] As chief planner, he oversaw the program to ring the city with a green belt of forests and meadows, and he had worked closely with Wagner in the 1890s to carry out the construction of the city rail network and the regulation of the Wien River. For much of the protracted fight over the Michaelerplatz he had remained above the fray. But now he became fully involved, urging the council to reconsider its position.

Goldman and Aufricht, in the meantime, maneuvered behind the scenes in an effort to influence the council. A few weeks before, they had shown Epstein's elevations with the vertically combined windows to the architects' association jury members, who had declared the design a "failure." Goldman and Aufricht then brought this to Goldemund's attention, hoping that the criticism would aid their case and prompt the officials to consider other solutions.[17]

Loos took a less conciliatory route. He continued to press his anti-ornament campaign. On July 13, the same day he showed his revised façade design to the press, he published a lengthy essay on Wagner in the *Reichspost*. Written for the occasion of Wagner's seventieth birthday, it chronicled his long career and his many successes and trials. But Loos also took the opportunity to trumpet his own ideas. Wagner, he wrote, had celebrated the traditions of classical antiquity and Viennese building in his work until just before the turn of the century, when he had "passionately embraced the Belgian efforts to invent a new ornamental language."[18] Wagner's newfound ardor for the Art Nouveau, he insisted,

was and is an error. One is familiar with my beliefs on this point. Already thirteen years ago I raised my voice of warning and expressed my conviction that we are no longer in the position to invent new ornament. (My enemies always want to assume from this sentence that I oppose ornament in general, but I only oppose so-called modern ornament and imitation materials). He who wants to decorate therefore should use old ornament. I believe that the invention of new ornament is not a symbol of power, but — for cultivated people — a sign of degeneration.[19]

Why Loos thought it necessary to take a stab at Wagner on the sort of occasion that is normally reserved for polite and fulsome praise — especially in light of the fact that Wagner had spoken up for him at the architects' association only a few weeks before — is open to question. Perhaps he had taken offense at Wagner's remarks about the alleged flaws in his design: Loos was always acutely sensitive to criticism. But he also genuinely believed that Wagner, by adopting the Jugendstil, had wandered from the path of true modernism. And, because of his great influence, he had led many of the younger architects and designers astray. Loos would not make that mistake.

A few days later, on July 18, Arthur Roessler, the art critic for the socialist *Arbeiter-Zeitung,* wrote a lengthy commentary on the Michaelerplatz controversy. Roessler was an outspoken defender of the modernist cause. He was a close friend and avid supporter of Egon Schiele's and, in the years before World War I, championed the careers of a number of other young Viennese artists. He argued that the "Looshaus" required no further elaboration: "It is complete as it is, there is nothing to affix." Just as some of the other buildings on the square rightly had plain façades, so, too, the Goldman & Salatsch Building needed no gaudy adornment. Those who wanted to "tart up" the building, he wrote, paraphrasing Loos, were no different from "those who had themselves tattooed." The real problem was that the authorities had overstepped their role: rather than merely assuring that the building was well constructed and safe, they had sought to make aesthetic judgments — a function that was well outside their capacities or proper responsibilities. Their need to be "right" in the controversy threatened to deface the build-

FIG. 78 Adolf Loos, Goldman & Salatsch Building, mid-summer 1911. *Der Bautechniker* 31, no. 33 (August 18, 1911).

FIG. 79 Goldman & Salatsch Building, entry, late summer or fall 1911. Bildarchiv Foto Marburg.

ing: appending ornament to the façade now would create an incongruous image — rather like a "man in a tuxedo forced to wear a Tyrolean hat with a feather."[20]

Schaukal, too, weighed in, writing in the *Reichspost* that "next to animal cruelty nothing was so painful to witness as the compulsion to beautify" the city's buildings. If the building could not stay "naked and smooth," then Loos's decision to install the boxes was a genial solution — even if the windows would lose their "squared" profile.[21]

By the end of July the interior of the store was nearly finished. Kokoschka wrote to Walden that it was "attracting throngs of visitors."[22] In mid-August, *Der Bautechniker* ran a photograph of the building (fig. 78). It showed the façade now complete except for the two large corner lamps, which would not be mounted until late summer. By then, the displays in the large show windows had also been installed (fig. 79).

All was now set for the next showdown with the authorities when the new deadline arrived on August 15.

But Loos was unable to carry on the fight. In mid-July, weakened by the continuous stress of the controversy, he experienced a severe ulcer attack.

Over the preceding years he had had recurrent problems with his stomach. In 1905 and 1908 he had been forced to seek medical treatment for the problem. Throughout the extended struggle over the building, he had kept an imperturbable public face, but the incessant criticism was taking a toll on him.

In 1911, treatment for gastric ulcers was still ineffective. Though Vienna was then one of the leading centers for medicine in the world, there was little that could be done to help Loos. Antacid therapy was several years off. Doctors had nothing in their arsenal with which to treat the underlying causes of the problem, and gastric surgery, in the days before the advent of antibiotics, was a risky venture — and often fatal.

By the end of July, Loos, unable to eat and in constant pain, was incapacitated. His stomach was bleeding continuously. He said later that over the next weeks he was losing blood "by the liter."[23] Kraus reported to Walden that Loos was "very sick."[24] He was simply unable to carry on.

Loos went to a sanatorium outside Bad Vöslau, a small spa town south of Vienna noted for its healing waters.[25] His recovery was slow. Unable to eat, he lost a great deal of weight. He was also depressed, wounded by all the negative reviews and fearful that the council would require him to despoil the façade. For the first time, he began to question his own decisions. Kulka wrote later that Loos, overwrought by the incessant criticism, was "close to suicide": his struggle "seemed to him so hopeless."[26]

Kokoschka, in an effort to buoy Loos's flagging spirits, asked Walden to compose a "pointed critique of the Viennese authorities, who had forced an artist onto his sickbed."[27]

Walden responded with an editorial on the "Loos case," which appeared in *Der Sturm* in late July. He complained about the lack of reaction to the "injustice" being carried out against Loos: "When the censor bans some dreadful text, the intellectuals are beside themselves," yet there is "only silence in response to this unprecedented oppression of an artist." But Walden reserved his sharpest criticism for the "Viennese architects": it is "their responsibility to react with all their power against the patronizing attitude [of the authorities], even if they themselves cannot imagine living a life without ornament."[28]

Kokoschka and Kraus applauded the piece, though — predictably — there was no reply from the architectural community.[29] The council met once more on August 3 to consider the issue. Loos, still in the sanatorium, was unable to attend.[30]

Although Goldemund and the building authorities had at least been willing to consider the new proposal, the council took a much tougher line. An official from the building office showed Loos's drawing with the proposed window boxes and recommended its adoption. The council summarily rejected the idea. During the discussion Hans Schneider spoke out again, standing by the design that he had proposed and demanding that it be carried out.[31]

A little more than a week after the meeting, the deadline for the completion of the new façade passed without action from either side. The following day, Epstein, who had been content from the beginning to observe the fight from the sidelines, spoke out. He told a reporter that he intended to withdraw his design. He had prepared it hastily, he said, under pressure to comply with the council's demands. He had decided, upon further reflection, that he did not wish to see it executed. Since the design was his "intellectual property," it could not be carried out without his consent, and he threatened to bring suit if it were.[32]

Epstein undoubtedly wanted to force the council's hand. He knew very well that if the Schneider-Epstein plan could not be executed, the council would have to either sanction Loos's original approved design with the horizontal banding or permit him to come up with an alternative. Whether he did so at the behest of Loos or of Goldman and Aufricht or on his own initiative, it was an inspired tactical move that both removed Schneider's scheme and limited the council's options.

In the meantime, Loos and his clients acquired another important supporter. Hermann Bielohlawek, one of the Christian Socialist representatives to the parliament, spoke out publicly on the question, calling for the council to take up the matter once more.

Bielohlawek was an improbable ally. A veteran ward heeler, he was a rock-hard conservative and a virulent anti-Semite. In a noxious speech before the council in 1902 he had threatened to destroy the Jewish community. Bielohlawek's reputation for philistinism was also widely known — and richly deserved. Once, annoyed when a Social Democratic representative had cited numerous books as evidence, he exclaimed: "Another book! I've lost my appetite!"[33] But after years as a political thug he had undergone a transformation. He succeeded in getting elected to a seat representing Vienna's first district, which encompassed the old town and was home to the city's wealthiest constituents. Flushed with success, he began to sport elegant clothes, drive around in a fancy coach, and eat in the best restaurants.[34] He even gave qualified praise of some of the Secessionists' buildings, including Wagner's Postsparkasse, which had drawn criticism from other rank-and-file Christian Socialists. (His favorable attitude, however, may have been less the result of an artistic conversion than an attempt to curry the favor of Lueger, who held a high opinion of Wagner).[35] To the chagrin of many, he sided with Goldman and Aufricht, cautioning the building authorities not to reach a hasty decision that would lead to the "official despoiling" of the building: "Every objective thinking person," he declared, "should resist such action."[36]

The council met again on August 17. This time, the vice-mayor, Josef Porzer, took the lead, announcing his willingness to reconsider the building's design. Porzer, too, was an unlikely ally for Loos. Though half-Jewish, he had been fiercely loyal to Lueger and outspokenly anti-Semitic, and he had moved up in the Christian Socialist leadership as a result. After Lueger's death he had emerged as the most powerful figure on the council. A lawyer by training, he was a quiet, unassuming man and usually assented to most Christian Socialist policies — even those he disagreed with.[37] But occasionally Porzer demonstrated an independent streak. When the matter of the Michaelerplatz came up on the agenda, he moved quickly to undercut Schneider, Rykl, and the building's other critics, requesting that the deadline for the completion of the façade be postponed until May 1, 1912. The council approved his motion with no discussion.[38]

The move effectively ended the political debate. Why Porzer decided to intercede remains yet another mystery. Perhaps he was convinced by Bielohlawek's appeal; perhaps he genuinely liked the building or had sympathy for Loos; perhaps either Goldman or Aufricht — or one of their supporters — had influenced him in some way. Whatever his reason, it was a great victory for Loos.

He said later that Porzer had saved his life.[39]

13

MY BUILDING ON MICHAELERPLATZ

FIG. 80 Max Oppenheimer, *Portrait of Adolf Loos*, 1910. Oil on canvas, 33 ½ × 31 ¾ in. (85 × 80.5 cm). Wien Museum.

Throughout August and the first weeks of September, Loos remained in Bad Vöslau. For a time he stayed in a less expensive boardinghouse in town. But by the beginning of September he was forced to return to the sanatorium. His condition had worsened; his stomach, he wrote to Kraus, had begun bleeding again.[1] In late August he had made plans to visit Kraus, who was vacationing in Bad Ischl in the Alps, but he was still so weak, he told his friend, that he was afraid to undertake the exertion of a train journey."[2] Bessie, who came to visit him on September 8, found him bedridden, unable to get up for more than a few hours at a time.[3]

By the middle of September Loos's health finally had begun to rebound. Kraus reported to Walden that Loos was "now really much better."[4] His recovery, though, was slow. Two weeks later, Stoessl wrote that Loos still looked "very sick and tired."[5] He had already shown the stress of the controversy when he sat for a portrait by the young artist Max Oppenheimer the previous year (fig. 80). But he now appeared gaunt and exhausted—visibly aged by the burdens of the past year. It was not until the end of September that he was finally well enough to travel to the Semmering to visit Altenberg, also recovering.[6]

In the wake of the council meeting in August, the controversy entered another period of relative calm. There was little public comment on the decision to postpone the final approval of the building's upper façade; the newspapers adopted a wait-and-see attitude. The commentaries in the press over the next two months were mostly favorable or, at least, less overtly hostile. An editorial in the *Publizistische Blätter,* a week after the meeting, even brought the novel argument that the building should be left as it was because it would "promote tourism."[7]

But Loos still faced strong opposition. At the end of August the architect Hans Berger wrote a scathing assessment of his design in the *Neue Freie Presse.* His comments came in an extended review summarizing what he thought were the merits and shortcomings of the city's recent modern buildings.

Among the works Berger discussed was the Residenzpalast, at the corner of Fleischmarkt and Rotenturm Straße (fig. 81). The construction of the building, designed by Arthur Baron, who had been a student of König's at the Technical

FIG. 81 Arthur Baron, Residenzpalast, Fleischmarkt 1, Vienna, 1909–10. Photo by author.

University, had paralleled almost exactly the erection of the Looshaus. It, too, replaced several older structures that had extended farther into the street, impeding traffic, and it was carried out as part of the city's ongoing street-widening effort.[8] Berger described it as a "valuable contribution to the problem of the artistic development of the modern city." He was especially taken with Baron's attempt, by means of geometries and simple ornament (borrowed in large part, it seems, from Wagner and his acolytes), to link the lower and upper sections while not obscuring its tectonic expression.[9]

Berger also applauded the design of another new commercial building a few blocks away, at Bognergasse 2 (fig. 82). It was the work of two other students of König's, Emmerich Spielmann and Alfred Teller.

All three architects — Baron, Spielmann, and Teller — were Jewish, part of a sizable group of young Jewish designers who had emerged in Vienna after the turn of the century. Prior to this time Jews had been mostly excluded from the ranks of the city's architects. There were a few exceptions — among them König, who came onto the scene in the 1860s and was the first Jewish architect to experience marked success. But many of the older architecture professors either did not accept Jewish students or actively discouraged them. The situation began to change only in the later 1890s, when growing numbers of young Jews entered the architecture faculties. Wagner, who was a German nationalist, was known to refuse almost all Jewish applicants to his master class, but several other professors — Friedrich Ohmann at the Academy of Fine Arts and König at the Technical University, in particular — welcomed and supported them.[10] By the time the Looshaus controversy erupted, young Jewish architects were beginning to have a noticeable impact on the cityscape.

Yet, as elsewhere in Vienna's social and cultural order, Jews found that full assimilation remained elusive. Even within Vienna's modernist camp there was a discernable cleavage between Wagner's adherents, almost all of whom were non-Jews, and the small but rising band of Jewish architects that included, in addition to Baron, Spielmann, and Teller, figures like Oskar Strnad, Oskar Wlach, Hugo Gorge, and Josef Frank. The split played out in the ways in which the various groups of Viennese modernists sought to convey the message of the new architecture: many of the younger Jewish architects demonstrated greater determination in their embrace of the new functionalism, adopting a language less reliant on traditional ornament, massing, and arrangement.

Given their interest in the new functionalism, the younger Jewish architects were, in fact, closely aligned with Loos's aesthetic. A number of them — Strnad and Frank, in particular — had been strongly influenced by his coffeehouse lectures. But Loos maintained a measured distance from them, preferring, as always, to keep his independence.[11] He was sympathetic to their ideas, but he preferred his insularity.

Spielmann and Teller's new building on the Bognergasse incorporated a number of common modernist ideas. Still, its straightforward imagery was an exception in Vienna, where, as late as 1910, the city's legions of modernists — aside from Loos and Örley — continued to rely on more elaboration. Berger found the Bognergasse building to be a good and representative solution to the new functionalism. It consists, he observed, "of not much more than its own façade." He complimented the two designers on their "architectonic" handling of the surfaces, which, he thought, "made an elegant, urbane impression."[12]

Berger reserved his strongest praise for the new Urania Building, located on the eastern edge of the Ringstrasse at the Aspern Bridge (fig. 83). Its architect

FIG. 82 Emmerich Spielmann and Alfred Teller, residential and commercial building at Bognergasse 2, Vienna, 1909 – 10. Photo by author.

FIG. 83 Max Fabiani, Urania Building, Urania Straße 1, Vienna, 1909 – 10. Private collection.

was Max Fabiani, who was now teaching at the Technical University as König's assistant. Over the course of the first decade of the new century, Fabiani had gradually found his way back to a modified historic revivalism, and his design for the Urania, an adult education center, was replete with classical moldings, pilasters, and detailing. Some at the time saw the building as a repudiation of his early works. Berger argued, however, that it was the most original of the city's new structures—in large measure because Fabiani had taken great liberties with the classical form language, altering its syntax and recasting the scale of its various elements.[13]

He failed to mention what, in retrospect, is the most remarkable feature of the building: the complex disposition of its interiors. To accommodate a large theater and other public spaces, Fabiani sliced the building into a series of volumes, which he pushed up and down in relation to each other, much like Loos did with his Raumplan. The result was a sequence of intricate interlocking rooms that offered a striking—and very modern—spatial experience.

Berger was seemingly untroubled by the disconnect between the building's outer envelope, which suggested a more or less conventional load-bearing structure, and its concrete and steel framing system. Yet it was precisely on this point that he condemned Loos's Michaelerplatz design. He charged that Loos, by concealing the actual structure of the building "under decoration," had produced a "sham construction" (*Scheinkonstruktion*). Moreover, Loos's use of a heavy cornice to differentiate the lower and upper sections, he wrote, had been "very amateurishly" executed: "What should always be avoided, is quite evident here: the plump, undifferentiated mass of the upper stories seems to crush the marble and brass grandeur of the lower portion."[14]

For Berger, then, the problem with the new Looshaus rested not in its unabashed modernism but in its expression—in essence, he suggested that Loos's skills as a designer had been unequal to the task. It was a verdict not very different from Wagner's, and it points to one of the reasons Loos received little support from the city's other modernists, many of whom held the same opinion.

Loos's critics also found other reasons to attack him. Just as repellent to many was his overt self-righteousness. Most of the city's architects and critics, both within and outside the modernist camp, regarded him as crusading, vain, and blindly uncompromising. (Even Kraus and Altenberg, though they did not state it publicly, thought that Loos's inflexibility sometimes clouded his judgment.)

In early October, in an essay in the *Fremden-Blatt,* the young playwright and director Georg Terramare assailed Loos for his purported fanaticism. While acceding to Loos's argument that the building's upper façades and roof resembled the city's Biedermeier-era structures, Terramare charged that Loos had failed to take into consideration the ways in which early nineteenth-century designers had used minimal moldings and other devices to avoid "leaving the surfaces completely smooth and the windows looking like they had been cut into the surface." In Loos's zeal to make a modern statement he had ignored history, not embraced it; in so doing, Terramare wrote, he had advanced his ideological agenda at the expense of making a fully realized architectural statement.[15]

Others found Loos's singlemindedness a source of amusement. In mid-October the satirical magazine *Kikeriki* poked fun at him, offering its own unique solution to the controversy: "The Looshaus on Michaelerplatz by itself would be quite beautiful. It's just that the imperial palace doesn't fit with it very well. So, away with the palace!"[16] The same month, a piece summarizing the controversy in the Munich literary and culture magazine *Der Zwiebelfisch* also made light of Loos's fanaticism: "On Michaelerplatz in Vienna Adolf Loos has erected a building" that is "completely naked and yet assembled from the finest materials: neither Baroque mayonnaise nor a Rococo hairnet, nor even little modernist squares from one of the Werkstätten have been glued onto the façade. Naturally, people like Stoessl and Kraus, little magazines like *Fackel* and *Sturm,* [and] other arty types are elated."[17]

At the end of October, Kraus again came to Loos's defense. A woman, he wrote in *Die Fackel,* had related to him that she had overheard the following about the Looshaus: "The building, which most saw as a portent of the future, was in fact a return to the best of tradition." It had achieved "complete harmony of idea and form, which bestowed it the power of a classical work. Who was the speaker? Adolf Loos? No, Mr. Josef Hoffmann."[18]

For Kraus, the story served a double purpose. Citing Hoffmann's unabashed praise was, of course, a means of supporting his friend. It also allowed him to get in a not very subtle dig at Hoffmann, who had been notably reticent throughout the debate.

By 1911, Hoffmann was, after Wagner, the most renowned of the Viennese modernists, both at home and abroad; his silence spoke volumes about the attitude of the majority of the Viennese reformers toward Loos and his building. Hoffmann's dislike of the design had its roots in part in his objections to Loos's use of historical elements: Loos's application of "classical columns and window surrounds," he later wrote, "was hardly consistent with our ideas."[19] But the long-standing antipathy between the two men also played a role.[20] Over the years, Hoffmann wrote, whenever they met, "there were often conflicts and differences of opinion."[21] That Hoffmann did not speak out, however, had only partly to do with his opposition: his reluctance to enter the discussion publicly stemmed from his usual reserve — he was anything but a polished speaker or writer — and throughout the years he showed a consistent unwillingness to engage Loos directly. But he was certainly also aware that his lack of commentary would be understood as criticism.

By mid-October, Loos was well enough to resume work. The episode with his stomach, though, had taken its toll. He was no longer able to eat normally. For years afterward he subsisted entirely on ham and cream, which he consumed in small portions throughout the day. Each morning he put a piece of ham in one of his pockets, and he would take a bite when he was hungry; in a second pocket he kept a small bottle of cream, which he refilled several times each day.[22] For a gourmand, who relished fine food and dining, it was an especially cruel blow.

Throughout this time Loos had continued to ponder the problem of the upper façades. An article in the *Frankfurter Zeitung* on October 17 quoted him saying that "he did not consider the building finished," and that he was still working out

FIG. 84 Goldman & Salatsch Building, late fall 1911, with the five test window boxes. Bildarchiv Foto Marburg.

a solution.[23] But only a week later, on October 24, he had workmen mount five bronze window boxes to the front façade, just below the windows on the second of the upper floors (fig. 84). His idea was to test their effect and to see how the public would react.

Most of the newspapers responded favorably.[24] A reporter for the *Fremden-Blatt* observed: "The general impression . . . is that the building's façade no longer disturbs anyone, and that it would be best not to conduct any further experiments."[25] The *Deutsches Volksblatt* wrote that the addition of the boxes "had met with great interest." The controversy was now over: "The battle of the façade . . . has been decided."[26]

Notwithstanding the friendly response in the press, the building authorities issued an order a few days later, demanding that the boxes, which had not been sanctioned, be removed immediately. Loos and the clients ignored it. They recognized that the public was coming to their side; leaving the boxes in place, they hoped, would win over those still on the fence and quell further criticism.

The move turned out to be even more effective than they dared hope. On November 13, although Loos and the clients had neither taken the boxes down nor complied with the earlier order to alter the façade, the authorities — evidently at Porzer's behest — acquiesced and issued an occupancy permit for the entire building.[27] Goldman and Aufricht were now free to operate their business and to rent out or sell the spaces on the upper floors.

At the same time, out of the glare of pubic scrutiny, workmen were putting the finishing touches on Goldman's new house on the Hardtgasse. Loos's design for the exterior of the three-story structure echoed many features of the Michaelerplatz building: simple, smooth surfaces, classical moldings, and robust columns framing the entry (fig. 85). The Goldmans' large apartment filled the two lower floors. Its principal living areas were situated on the second-story piano nobile, arranged around a central atrium that gave access to the main rooms.

Goldman also asked Loos to execute the interiors. He responded with what were now his customary elements for domestic spaces: a built-in inglenook in the living room, beamed ceilings, marble revetment, Oriental carpets, and English-inspired furnishings (fig. 86).[28] (Deeply grateful, Goldman expressed his appreciation and admiration by commissioning the sculptor Arthur Imanuel Löwenthal to make a bust of Loos, which he placed in a niche in the dining room [fig. 87].)[29]

Loos made no attempts to publish the building. Though it was, aside from the Michaelerplatz commission, his largest work to date, he kept silent about his involvement. His long-standing aversion to having his works photographed was doubtless part of the reason, but he and Goldman doubtless also wished to avoid any further publicity or the sort of acts of vandalism that had plagued the Steiner House.[30]

FIG. 85 Adolf Loos, Leopold Goldman House, Hardtgasse 27 – 29, Vienna, 1909 – 11. Photo by Wolfgang Thaler.

Loos was at work during this time, too, on the design of a diminutive house in the Viennese suburb of Ober-St. Veit for Stoessl and the interiors of a perfume shop for one of the small ground-floor retail spaces in the Goldman & Salatsch building on the side facing Kohlmarkt. For the latter he reused the snakewood vitrines and display cases from the former Goldman & Salatsch store on the Graben, which the owners had now closed.[31]

After this flurry of work Loos went to the Semmering with Bessie to visit Altenberg and take a much-needed break. But he simply could not distance himself from the controversy. In a postcard he sent to Kraus from the hotel, he mentioned that he had spoken to "Benedikt" — presumably Moriz Benedikt, chief editor of the *Neue Freie Presse* — protesting Berger's article, which he thought particularly unfair.[32]

Loos now felt well enough to resume his public lectures. Walden invited him to speak in Berlin at the end of November. Loos agreed. This time he proposed to repeat his lecture "Vom Gehen, Stehen, Sitzen, Liegen, Schlafen, Essen, Trinken." The talk took place on November 25 in the Architektenhaus, part of the annual lecture series organized by Walden's Verein für Kunst (fig. 88).

Loos presented his familiar argument about the modernism of everyday objects. He also used the occasion, as Walden had suggested, to discuss at length his ideas for the Michaelerplatz building.[33] The talk turned out to be a resounding success: many of the Berlin avant-gardists turned out, and the large hall was nearly

FIG. 86 Leopold Goldman House, living room. Graphische Sammlung Albertina, Vienna, ALA 3107.

FIG. 87 Leopold Goldman House, dining room. Graphische Sammlung Albertina, Vienna, ALA 3108.

filled to capacity. When Loos finished speaking, the audience responded with boisterous applause.[34] Afterward he met Schönberg, Webern, Walden, the artist Emil Nolde and his wife, Ada, and the writers Alfred Döblin, Albert Ehrenstein, and Karin Michaelis at the Rheingold Restaurant for a celebratory dinner.[35]

His mood, though, was anything but jubilant. Before the event he had written to Schönberg, who had moved back to Berlin because he had been unable to

FIG. 88 Advertisement for Loos's lecture "Vom Gehen, Stehen, Sitzen, Liegen, Schlafen, Essen, Trinken," November 25, 1911. Der Sturm, November 1911, 689.

FIG. 89 Loos (in the front of the bobsled) in Davos, December 3, 1911. Graphische Sammlung Albertina, Vienna, ALA 2065.

make ends meet in Vienna, that he was weary of the public scrutiny of his work —especially from the critics. He was certain Schönberg felt the same way: "We architects and musicians can't keep the dirty scribbling dogs off our backs. Yes, I stay as far away from the architects as possible, as you certainly do the musicians." He complained that Kraus, who was financially secure and had complete control over his journal, had no one to please but himself: he could not understand how difficult it was for those who relied on others to carry out their work. If I fail to please people, Loos groused, "it means going hungry."[36]

When he arrived back in Vienna, Loos was confronted with a new crisis. Bessie, who had been living in their apartment since returning from Algeria in May, had taken a turn for the worse. During her time in Biskra her health had shown a little improvement, but the damp autumn weather in Austria aggravated her condition once more. The doctors now recommended that she spend at least two years in a sanatorium.[37]

Loos took her to Davos, Switzerland, for treatment. Perched in the high Alps, the town had long been a favored destination for the well heeled and ailing, renowned for its cool, dry climate. (The following spring, Thomas Mann would accompany his sick wife to a sanatorium there: not long afterward, moved by the experience and the cosmopolitan atmosphere, he began writing the first version of *The Magic Mountain*.)

The experience for Loos, though, was anything but inspiring. He was concerned for Bessie, but he also had to face the reality of paying for her treatment. He had been forced to lay out a large amount of money for his own convalescence, and he had contributed to Altenberg's sanatorium bill. And for much of the late summer and early fall he had been unable to work. Now he had to find a way to finance Bessie's stay.

He stayed in Davos only a few days—just long enough to help Bessie settle in. Remarkably, he managed to find time for a little diversion. Though he had been gravely ill only months before, Loos, now sporting longer hair and a thick mustache and looking fit, took part in a bobsled race (fig. 89). Soon thereafter, he departed. Arrangements were already under way for him to deliver a major address in Vienna a little more than a week later.[38]

The idea to present the lecture, which took place on December 11, 1911, may have been Loos's. He knew that his best chance for winning his struggle with the council and building authorities was to bring the public over to his side. It is possible, though, that the initiative came from Philipp Berger, director of the Akademischer Verband für Literatur und Musik. Berger had a central role in organizing the lecture. He was an outspoken supporter of Loos, and he wanted to aid him in his fight. It was he who came up with the text for the poster—and the idea of including Rykl's epithet, "A Monstrosity of a Building" (Ein Scheusal von einem Haus) (fig. 90).[39]

Wishing to fan the flames of controversy — and ensure a massive turnout — Berger had a thousand copies of the poster printed, as well as a large number of handbills.[40] "A furious propaganda campaign ensued," the young Expressionist poet Heinrich Nowak recalled.[41] Students from the universities, who formed much of the Verband's membership, took up Loos's cause, distributing the handbills around the city and getting out the word to friends and acquaintances.[42]

The lecture took place in the Sophiensaal, on Marxergasse, in the third district. The old hall, one of the city's largest, seated more than 2,700. Designed in 1826 by Sicard von Sicardsburg and Van der Nüll, it had originally been a steam bath; later, in the 1840s, it had been converted into a concert and dance hall. Johann Strauss conducted the opening ball in 1849, and he and his sons subsequently premiered many of their waltzes there. The building's high vaulted ceilings and the pool beneath the floor provided superb acoustics. (Until 2001, when a fire destroyed it, it was a favored recording site.)

The lecture took place on a cold and foggy Monday evening. But the uncongenial weather and timing did nothing to lessen the enthusiasm of the large crowd. The publicity effort had proved wildly successful. The hall, a reporter for the *Reichspost* wrote the following day, "was filled to the last seat." The audience members, "familiar with the entire contentious and emotional" struggle Loos had fought over the preceding months, "followed every word with rapt attention."[43]

Among those in attendance were Porzer and Bielohlawek. Most of Loos's close friends and supporters also came. Walden even made the trip from Berlin to hear his friend.[44] Of the city's leading architects, however, the newspapers mentioned by name only Örley; Wagner, Hoffmann, and most of the other Secessionists, it seems, stayed away.[45]

Loos spoke, as he had for almost all of his public lectures since 1909, with slides to illustrate his points. The showing of the slides, first without commentary, began at 7:30; Loos came onto the stage promptly at 8.[46] The *Reichspost* reporter noted that he lectured in a "resounding voice" — too loud for the building — evidence, he thought, that Loos was not an experienced public speaker and had overestimated the size of the space. (In fact, Loos probably spoke too loudly because his growing deafness rendered him unable to gauge the sound in the hall.)

The lecture lasted nearly two hours.[47] Loos first discussed the original competition Goldman and Aufricht had mounted, and how he had come to receive the commission for the building. His design, he told the audience, had differed greatly from those of the other participants, and he outlined his reasons for adopting the pushed-back building line, his use of a single courtyard, and his intentions for the shop's complex interior arrangement. He also explained why

FIG. 90 Poster for Loos's talk "Mein Haus am Michaelerplatz" at the Sophiensaal, December 11, 1911. Wien Museum.

the plan he initially submitted to the building authorities deviated from the final version of the building: "I requested that the four [upper] stories be left out of consideration. I did not know yet what sort of stone, which I wanted to look for in Greece, would be available to me. In the meantime, the builder, architect Epstein, drew a proposed design for the four stories. I knew that I would select Cipollino marble. But every block has a different character. Thus, I deferred the decision."[48]

Loos then took up the question of why the windows on the lower floor of the building did not line up with those above, a feature that had been the source of much consternation. It was his solution, he said, for establishing a clear separation between the commercial and residential zones: "The discord between the two [vertical] axes underscores this effort."

Loos also tried to answer those who had found fault with his use of the four nonstructural columns at the entry. It was true, he admitted, that the columns are not necessary to support the lintel: "But the ground floor required large windows, and the columns carry over to the residential stories above, showing that, in the mezzanine story in between them, there is not a storage space, but an exclusive store." The columns helped to carry the visual weight of the large lintel and upper stories and corresponded to the way that supporting such loads was traditionally expressed.[49]

But all this careful planning, he said, had almost come to naught. When the council had interceded and had turned to Schneider, who had hastily sketched his "solution," the result had undermined Loos's design. The vertical arrangement of the windows he proposed, Loos protested, "was impossible: with a few ill-considered pencil strokes he rendered my painstakingly thought-out design for the lower stories into an absurdity." The stress of the controversy had made him sick. "I'm a resilient person, I held up fine, but not my stomach."[50]

Loos then went on the attack. "From time to time," he told the audience, "I have thought about whether Councilman Schneider was really the one who should be correcting my façade. He did win the competition for the Technical Museum and executed his design." While still recovering from his ulcer, Loos had sought out other opinions: "Since everyone knows that I understand nothing about architecture, I turned to two German architects . . . Ludwig Hoffmann, the most important architect in Berlin, and Martin Dülfer, the most important architect in Dresden." Both savaged Schneider's design. Dülfer wrote that "it was evidence of the poor state of our contemporary architecture." The verdict, Loos told the audience, buoyed his flagging spirits: "When I read that, I became happy again and my health returned."[51]

He saved a few barbs for Rykl and Berger. After Rykl had denigrated his building, Loos told his listeners, he had thought that he might be able to "personally persuade him of the merits of the marble facing." Not knowing who Rykl was, he looked up his name in the city directory and discovered the reason for his reaction: he was a major producer of artificial stone. With that, Loos said, "I dispensed with the idea." Berger's critique, he continued, was simply personal pique, the result of a private matter he "did not want to discuss publicly." But, he added, he found it troubling that Berger had misused the public platform of the *Neue Freie Presse* to get even.[52]

Finally, Loos addressed the question of how the building fit into contemporary Viennese design:

Which style is the building? The Viennese style of the year 1910. But people do not understand that. They search for strange models in far-off lands, just as they looked for American models for the Café Museum. And here, as I did with the café, I collected elements from the old Viennese coffeehouses and building façades to find the modern, the truly modern style.[53]

Loos thanked several people for their support: Porzer, Bielohlawek, and the two clients. He concluded by observing that the uproar over his building was merely business as usual in Vienna:

So it has been with all the buildings the Viennese are now proud of. So it was with the Opera House. One of its designers, who had been made ill by the ceaseless attacks, ended up in the insane asylum; the other committed suicide. I'm made of tougher stuff. I'm not afraid for myself. I fear instead for architects one hundred years in the future. Who will they kill in one hundred years with comparisons to the Haus am Michaelerplatz?[54]

14

TRIUMPH

The large audience in the Sophiensaal, which had interrupted Loos repeatedly with cheers and clapping, erupted into a torrent of applause when he finished speaking. A few people jeered, but their whistles and catcalls were all but drowned out.[1] Visibly moved, Loos returned to the podium several times to acknowledge the appreciation.[2]

In the lecture's aftermath, almost all of the newspapers hailed Loos, recounting the evening's events in detail.[3] A reporter for the *Wiener Mittags-Zeitung* wrote that the lecture had been a "sensation." The arrival of celebrities had been tantamount, he claimed, to the excitement that preceded the Metternich-Redoute, the city's most illustrious masquerade ball, held each year during Mardi Gras week.[4] Only the *Wiener Montags-Journal* responded negatively. Loos's answer to criticism, its editors wrote, was "cheeky" and ill-considered: It was typical of the "school of Karl Kraus. One rents a hall, fills it full of impudence, and makes some money along the way." (With the auditorium at capacity, Loos had indeed made a tidy sum from the event.) The only thing he had gotten right was that "people would eventually grow accustomed to the building: that, however, speaks not for the aesthetic qualities of his art. A man married to a humpbacked woman may grow used to her appearance, but that doesn't make her beautiful."[5]

Loos was unfazed. He knew he was now winning the struggle. The lecture, in fact, was only one prong of his campaign to secure public support. Beforehand, he had arranged for a series of tours of the now complete Goldman & Salatsch store. Beginning December 4, those who held tickets for the lecture could walk though the spaces with Loos, who would patiently explain his design and point out its innovative features.[6]

The new store was stunning (figs. 91 – 94). The exquisite marble cladding and the brass mullions, and Loos's meticulous attention to the detailing, raised it well above the norm. The four marble columns across the front lent the building a quiet dignity — quite unlike the Viennese department stores, or, even, the city's other upscale retail establishments. The columns and the deep-set porch served precisely as Loos intended: to screen the entry doors, developing a separation between the store and the busy surrounding square. Even window-shoppers were required to walk into the porch area, deviating from the usual traffic flow along and around the building.

The columns, as Loos had suggested, were also a gesture of historical continuity. But by being pressed into the mass of the structure they fostered a sleek, modern image, an impression he reinforced with the brass-framed lintel, which resembled an iron I-beam. In this way the porch both affirmed and denied its connection with the past.

The large plates of curving glass framing either side of the doors were a novelty (fig. 95). The rolled plate process required to fashion such massive sheets

FIG. 91 Detail of the Looshaus showing the corner of the entry and the mezzanine. Photo by Wolfgang Thaler.

FIG. 92 Front of the Looshaus, summer 1912. *Charakteristische Details von ausgeführten Bauten* (Berlin: Ernst Wasmuth, [1914]), plate 46.

FIG. 93 Postcard showing the Looshaus and Michaelerplatz soon after the building's completion. Author's collection.

FIG. 94 Goldman & Salatsch Building, detail of the second-story bay windows. Photo by Wolfgang Thaler.

had been perfected only in the 1880s, and the manufacture of rounded panels was still a new technology in 1910. Here, once more, Loos presented a manifest opposition between modernity and tradition: the monolithic columns, solid and staid, offering a pointed contrast with the transparency, lightness, and inherent newness of the windows.

The curved glass produced a shimmering effect, reflecting light from the square. Loos enhanced it by interrupting the concave membrane of glass that ran along the inside edge of the porch with bow windows on either side of the doors. The smaller beveled squares of glass above the display windows acted like prisms, further refracting and distributing the light. It was a technique that he had developed in the first Goldman & Salatsch shop, and here he accentuated it with a grid of electric lights in the soffit, which amplified the light and its reflective qualities.

Inside, the new shop was arranged on four principal levels. From the front doors, customers arrived directly in the outfitting and accessories area. Immediately before them was a broad staircase leading up to the tailor department on the mezzanine (fig. 96). The room, perfectly square, was framed by massive piers; set into the spaces between them was a series of display cases edged in brass (fig. 97).

The vitrines and sales counters divided up the large space, reducing its scale. The areas along and between the counters were in fact quite compressed, preserving some of the intimacy of the original Goldman & Salatsch store. Dominating the room were four freestanding columns, which, like those along the

OPPOSITE
FIG. 95 Goldman & Salatsch Building, view of the porch. Photo by Wolfgang Thaler.

FROM TOP
FIG. 96 Goldman & Salatsch Building, main stair within the store. Photo by Martin Gerlach, c. 1930. Heinrich Kulka, *Adolf Loos: Das Werk des Architekten* (Vienna: Anton Schroll, 1931), plate 45.

FIG. 97 Goldman & Salatsch Building, sportswear department on the ground floor. Brochure for Goldman & Salatsch, c. 1911. Graphische Sammlung Albertina, Vienna, ALA 1526/4.

FIG. 98 Goldman & Salatsch Building, winter sports department. Brochure for Goldman & Salatsch, c. 1911. Graphische Sammlung Albertina, Vienna, ALA 1526/6.

walls, were encased in polished mahogany. On either side of the inner front columns were two pairs of terraced vitrines, directing customers to the center of the room and the stair; just above, on the first landing, were the two cashiers.

Downstairs, in the basement, customers found the sports department (fig. 98). Its spatial configuration matched the main sales area above, but its surfaces were treated more sparingly: the great concrete piers and carrying beams were merely painted, yielding at once an elemental and modern appearance.

By contrast, the stair leading from the ground floor to the mezzanine offered an image of refinement and visual complexity (fig. 99). At the top of the first flight of stairs the path diverged into two smaller stairways extending up on either side. The space here was compressed as well, but the skylight and panels of mirrors along the back wall created an illusion of openness. The mirrors gave a preview of the rooms above, which became visible only as one ascended the stairs (fig.100). At the same time, the dark mahogany paneling established a shift of mood, a sense of exclusivity and privacy, notably distinct from the more public area below.

The mezzanine was subdivided into two principal levels: on the lower portion, immediately in front of the stairs, were the accounting department and a part of the material storage area (fig. 101). Above, on the upper mezzanine, customers found a waiting lounge, a small office, the upper part of the material storage area, and three large fitting rooms (figs. 102 – 106).

FIGS. 99 AND 100 Goldman & Salatsch Building, views of the stair leading to the mezzanine. Photos by Wolfgang Thaler.

FIG. 101 Goldman & Salatsch Building, contemporary view of the mezzanine. Photo by Wolfgang Thaler.

FIG. 102 Goldman & Salatsch Building, contemporary view from the mezzanine office looking back toward the stair and the material storage area. Photo by Wolfgang Thaler.

FIG. 103 Goldman & Salatsch Building, contemporary view of the reception space on the mezzanine. Photo by Wolfgang Thaler.

FIG. 104 Goldman & Salatsch Building, reception space on the mezzanine. Brochure for Goldman & Salatsch, c. 1911. Graphische Sammlung Albertina, Vienna, ALA 1526/8.

FIG. 105 Goldman & Salatsch Building, fitting rooms on the mezzanine level. Brochure for Goldman & Salatsch, c. 1911. Graphische Sammlung Albertina, Vienna, ALA 1526/10.

FIG. 106 Goldman & Salatsch Building, material storage and ordering area on the mezzanine. Brochure for Goldman & Salatsch, c. 1911. Graphische Sammlung Albertina, Vienna, ALA 1526/9.

Loos took particular pains with this part of the salon, adapting some of his now standard ideas for domestic design to fashion a series of spaces appropriate for the store's well-to-do clientele. The lounge, with its low, beamed ceilings, dark paneling, and upholstered furniture — evoking an English gentlemen's club — was especially luxurious.

The adjoining work areas, arrayed along the Herrengasse side of the building, on the other hand, might be best described as Spartan. The largest portion of this zone was taken up by the two-story tailor workshop (figs. 107, 108). To the rear, on the lower mezzanine, was the double-height ironing room and a cramped shirt workshop, the only area in the store where women were employed (figs. 109, 110). In another space concealed from customers, Goldman & Salatsch

FIG. 107 Goldman & Salatsch Building, repair workshop on the lower mezzanine level. Brochure for Goldman & Salatsch, c. 1911. Graphische Sammlung Albertina, Vienna, ALA 1526/13.

FIG. 108 Goldman & Salatsch Building, suit workshop. Brochure for Goldman & Salatsch, c. 1911. Graphische Sammlung Albertina, Vienna, ALA 1526/12.

FIG. 109 Goldman & Salatsch Building, ironing workshop. Brochure for Goldman & Salatsch, c. 1911. Graphische Sammlung Albertina, Vienna, ALA 1526/14.

operated a school for apprentices. Situated in the attic story, it included, in addition to a classroom, a sizable work area illuminated with large expanses of glass facing into the rear courtyard (figs. 111, 112).

It is a keen irony that this room, its fittings and forms wholly determined by its function, was the most unabashedly modern in the building. It achieved what Loos had taken pains to avoid: the building's exterior and the main store denied any direct expression of their underlying structure. By cloaking the concrete frame and cunningly obscuring the functional form of the rooms, he had concocted a picture of respectability and decorum — one that was modern to be sure, but moderated through the application of traditional devices and elements. The school for apprentices, conceived and executed without any concession to pro-

FIG. 110 Goldman & Salatsch Building, shirt workshop. Brochure for Goldman & Salatsch, c. 1911. Graphische Sammlung Albertina, Vienna, ALA 1526/11.

FIG. 111 Goldman & Salatsch Building, classroom for the apprentice school in the attic. Brochure for Goldman & Salatsch, c. 1911. Graphische Sammlung Albertina, Vienna, ALA 1526/16.

FIG. 112 Goldman & Salatsch Building, workshop of the apprentice school. Brochure for Goldman & Salatsch, c. 1911. Graphische Sammlung Albertina, Vienna, ALA 1526/15.

priety, evoked what some commentators had missed in the building: a straight-forward expression of modern reality.

To judge from the few accounts we have of those who went on the tours, most were impressed with the building. Karin Michaelis, who had traveled from

FIG. 113 Goldman & Salatsch Building, entry to the apartments. Photo by Wolfgang Thaler.

Berlin to hear Loos's lecture, joined one of the tours and wrote afterward in the guestbook that the building was an "artist's dream made real."[7]

The newspaper of the Lower Austrian Trades Association included the only report of what Loos had said during one of the tours, alluding to his ideas about using quality materials and finishes in lieu of ornament to produce a "distinguished effect."[8]

The write-up in the paper also made mention of his Raumplan ideas — one of the only references at the time to the building's innovative spatial design. Looking back, it is remarkable how little the interiors figured into the debate about the building. The radical nature of Loos's spatial ordering and his idiosyncratic handling of the public and work areas remained outside the discussion — a fact that is all the more striking when one considers that the arrangement of the shop's interiors had been Loos's primary focus from the beginning.

And nowhere in the debate was any discussion of Loos's treatment of those areas devoted to living spaces on the upper floors. The entry sequence and stair leading off the Herrengasse to the upper stories make up one of his most characteristic and aesthetically appealing designs (figs. 113 – 116). As in the store, he lavished attention on these spaces, employing an array of stones (smoky white Carrara marble for the entry, vibrant Skyros and Cipollino marble for the staircase walls), brass, wood, and other materials to contrive an image of luxury and modernist clarity.

FIGS. 114–116 Goldman & Salatsch Building, stair to the apartments with detail of railing. Photos by Wolfgang Thaler.

In the weeks after "My House on Michaelerplatz," Loos bided his time. The great success of the lecture, almost all observers acknowledged, had nearly ended the affair. With the new deadline to submit an acceptable façade design postponed until May 1912, he had five months to find a means to end the impasse with the city.

After the lecture, Loos traveled back to Switzerland to visit Bessie.[9] They spent the Christmas holidays at the Hotel Palace in Montreux. Sporting a mustache and beard, he was now visibly more vital (fig. 117). Success had reinvigorated him: he had managed to gain weight, and the lull in the controversy had allowed him to relax fully for the first time in months.

Just after the start of the new year Loos returned to Vienna. A few days later he escorted Altenberg — recently released from the sanatorium in Inzersdorf — on a vacation on the Semmering.[10] Altenberg was still sick, suffering from periodic mania and delusions. Outwardly he was amiable and gracious, but his mounting paranoia fueled a jealous rage toward his old friend. The day after Loos spoke at the Sophiensaal he wrote to Lilly Steiner that he could no longer bear Loos's egoism and single-minded promotion of himself and his ideas: "I can stand Loos only in his better moments, but his toothpaste-Barnum and Bayley [sic] advertising campaign for his own personal cause was Jewish, inartistic, and disgusts me."[11]

With the money he received from his persistent appeals to friends and supporters, Altenberg found lodging at the exclusive Hotel Panhans. There he devel-

FIG. 117 Adolf Loos, spring or summer 1912. Private collection.

oped a fixation on the owner's eleven-year-old daughter—part of his pattern of obsession with prepubescent girls. But he was writing again; by summer's end he had completed a new book of prose sketches and poems, which he published under the title *Semmering 1912*.[12] It was among his most accomplished works, by turns eloquent, ardent, and moving. His fleeting moments of lucidity ended not long thereafter; in December his brother Georg had him committed to the Steinhof psychiatric hospital in Vienna.[13]

After a restful time spent hiking and sledding in the mountains, Loos returned to Vienna. During this period he was engaged with several other projects. Workmen were putting the final touches on the Stoessl House, and they were making progress on fitting out the interiors of another store, the Kniže tailor shop on the Graben (fig. 118). Loos was also involved in the design of two other residences, one for Andreas Horner, concierge of the Hotel Krantz, and his wife, Helene, and a second house for the lawyer and Social Democratic party functionary Gustav Scheu and his wife, Helene Scheu-Riesz, an author, translator, and editor (figs. 119, 120).

   The two houses, completed over the next year and a half, were to be exalted in the literature of modernism as progenitors of the new functionalism. At the time, however, they caused barely a ripple of interest. Neither house was widely published—again, because Loos refused to promote them. A few cognoscenti and

FIG. 118 Adolf Loos, Kniže Store, Graben 13, Vienna, 1910–13. Photo by Wolfgang Thaler.

FIG. 119 Adolf Loos, Helene Horner House, Nothartgasse 7, Vienna, 1912. Bildarchiv der österreichischen Nationalbibliothek, Vienna.

FIG. 120 Adolf Loos, Gustav and Helene Scheu House, Larochegasse 3, Vienna, 1912–13. Graphische Sammlung Albertina, Vienna, ALA 2530.

enthusiastic young architects found their way to Vienna's outer districts to view the villas, but they remained for some time nearly silent witnesses to his vision of an architecture of simplicity and immediacy.

At the beginning of February, Loos traveled to Berlin to hear a concert of Schönberg's music.[14] The program included some of Schönberg's older songs as well as several new pieces. The audience greeted it with rapt enthusiasm, though most of the critics — unsurprisingly — panned it.[15]

Loos made the journey with the progressive educator Eugenie Schwarzwald. The two had met at the turn of the century, and over the intervening decade they had developed a close friendship. Some years before, Schwarzwald had opened a private school aimed at providing girls with high-quality secondary school training. She had Kokoschka give drawing lessons to her students, and she enlisted Schönberg to teach music and Loos to lecture on architecture. She also asked Loos, who had furnished her apartment in 1905, to design a new building for her planned school on the Semmering.

He was already at work on it by the time they left for Berlin. He conceived an expansive eight-story, U-shaped structure perched on a hillside (fig. 121).[16] Powerfully massed, with basic windows set nearly flush into its unadorned walls, it bore witness to Loos's preoccupation with a radical simplicity. The design suggested, even more than the Michaelerplatz building, the possibilities of a realist idiom — forthright and unencumbered by notions of embellishment. Had it been

realized, it would have announced an even more jarring image of the new. Schwarzwald, however, was unable to put together the financing. Loos produced two other smaller variants of the design for sites in Vienna, but, in the end, it remained unrealized.

The late winter months brought Loos new concerns. He was worried about Kokoschka, who was agitated and emotionally fragile. After returning from Berlin, Kokoschka had found a position as a teaching assistant at the Kunstgewerbeschule. In early January he presented a lecture about his work under the auspices of the Akademischer Verband für Literatur und Musik. It was his intention to offer an important statement of his ideas and explain his recent work. But the event was poorly attended, and Kokoschka, who rambled on incomprehensibly, left much of the audience bewildered.[17]

It was during this period that Kokoschka met Alma Mahler, the widow of Gustav Mahler.[18] The two began an impassioned affair. Loos believed — correctly, as it turned out — that the relationship posed a real threat to Kokoschka's spiritual and emotional stability. He warned his young protégé not to become too involved, but Kokoschka, obsessed with Alma, paid no heed. The tumultuous relationship went on for three years, until Alma left Kokoschka for Walter Gropius. Kokoschka was devastated.

In late January or early February, Bessie, who could no longer abide her isolation in Davos, returned to Vienna. Loos took her to the Semmering, lodging at the Hotel Panhans. They visited Altenberg and spent time hiking and sledding in the mountains.[19] All this activity was too much for Loos. On March 6, Kraus reported to Walden that Loos was "sick" again.[20] This time, however, he recuperated quickly. Kokoschka, who paid both Loos and Altenberg a visit a few days later, found his friend already on the mend; by the middle of March, when Loos returned to Vienna, he had fully recovered.[21]

Loos now took up the problem of the Michaelerplatz building once more. Here, though, there is a gap in the story. He must have met with the officials in the building office sometime in March in an effort to negotiate an end to the matter, but there is no record of the meeting. What happened occurred off stage, out of the glare of the media. We can surmise from later events some of what must have taken place.

It appears that he spoke with Goldemund, who decided to drop the require-ment that Loos complete a new façade and accept his proposal to add the window boxes. To ensure that the building's final form fit as well as possible into the square, they discussed the distribution of the new boxes. A draftsman in the office prepared — evidently with Loos's input — a revised drawing of the façade, with five additional window boxes on the front and a continuous row of boxes under the second of the upper stories facing the two side streets (fig. 122).[22]

On March 29 the council met to discuss the issue. Porzer presided at the meeting; Schneider, too, was in attendance. Mayor Neumayer himself pre-

FIG. 122 Elevation of the Looshaus showing the placement of the window boxes, drawn by a staff memberof the building office, approved May 3, 1912. Pencil on tracing paper, 196 ⅞ × 171 ¼ in. (500 × 435 cm). Plan- und Schriftenkammer der Magistratsamt (MA 37), Vienna.

sented a short summary of the proposed changes, with a recommendation to accept the new design. Without debate the council voted to sanction the new façade provided that the extra window boxes be added permanently and filled with live plants throughout the year.[23] On April 19 the Looshaus was added to the building register, signaling that it was officially complete, and on the 29th the two security deposits were returned to the clients. A short time afterward, on May 12, 1912, the council's decision was formally issued.[24]

It was an all-too-quiet ending to the controversy. The newspapers paid almost no attention to the proceedings.[25] By that time, everyone considered Loos's victory a fait accompli. With the council's decision, the matter was finally closed.

What began with great public outcry ended with hardly a sound — a response as muted as the bare surfaces of the Looshaus's upper façades.

15

A BUILDING AND ITS TIME

Loos's victory in many ways was a Pyrrhic one. Between 1909 and 1911 he made a meteoric rise within the modernist ranks. He was, ever after, famous or infamous. But in the pursuit of his beliefs, he paid a real price: he would suffer the ill effects of his stomach ulcers for years to come, and, as subsequent events would show, the controversy had taken much of the fight out of him. In the early 1920s, when called to head the municipal housing office for the new Socialist government, he resigned in the face of political and official opposition after a short tenure and took up exile in Paris. Never again would he have the opportunity to build a large building. And he had had to compromise: the Looshaus as it appeared in the summer of 1912, with its window boxes fully installed and planted, was not as he had intended. The flowers gave it an air of dulcet domesticity, diminishing noticeably its hard edged appearance (fig. 123). The new building was *echt* modern, but it was a tempered and reconsidered modernism.

In the years after its completion, the Looshaus was extolled, condemned, misrepresented, and, just as often, ignored. When Loos turned sixty, in 1930, Karin Michaelis wrote a tribute for the *Neue Freie Presse* lauding the building's merits and its signal import for his work.[1] Yet for many later modernists it remained an inconvenient apparition. Those who wanted to view Loos as the founder of the new functionalism found it awkward, if not impossible, to reconcile the Looshaus's undeniable classicism with its more progressive features; the commanding Tuscan columns, moldings, and cornice were hard to explain away. Many did not

FIG. 123 Goldman & Salatsch Building, 1912, with newly installed window boxes. Bildarchiv Foto Marburg.

even try. When Nikolaus Pevsner published his *Pioneers of the Modern Movement* in 1936, he cast Loos — not very accurately — as one of the first to "admire the machine and to understand its essential character and consequences in the relation of architecture and design to ornamentation."[2] Rather than illustrating the Michaelerplatz building — it is never even mentioned in his text — he showed the rear of the Steiner House, which had, he remarked, "achieved the style of 1930 completely and without any limitation."[3]

Pevsner was not alone. In *Der moderne Zweckbau* (The Modern Functional Building, 1926), one of the first reckonings with the phenomenon of the Neue Sachlichkeit in architecture, Adolf Behne passed over Loos's prewar works in silence. Walter Curt Behrendt, in *Der Sieg der neuen Baustils* (The Victory of the New Building Style), published the following year, claimed for Loos a place in the "first rank" of the "courageous champions of the new building spirit."[4] Yet he, too, included only a photograph of the rear and side views of the Steiner House, its plain surfaces selected to offer evidence of Loos's prescience; the Looshaus was nowhere to be found in his tale of modernism's ascent. In recent decades it has become a commonplace for historians to write what are known as "reception histories" — inquiries into how a particular work or event has been reinterpreted or reinvented over time. For the Looshaus in the 1920s and 1930s, more fitting would be an "avoidance history."

There were occasional exceptions. In one of his articles on the new architecture in *Het bouwbedrijf* in the 1920s, Théo van Doesburg included two photographs of the building's mezzanine; the Goldman & Salatsch store, he claimed, was "important in particular because of the interior arrangement and a new application of materials."[5] Missing from his account was any appraisal of the Looshaus's exterior or its larger meanings. More usual and more telling was Henry-Russell Hitchcock and Philip Johnson's catalogue for the 1932 "Modern Architecture" exhibition at the Museum of Modern Art: it omitted Loos entirely. (The only Austrian architects who made the cut were the Tyrolean Lois Welzenbacher, and Frederick Kiesler and Richard Neutra — by then, both living in the United States.)[6] For the younger modernists of the interwar years, the Looshaus was at best problematic; at worst, it was an embarrassment.

In Vienna, the verdict on the building remained split. The critic Franz Ottmann observed in 1919 that many Viennese were "still unable to come to terms with it."[7] Karl Marilaun, in a little booklet on Loos he published in the early 1920s, gave it no attention whatsoever.[8] Loos's supporters naturally were enthusiastic. Kulka wrote in his 1931 monograph on Loos that the "history of the Michaelerplatz building was the story of the painful birth of the modern style," its maker, a martyr for the modernist cause: "The man, who bled for it, who was nearly tortured to death by a pack of philistines both outside and within the architectural profession, made it possible, through his heroic perseverance against a whole nation, to enable us to build as we build now."[9] The critic and historian Ludwig Münz, who was also close to Loos, counted (with much less hyperbole) the Michaelerplatz building as his most significant achievement.[10]

There was little between the hagiographers and the naysayers: attempts to render an unemotional and nuanced assessment were all but nonexistent. One of the very few issued from Alfred von Baldass, a writer from outside the architectural establishment. In his guide to Vienna and its environs, first published in 1925, Baldass praised the Looshaus's "exemplary and frankly refined distribution and use of space." Even more perceptive was his judgment of Loos's effort to adapt the building to its context, "thanks to his honesty, his avoidance of creative architectural ideas, his subordination of the building's character, and his clever matching of the cornices" to the square's older houses. And all this stood, he wrote, in notable "contrast to the Palais Herberstein, with its bombastic aggregation of empty decoration."[11]

It was Kulka, though, who added the most to the understanding of the building in this period with his discussion of Loos's Raumplan idea. The term was in fact Kulka's — at least, he was the first to put it into print; Loos never used it in any of his writings. He asserted that Loos was the true pioneer of the new spatial thinking in architecture. He had "introduced a fundamentally new and higher spatial concept: thinking in space, the planning of rooms of differing heights, composing with these interlocking volumes to create a harmonious, inseparable unit that formed a single spatially economical whole." Modern engineering had brought the ability "to calculate the dimensions of columns and beams with extreme accuracy," but no one had "considered the space itself, which was being blithely wasted." What had preceded Loos's great innovation was "empty façade architecture." He had transformed the way architects approached the problem of design: "For Loos, the interior is primary. It determines the exterior form."[12]

Kulka's implicit argument was that Loos's critics, and, indeed, his admirers, had missed the real worth of the Michaelerplatz building. Its essential meaning, as he saw it, lay not in its controversial façades but in its radical new spatial conception.

Loos had curiously little to say about his own achievement. One of his few pronouncements came two years before the appearance of Kulka's book, in an essay written after the death of his favorite cabinetmaker, Josef Veillich. In a footnote, he exclaimed that his new approach to spatial design was the "greatest revolution in architecture" — architects in the future would all "find spatial solutions for the ground plan."[13]

Yet the spatial argument — at least as it related to the Looshaus itself — was mainly lost on his contemporaries. Most writers on modernism in the interwar years seemed strangely oblivious to its spatial innovations. If they wrote about the Raumplan at all, it was in connection with the later villas.

Throughout this period, of course, Loos was lionized as the great slayer of ornament, the knight errant who had freed young architects from the burdens of bygone adornments. Loos did much to promote this image. As early as 1915, in an autobiographical sketch, he had written: "Adolf Loos is the philosopher among contemporary architects, and by means of his defiant declaration against the persistence of ornament he achieved a special position."[14] In his foreword to *Trotzdem* a decade and a half later, he added: "I have emerged from my thirty-year-long struggle as victor: I have freed humankind of superfluous ornament. 'Ornament' was once the epithet for 'beauty.' Today, thanks to my life's work, it is synonymous with 'mediocrity.'"[15]

But most modernist critics and historians could not reconcile Loos's application of classical elements with his anti-ornament pronouncements. The paradox was all the more glaring in Loos's house and apartment interiors — one reason, no doubt, why they appeared so infrequently in the modernist books and journals of the day. Loos was acclaimed for his ideas and, sometimes, for his Raumplan villas of the 1920s, but his work was always very selectively depicted. It was easier to regard him as a spiritual father of the modern movement than as a model practitioner of the new architecture.

The obituaries after his death in late August 1933 stressed his campaign against ornament, his commitment to craft and to the modernist ideal. They generally passed over the Michaelerplatz building.[16] Only after World War II did interest in the Looshaus begin to revive. By the mid-fifties, the architectural terrain had shifted. The earlier, seemingly unbreakable faith in the tenets of the new functionalism started to exhibit subtle cracks: a new appraisal of modernism and its meanings was in the offing.

In 1955, Münz published a short monograph on Loos in Italian for the Milan publisher Il Balcone.[17] It was mostly a picture book, but in the short, accompanying text he sought to correct some of the myths and misperceptions surrounding Loos and his designs. Like Kulka, Münz put special emphasis on the Michaelerplatz building's interiors. He proclaimed the salesroom and its stair one of the most important spaces of functionalist architecture. And he wrote at length about Loos's Raumplan idea and its implications.

It was not until the 1960s, however, that the critical and historical establishment started to devote real attention to Loos. The Galerie Würthle in Vienna mounted an exhibition in 1961, organized and curated by the architect Johann Georg Gsteu, featuring original drawings and photographs from his archive, and the following year, Glück put out the first of two promised volumes of Loos's complete writings. (The second volume, which was to have contained his later texts, never appeared.)[18] In 1964, Münz and Gustav Künstler produced the first comprehensive study of Loos and his work since the early 1930s. *Der Architekt Adolf Loos* focused on his buildings by typology; a section on Loos's "urban multi-purpose structures" included the first extensive analysis of the Michaelerplatz building in decades.

Künstler, who was responsible for most of the text (Münz had died in 1957), recounted in detail how the interior spaces (now destroyed) had been arranged, how Loos had subtracted height from some rooms to make others grander or more serviceable, and how he had fit together the varied volumes.[19] He described Loos's striving for material honesty ("because in much of his aesthetic he is influenced by Gottfried Semper"). He traced Loos's ideas for drawing a separation between the upper and lower portions of the building. He sought to explain why the columns and openings below failed to align with the upper grid.[20] He observed that Loos's emphasis on the two corners and his reduction of the distance between the front outside windows and the building's edges — a technique he compared to Palladio's Basilica in Vicenza — though "inconspicuous and yet suggestive," appeared to render the entire façade slightly concave.[21] And he noted and admired Loos's artful handling of the slight slope on the building's right side of the Michaelerplatz front where the Herrengasse and Kohlmarkt met, a problem, Künstler contended, that he had solved with greater refinement than any of the competition designs (fig. 124).[22]

It was a masterful reading, one informed by an acutely sensitive understanding of Loos's ideas and intentions. For some of the older modernists, however, it was difficult to take. An unsigned review in the *Times Literary Supplement* dismissed much of it: the book was "not ideal, partly because it was written by two authors," Münz, "who contributed only a few (very interesting) passages[,] and by Herr Künstler[,] who did the rest, uncritically and in a tone of almost unqualified praise."[23] The problem was that too many of Loos's designs (and here one may safely assume that the reviewer included the Michaelerplatz building) fell outside the accepted norms of the modernist canon: "It is precisely their uneven value and contradictory principles that baffle. After scrutiny of all that is available of Loos's work, he remains enigmatic. His revolutionary role in the architectural thought of the first quarter of our century is beyond all doubt. But he was a traditionalist as well, and certain traditional designs are hard to stomach."[24]

Loos continued to pay for the sin of traditionalism even after the first modernist generation passed from the scene. The elderly masters died off one by one in the 1960s and 1970s; the modernist credo, however, proved more resilient. The new historians and critics who appeared at this time still saw the built world through modernist eyes — even as they questioned its dogmas. For Reyner Banham, Loos was a "traditionalist" and a "classicist," who "tended to look backward, not forward."[25] Leonardo Benevolo decreed that the house on the Michaelerplatz and the Steiner House were the "first examples of European rationalism" and "certainly influenced the work of Gropius, Oud, Le Corbusier and other post-war masters." But, he added, with more than a whiff of condescension, "the terms of

FIG. 124 Goldman & Salatsch Building, detail of the front portico. Photo by Wolfgang Thaler.

Loos's argument were those of traditional culture; he accepted *a priori* the antithesis between beauty and utility, between decorated and undecorated objects." The later modernists "cast doubt on the meaning of these very terms," Benevolo charged, "and within its ambit a theory like Loos's became an irrelevance."[26]

Others resorted to the old strategy of denouncing the Looshaus through omission. Vincent Scully, in *Modern Architecture,* accused Loos and his fellow Viennese modernists of "obsessive puritanism" (ignoring, it seems, the important differences between his approach and that of Wagner and Hoffmann). Loos's designs of the period carried "further the stripped, linear, taut, and planar character" Wagner had introduced. His exemplar was once more the standard rear photo of the Steiner House; the Michaelerplatz building is neither mentioned nor depicted in the book.[27] Likewise, in his *Modern Architecture: A Critical History,* Kenneth Frampton made only a passing mention of Looshaus: he claimed instead that the Steiner House "initiated a series of houses in which Loos gradually evolved his conception of the Raumplan."[28]

The task of coming to terms with Loos's legacy fell to a small group of Austrian architects and scholars reared during and just after the Second World War. Most, including Friedrich Achleitner, Johann Georg Gsteu, Friedrich Kurrent, and Johannes Spalt, had studied at the Vienna Academy of Fine Arts or at the Technical University. It was a dismal period in the country's architectural fortunes. Many of the best modernists of the prewar years had been Jewish or Socialist (or both) and had emigrated or been killed. A whole generation of younger architecture students, who should have taken their place, had been ground up in the war. Only a few of the leading lights of the old guard — Clemens Holzmeister and Ernst A. Plischke were the most prominent — remained or returned. The country faced daunting problems. Vienna had suffered extensive damage during the war's later years and continued to be plagued by a housing shortage. The small cadre of architects who had endured were consumed with the rebuilding effort; they had neither time nor interest to revisit the early years of the century. The late 1950s and early 1960s, when Achleitner, Spalt, and the others came on the scene, also marked a low ebb for architectural history itself: the modernist conviction that little or nothing could be gleaned from the past was then in its ascendancy.

Gradually, these young Austrians began to recover their own recent past. Much had already been lost. A substantial portion of Otto Wagner's archive had ended up in a dumpster, discarded by the family after the war. A significant part of Loos's papers, however, had been preserved by Glück and Münz. (After their deaths, Münz's heirs sold the archive to the Albertina, even though Loos's third wife, Elise Altmann-Loos, was his sole heir and the material rightfully hers; a series of legal battles eventually ensued that spanned more than a decade.)[29]

Hermann Czech and another young architect, Wolfgang Mistelbauer, under-took a systematic study of the Looshaus from 1962 to 1965. They had no luck finding a publisher, however, and the work circulated in mimeographed form until 1976, when Löcker & Wögenstein Verlag finally published it.[30]

Their book, *Das Looshaus,* retold the story of the building's genesis and the controversy surrounding it. It sought to put the Looshaus into the context of Vienna's building history, and to reassess it meanings. They confronted many of the old sources of dispute: Loos, they wrote, "did not destroy the Michaelerplatz" — the square as such had never formed a cohesive image in the first place; the building stood entirely outside the tradition of the city's retail establishments — it made no sense to examine it in such terms; and Loos's understanding of the function of its spaces was wholly different from that of his contemporaries.[31]

Two of their arguments stand out. One has to do with the attacks on Loos for concealing the building's structure. It was not that Loos failed to understand the possibilities of tectonic expression, they claimed; indeed, in the building's court-yard, as a number of later critics would point out, the *Skelettbau* — the frame-work of columns and beams — is expressed with a directness rarely matched in the architecture of the pre–World War I period (fig. 125). Loos simply had no interest in such issues: he thought instead in terms of a "shaped materiality" — of

FIG. 125 Goldman & Salatsch Building, elevator shaft and courtyard façade. Photo by Wolfgang Thaler.

the relationship between the hand of the craftsperson and cultural expression. The reason the columns and openings on the street-side façades did not align vertically was a consequence of a distinct and divergent vision of propriety. Loos's approach, they wrote, was diametrically opposed to that of the French architect Auguste Perret, who had once said that "'he who concealed a support committed an error; he who employed a nonstructural column committed a crime.' Loos was guilty of both offenses. His design ethos — his concepts of truth and criminality — was rooted not in constructive but cultural ideals."[32]

Their second significant argument revolved around whether the building should be considered a precursor of the *Neue Sachlichkeit.* Part of the answer to this question, they insisted, went beyond the superficial similarities of the upper façades with the architecture of the 1920s. It rested instead with Loos's complex attitude toward history. He belonged to a generation — those who had come of age at the turn of the century — for whom the application of past forms had taken on a new value: "Wagner's relationship to classical antiquity — more precisely, the column — was something else; he had been an architect of Historicism and had liberated himself from it; he could not yet use a column as a mere quotation. Wagner had arrived at the smooth façade in his late work, not through discarding the past but by means of a gradual reduction of ornament. . . . His approach, in contrast to Loos's, was uncomplicated and easily repeatable."[33] In that sense, Wagner's method was closer to that of the functionalists than to Loos's: "To interpret the Looshaus as a forerunner of the *Neue Sachlichkeit* was to view only one of its aspects — and certainly not the most important one." It was "less about functionality and construction" than "intellectual will."[34]

By the time Czech and Mistelbauer's book appeared, several younger scholars had launched their own reexaminations of Loos and his work. Burkhardt Rukschcio, who wrote his dissertation on Loos's buildings and projects at the University of Vienna in the early 1970s, mostly followed Czech and Mistelbauer's account, though when he and Roland Schachel published the first full-fledged monograph on Loos's life and work in 1982, they added new details.[35]

When their *Adolf Loos: Leben und Werk* came out, the postmodernist trend was unleashing a torrent of new interpretations. Suddenly Loos's classicism, his stubborn clutching at tradition, seemed less retardaire than prescient. (His proposed giant column for the *Chicago Tribune* competition, for instance, often described as an emblem of his detachment from modernist doctrine, became an icon for the anti-modernists, a sign of his utter disregard of the new functionalism.) Some acclaimed the "Haus am Michaelerplatz" precisely for the logic of its inconsistencies: "The building might be perceived as a string of contradictory architectural decisions, but a closer interpretation might well conclude that Loos deployed the principle of differentiation in order to bridge the gaps between the character of the inside and outside, top and bottom, and the Imperial palace and the shopping street" — so wrote Yehuda Safran and Wilfried Wang in 1985.[36] The Swiss historian Werner Oechslin argued that it lay outside the standard dichotomy of modern versus historicist: "It followed from an entirely different kind of architectural tradition. Loos set himself apart from history. Necessity replaced history in his construct: necessity as the principle of immanent, logical coherence."[37] The Berlin historian Dietrich Worbs offered a less settled assessment: Loos's façades, he suggested, "oscillate between 'architecture parlante' and strict silence. Loos did not render it easy with his conception of the modern façade: on the one hand, [he believed] the façade should convey to the observer, even at a distance, the nature of building, on the other hand that buildings should be vessels of concealment and reveal their riches only in the interior. Is a dialectic unity somehow hidden within this contradictory approach?"[38]

For the Belgian scholar Hilde Heynen, the answer to this question lay in Loos's attempt to show all of the features of modern life — and to distinguish among them. The "dissonances and nihilistic aspects" that accompanied Loos's design were precisely what made it "true to life." Instead of "deceiving people with an illusory harmony," she argued, he had sought to reveal the full array of contemporary possibilities.[39]

The baffling nature of Loos's seeming inconsistencies prompted a good deal of intellectual handwringing. Joseph Rykwert, in London, insisted in the early 1970s that Loos's "own understanding of his modernity" was "already so remote as to need comment."[40] For many scholars, the most auspicious route back to Loos seemed to be a close reading of Viennese architecture and theory around the turn of the century. Panayotis Tournikiotis, a professor at the National Technical University in Athens, founded his argument, as Münz had, on Loos's underlying cultural reasoning: "Even the building's parti was neither traditional nor modern: it was determined by the cultural exigencies of the place and moment. Loos's work is more understandable," he claimed, "if it is not seen as a predecessor of the Modern Movement, but as a reaction to the theories of his Viennese contemporaries on the material essence of style, the thoughts of Gottfried Semper and the historic continuity of forms in the tradition of Alois Riegl and the Vienna School."[41]

Yet some questioned whether this sort of contextualized reading was possible — whether Loos himself was fully aware of the reasons behind his design decisions. In the mid-1990s, Princeton professor Beatriz Colomina challenged the notion of Loos as an "authority, a man in control, in charge of his own work, an undivided subject. In fact, he is constructed, controlled, and fractured by the work." This was especially true, she asserted, of his Raumplan designs, which only magnified the myriad oppositions in his buildings.[42]

Still, there were many who retained an unshakeable belief in the historian's ability to decipher Loos's intentions and the building's meanings. Richard Bösel, Corradino Corradi, and David Leatherbarrow, like Czech and Mistelbauer before them, all maintained that the form of the Looshaus was an exquisitely sensitive response to the immediate frame of Michaelerplatz.[43] The Italian historian Benedetto Gravagnuolo enlarged this argument: he was convinced that the key lay in interpreting the building's relationship to the wider city: "The fundamental character of the house in the Michaelerplatz derives from its quality as an element of urban design consciously placed in critical continuity. In the end [it] shows how it is possible to immerse oneself totally in the history of a city without drowning in vulgar mimicry." Loos's ultimate pursuit was in establishing a relationship not "with the Hofburg and the square but . . . with the city as a whole."[44]

Gravagnuolo relied on his urban argument to explain the "lack of congruity" between the Looshaus's "sculptural skeleton" and its architectural form: its shattering of "rational rules," he decided, sprang from Loos's "desire for a form that transcends banal functionalism in order to acknowledge . . . the urban scene."[45] For those at the time seeking an answer to the pressing question of how to rejoin modernism and history, such arguments provided a degree of solace. Yet the question of Loos's concealment of structure tugged relentlessly at scholars. It became an inexorable question in nearly every discussion about the building. How could a modernist have so blithely veiled and misrepresented construction in this way?

Leslie Topp, who teaches at Birkbeck, University of London, offered a novel response. The Looshaus, she protested, was never an attempt to issue a customary reading of modernist structure. "To debate over whether the building is true or false" was beside the point: "It was always intended to be both." The Looshaus could best be understood as an "honest mask."[46] It was honest in the sense that it was well dressed — "like a simple and correct Goldman & Salatsch tail coat inspired by Savile Row." Loos had relied on "some of the pragmatism and honest workmanship that he felt was particularly English." The interiors, too, were an honest effort to address the requirements of the clients. His fastidious "dressing" of the building according to its varied functions — exclusive store, commercial building, and bourgeois apartment house — concealed its tectonic nature. At the same time, its surfaces and materials revealed a deeper truth. They spoke of the reality of use and place and culture.[47]

What no one had considered was the role of the clients — Goldman and Aufricht — in "tailoring" the building. Elana Shapira, a young Israeli scholar in Vienna, wrote in her doctoral dissertation in 2004 that the Looshaus was a "modern architectural 'outfit' meticulously designed to 'fit'" its distinguished owners: "Loos's respect for his clients' position as assimilated Jews . . . determined the special semantics" of his design.[48] What he provided them was a "new 'cultured dress' representing a progressive Jewish assimilation." Loos's outfit for them "combined (traditional) European and (fashionable) local motifs" — the proper representation for the second generation of assimilated Jews.[49]

Shapira is doubtless right to remind us that Loos's special language conveyed messages not only about the city but also about its inhabitants. But the building spoke — or did not speak — in other ways. Achleitner, who has been perhaps the most sensitive observer of the architectural scene in Vienna over the past five decades, mused that Looshaus might have been about something else altogether: "Loos appeared to use his building to expound . . . on the architectural culture of Vienna around 1910"; in reality, he "built into it a radical critique" of Viennese modernism.[50] Even while he employed some of the standard tropes of Viennese design, including a widely shared interest in grafting the historical past onto the present, he did so in ways that departed from — indeed, were almost unintelligible to — his contemporaries.[51]

There are more than a few grains of truth in all of these interpretations. Stoessl, though, may have gotten it almost right in 1911: the Looshaus was nothing more, he wrote, "than a modern bourgeois commercial building" that was "modest" but "self-aware."[52] Loos gave his clients a design adapted to their needs and expectations. Like any good and responsible architect he had endeavored to find ways to respond to its setting, and he did so with an awareness that was more perceptive and penetrating than that of the great majority of his contemporaries.

There is more to it than that, of course. The Looshaus was a direct expression of Loos's ideas about the modernism of the everyday. From his time in America to the end of his life he relied on his conviction that architecture should express reality: the architect's task, as he saw it, was not to invent a modern language but to interpret modern life, to discern the inner nature of the new culture and reproduce it in a manner that was tangible and truthful.

A belief in the search for authenticity and newness was common to all of the modernists, of whatever stripe. What set Loos apart was his fervid respect for tradition and craft. He genuinely believed that history still held power and meaning and that those who still plied the crafts were the true keepers of the knowledge of past custom and practice. Accordingly, he despised the "artistic" aspects of the fin de siècle in which he lived — the headlong hunt for a "style," the pretentions of architectural virtuosity, the falsity and superficiality. If he shared a penchant for austerity and purity, his designs sprang from a distant and distinct intellectual terrain.

One of the routes to understanding the Michaelerplatz building undoubtedly lies with Loos's special view of the evolutionary nature of culture. When he wrote in "Ornament and Crime" that the "evolution of culture is synonymous with the removal of ornament from objects of everyday use," he implied not only that modernism was about expressing new traits — a new pared-down look — but also that it was part of a much longer process of development. As in nature, some earlier features would survive. Those characteristics would continue to be expressed, even if, as Darwin had suggested, they might have lost their original purpose. Such features were still very much part of the organism, just as for Loos they were still integral to a culture. Latin was a dead language outside the church, yet it remained firmly embedded in what it meant to be a cultured European. Loos's famous dictum, that "an architect was a bricklayer who had learned Latin," implied the perseverance of history and the fact that to build properly was to engage the past with a full understanding of what had come before.

Loos's application of classical elements to the Michaelerplatz building issued from two closely allied ideas: that the ancient parole of Western architecture was a sign of cultural continuity—and that it was still part of formal "attire." Loos "dressed" the lower floors for exactly the reasons he had given in his talks and writings: to make it appropriate for its purpose as a gentlemen's tailor shop. That the columns were not load-bearing, and that the cornices and other allied elements made no real tectonic sense, was for him of little consequence. They were symbols of what it meant to be cultured and urbane. They offered, too, a visual reminder of traditional statics, even if they did not function in that way.

In the same way, Loos had sought not to "match" the surrounding square but to build in a manner that was in keeping with the city's traditions. He was respectful of the Hofburg, but his true project was an endeavor to continue the visual dialogue of the Michaelerkirche. The language of the Looshaus's columns, moldings, and divisions was a colloquy with the church (fig. 126). It spoke in a complex fashion of the legacy of classicism and of the standing habits of Viennese bourgeois life—of what it meant to exist in the city and be rooted to place.

More radical—and, for most observers at the time, less forgivable—was Loos's interpretation of Viennese history in the building's upper façades. He claimed that the planar surfaces were a direct tie to the city's past—to the time of the Biedermeier. In truth, they were at best an homage. His smooth plaster finish may have been a reminder of the building practices of old Vienna, but missing were the other usual elements: window surrounds, stringcourses, and quoins or other corner detailing. Even the most humble Viennese buildings of the Josephine and Biedermeier eras showed some elaboration of this sort. And the buildings that evinced the simplest handling were in the former outlying villages, such as Grinzing, Sievering, or Nußdorf; they were not urban architecture.[53] Loos's critics at the time were quite justified in charging that the stripped façades, whatever else one might have thought of them, seemed out of place on Michaelerplatz.

Strangely, few commentators, then or later, noted that the windows Loos chose for the upper floors were also not representative of premodern Viennese architecture.[54] He specified so-called *Galgenfenster* (literally, gallows windows) made up of three lower vertical sections and a fixed upper panel. Windows of this type had been popular in the latter part of the nineteenth century, but normally they had two lower operable sections and a single transverse upper light.

FIG. 126 Goldman & Salatsch Building, Herrengasse façade and the adjacent Michaelerkirche. Photo by Wolfgang Thaler.

The configuration formed a "T," resembling a gallows — hence the name. Why Loos opted for a tripartite lower section is not clear. He may well have drawn inspiration from the three-piece Chicago windows he saw during his visit. Whatever their source, they were a departure from Biedermeier building.

More notable still was Loos's decision to set the windows well into the façade.[55] Viennese houses of the eighteenth and early nineteenth centuries almost always had their windows put flush or protruding slightly out from the wall, and the exterior windows were often hinged to open outward. This arrangement made it easier to air out the rooms. It also produced a shimmering effect as sunlight reflected off the buildings' glazed surfaces. In the Looshaus, the deep-set windows absorb much of the light. This, in turn, not only made the flat surface of the walls more conspicuous, but it also heightened the impression of a box with holes cut into it — the effect many observers at the time found so disturbing.

Whether or not Loos's solution for the windows was more or less modern than the original Biedermeier forms (the advent of curtain walls only a few years later would, in any event, render such fenestration patterns obsolete), his design for the upper façades was without question a decided departure from earlier practice. The reason so many found the building alien was that it truly was unfamiliar — and not only because of the differences from late nineteenth-century design.

A Building and Its Time   **193**

Loos's transmutation — and that is certainly the right word — of history sprang from his evolutionary ideas. His design of the façades arose from a considered reinterpretation of the past. Like the historicists, he sometimes reached directly into the treasure chest of earlier forms; the Looshaus's Tuscan columns are a perfect example of this sort of pure appropriation. More often, he worked in a different way: he recast older building elements and patterns, "updating" them in the process. When Loos writes that he drew on the Viennese Biedermeier for the upper façades, he is describing the forebears of his design; his own off-spring are closely related, but they are altered, sometimes subtly, sometimes more drastically. The process of evolutionary change in Loos's works occurred at varied speeds according to a formula he never outlined precisely.

His practice of careful historical manipulation was present in his work from the very beginning. It showed fine changes over time, but it remained a central element to his last days. The Looshaus was only one link, albeit a critical one, in the gradual unfolding of his design method. Many of its features were already present in his earlier works. In hindsight, it is easy to see that his initial attempts to present a new form of modernism readily predict what he would do when offered the opportunity to build his first building. For the handful of critics and devotees already familiar with his projects, the Michaelerplatz building came as little surprise. But most of Loos's previous works had appeared out of the public eye or in tiny spaces. One of the reasons for the shock and disquiet the Looshaus aroused was that most Viennese were unprepared for it. And, just as unsettling, it revealed his ideas at large scale: the sheer size of the building and the fact that it was so visible in the square magnified its strangeness, its otherness.

What was new for Loos was his introduction of the Raumplan in the main store. Therein resides another mystery. Had Loos been thinking about the pos-sibilities of a new spatial idea prior to this time? If so, when? And what prompted it? Was Loos's development of the Raumplan a direct consequence of his attempts to work out an appropriate suite of rooms for the salon? What role, if any, did Goldman have? Did Loos's ideas for a multilevel interior emanate from the problems Goldman set out for him? Here again, we have no firm answers.

Certain, however, is that Loos's introduction of the Raumplan was bound up with his concept of functionality. If there is an arena, aside from his attitude toward ornament, where misunderstandings about Loos's intentions have been the most tenacious, it resides with his beliefs about utility and form. The mod-ernists of the 1920s and 1930s were all too eager to find in Loos's buildings evidence of their own views of functionalism. They sought signs of architectural purism, of stark and undifferentiated surfaces and masses. They were looking for an *image* of modernism. For the modernists of the interwar years, of course, functionalism also implied the response to need, especially to social need. But for Loos, functionality was neither a visual Platonic ideal nor tied solely to social mission (even though he harbored strong leftist sympathies). The role of the architect, he believed, was simply to build sound buildings, in "good taste," that served "some practical purpose" — ideas he spelled out most explicitly in "On Architecture." It was especially important, he wrote, that buildings communicate their purposes: "Architecture arouses moods in people. The task of the architect, therefore, is to give these moods concrete expression. A room must look cozy, a house comfortable to live in. A court of law must appear threatening to those harboring secret vices. A bank must say: 'here your money is held in safekeeping by honest people.'"[56]

The Looshaus fulfilled these precepts. The elegantly "dressed" exterior announced its role as a tailor shop for gentlemen; the upper stories expressed their function as housing for the middle class. Loos's words in this passage speak, too, of mood and emotion. Here, the interiors of the store were especially carefully calibrated: they were not only refined but intimate. His constriction of the spaces implied privacy and personal service — precisely what clients of such an establishment expected.

Loos addressed the issue of functionality in other ways: the rooms were ordered in ways that facilitated the work of fitting and making clothing. He paid minute attention to issues such as proper lighting and storage. By establishing a clear demarcation between service spaces and those reserved for the gentlemen clients, he signaled the express purpose of each room or area. The building's façades further delineated these functions. Yet they did so with strategies that departed from later functionalist precepts. The windows and other architectonic elements relied on the interiors, not the other way around. The design of the lower façades was the outcome of Loos's decisions about how to configure the shop and work areas. The discontinuities and shifting of the vertical and horizontal lines reflected the salon's inner organization.

Few understood that at the time. Loos's critics charged him with incompetence (Berger and Seligmann) or poor judgment (Wagner). But the "disorder" of the lower façades was really neither. Loos knew very well how to elucidate modern construction: the wall and elevator shaft on the rear of the building are more than ample evidence of his facility. The façades are instead the expression of two other intentions. One was a different approach to showing function. Loos, ever the realist, rendered a mostly literal representation of what the store was inside. The Raumplan is sketched out on the surface like a diagram; it is unavoidable, even if it is challenging to decipher.

But there is a second reason for the composition of the façades. It is hard to imagine that Loos did not take a certain perverse pleasure in crafting a look he knew would offend many — especially his fellow architects. Achleitner is undoubtedly correct when he writes that the Michaelerplatz building was a "commentary" on the "Viennese architectural situation around 1910."[57] With the building,

Loos sought to assail not only the conservatives but also the other moderns. It was a pointed critique of the stylistic pretensions of the Ringstrasse, of the Jugendstil, and of those modernists making superficial associations between structure and form. It was, to use Stoessl's formulation, a "self-aware" gesture of defiance hurled at his fellow architects, of whatever stripe. He despised almost all of them. With the Michaelerplatz building, he laid bare his contempt.

As the parade of modernist bands passed by before and after the First World War — Art Nouveau, Jugendstil, Cubism, Futurism, Expressionism, De Stijl, the Neue Sachlichkeit — it became ever more evident that Loos belonged to none of them. Yet his works and ideas illuminate well the concerns and preoccupations of his time. The Looshaus and the controversy that once spun around it are pure products of the unfolding of Viennese modernism: they offer glimpses of a special moment in its history, a juncture between old and new, between tradition and the future.

What set Loos's effort apart was not a striving for novelty but his attempt to retrieve the old, to recast local tradition in a new, manifestly modern spirit. Propelling his quest was a desire to ally two opposing forces: permanence — a firm connection with the past — and contemporaneity — the fleeting, almost ineffable tide of everyday life. Embedded in the Looshaus is a frozen image of Vienna during a moment in time and a glance into the deep well of its culture.

EPILOGUE

FIG. 127 Looshaus after 1913. Bildarchiv der österreichischen Nationalbibliothek, Vienna

In February 1915, not long before being posted to the Russian front, Kokoschka wrote in the Looshaus's guestbook that he "hoped the building would survive the war."[1] The building, as it turned out, fared much better than Kokoschka, who was grievously wounded a short time afterward. Shot in the head, bayoneted in the lung, and left for dead, he would spend many months recuperating. The Looshaus emerged from the war unscathed. But it and the surrounding district had begun to exhibit changes even before the outbreak of the conflict.

In 1913, the Palais Liechtenstein, which adjoined the Looshaus on the Herrengasse side, was torn down (fig.127). Loos and many others publicly decried the destruction of the old building, one of the city's landmarks. Built in 1685, it had housed, in addition to the Liechtenstein family library and offices, an indoor equestrian arena. In 1872, at the suggestion of the piano maker Ludwig Bösendorfer, the arena had been converted into a concert hall, the famed Bösendorfersaal, renowned for its splendid acoustics.[2] Loos, reacting to news that the hall would be demolished along with the rest of the palace, wrote an impassioned plea to save it.[3] The old structure protruded well out into the Herrengasse, however, and when Prince Liechtenstein sold it to a developer, it was razed and the legal building line moved well back to match that of the outer wall of the Looshaus.

Some took the destruction of the palace as another indication that the old city — and with it, its artistic traditions — was doomed. A cartoon in the satirical magazine *Kikeriki* blamed the proliferation of the new "showy boxes," like the

Looshaus, for the demise of the city's landmarks (fig. 128). Worse yet, in the eyes of many, was the fact that after the palace was razed, it was not replaced. The eruption of the war a short time later postponed any plans to erect a new structure. The land changed hands several times, but the financial collapse in Austria after 1918 forestalled all efforts to redevelop the site. For more than a decade and a half the space remained a gash in the city's fabric.

The Looshaus itself began to undergo alterations soon after its completion. For two or three years after the council granted final approval to the façades, the owners complied with their directive to keep the window boxes planted and tended. During the war years, however, they remained empty. The impact of the bare planters offered a very different impression — austere and doubtless much nearer to what Loos had intended. But another change detracted from his original conception: sometime in the late 1910s or early 1920s the upper façades were repainted — a pale yellow that diminished the building's crisp look.

The war and its aftermath also brought changes to Loos's personal life. During the conflict he had worked little, and afterward he became preoccupied with the housing problem in Vienna. Aside from several housing complexes, he would execute only a few, mostly small, commissions before moving to Paris. Bessie returned to London when the conflict ended (her relationship with Loos had begun to deteriorate even before the war); she finally succumbed to tuberculosis in 1921. Altenberg, too, died, in 1919, of a lung infection, after a long downward slide brought on by alcoholism and mental illness. During this time Loos also started to meet less often with Kraus, who was obsessed with writing his great antiwar play *Die letzten Tage der Menschheit* (The Last Days of Mankind), which first appeared in a series of special *Fackel* issues in 1919.

Beim Loos-Haus auf dem Michaelerplatz.

Kikeriki: Trauerig g'nug, Herr von Bösendorfer: Solche Prahenkasten dürfen sich breit machen, und für an alten Wiener und sei' Kunst is ka' Platz mehr.

FIG. 128 Cartoon making light of the role of the Looshaus and other new buildings in the destruction of the Bösendorfersaal. *Kikeriki,* November 30, 1911. The caption reads: "That's certainly sad, Herr von Bösendorfer. Such overblown boxes are allowed to proliferate, and for an old Viennese and his art there is no longer a place."

The firm of Goldman & Salatsch began to experience financial problems in the early 1920s. The war had siphoned off and then obliterated all too many sons of the city's elite, and the postwar inflation devoured the fortunes of the upper middle class and aristocracy. The company's client base shriveled up. In the mid-1920s Goldman and Aufricht were forced into bankruptcy. A number of the company's employees subsequently opened their own firms; Goldman continued to operate a small shop on the ground floor through the late 1930s.[4] The building itself was sold to a Dutch investment company; much of the first-floor retail area and many of the grand apartments above remained empty.

There was discussion at the time about converting the bottom floors into a showroom for new building technologies and into smaller apartments, but nothing came of the idea.[5] In 1934 an Austrian real estate firm, the Österreichische Realitäten AG, acquired the building, and plans were made to open a coffeehouse in the space formerly occupied by the Goldman & Salatsch salon.[6]

Upon catching wind of this news, fearing that the interiors would be destroyed, Münz published an anonymous appeal calling for the building to be protected as a historic monument; if the installation of the coffeehouse were to come to pass, he pleaded, the work to modify the space should be undertaken by Kulka, who was "wholly familiar" with Loos's ideas.[7] The coffeehouse never became reality, and the space remained unused for several more years.

In the meantime, plans were formulated for the site of the former Palais Liechtenstein. Between 1931 and 1933 the Hochhaus, the city's first skyscraper, was constructed there.[8] The massive building, the work of the firm Theiss & Jaksch, turned out to be one of the very few high modern works erected in Vienna during the interwar years. Spare and forthright, adumbrating accurately the new style, it presented a fitting annex to the Looshaus (fig. 129). Its lower portion established an understated and sympathetic continuation of Loos's planar aesthetic, though its mass overwhelmed its smaller neighbor (figs. 130, 131).

Less felicitous were modifications to Carl König's Palais Herberstein, which received an additional story in 1936. Clad in cooper-surfaced sheet metal siding, with "quiet lines," as a newspaper report suggested, that allowed it "to match the form of the Loos-Haus," it emerged with a more modern cast, but one, as Josef Frank (who had been a student of König's at the Technical University) noted in a speech before the Austrian Werkbund, that manifestly violated its original design.[9]

For the Looshaus itself, more momentous were the events of 1938. After the Nazi takeover of Austria in March, Jewish-owned properties throughout the country were seized. Because the president of the Österreichische Realitäten AG, Franz Rottenberg, was Jewish, all of the company's assets, including the Looshaus, were confiscated.[10] Many of Loos's other buildings still in the hands of their original Jewish owners, including the Steiner and Scheu houses, the Kniže store on the Graben, and the apartments for Kraus's brothers Alfred and Rudolf, were

FIG. 129 Siegfried Theiss and Hans Jaksch, Hochhaus, Herrengasse 6–8, Vienna, 1931–32. Postcard from the 1930s. Author's collection.

FIG. 130 Hochhaus (left). Photo by Wolfgang Thaler.

FIG. 131 View of the Hochaus (left) and Looshaus (right), where the buildings abut. Photo by Wolfgang Thaler.

"aryanized." Among the innumerable victims of the first wave of persecutions was Epstein. In May, despondent over the hectoring of Jews in the streets and the recent death of his wife, he committed suicide with an overdose of sleeping pills.[11]

In preparation for the plebiscite to sanction the annexation of Austria into Germany, the Looshaus once more became the center of attention. The building was festooned with a banner reading "Gleiches Blut gehört in ein gemeinsames Reich" (Those of the same blood belong together in the same empire) and other Nazi paraphernalia (fig. 132). Swastikas replaced the lights on the brass lamps on the two corners of the building; immediately inside was what one newspaper described as an "altar of our time"—a monumental bust of Hitler on a dais flanked on each side by SS sentries.[12]

The same year, the former Goldman & Salatsch shop on the ground floor was transformed into a showroom for an Opel automobile dealership. To accommodate the new sales area the original show windows and all the fittings were torn out. The remodeled display windows were moved up immediately behind the columns, enclosing most of the porch. Another company, the Modellhaus Prodinger, a builder of affordable housing, occupied the mezzanine level.[13]

The building suffered minor damage in World War II. During an Allied raid in September 1944, two bombs hit the adjacent Hochhaus, one of which damaged the upper corner of the Looshaus where the two buildings joined. In 1947 the Looshaus was declared a historic landmark, though it continued to undergo further changes. A new portal was added that year, positioned somewhat behind the 1938 one. The new windows were framed with strips of wood in place of the

FIG. 132 The Looshaus shortly after the Anschluss, 1938. Corbis, New York.

original brass mullions. The following year, the opening between the upper and lower mezzanine on the Herrengasse side was enclosed. Other changes followed: in 1959, some of the exterior marble cladding was replaced with inferior Italian marble; in 1960, the two consoles that the Nazis had mounted in 1938 in place of the corner lamps were removed; and, in 1966, the front portal was rebuilt again following the lines of the 1947 design.[14]

During the 1950s the building started to age visibly; by the early 1960s it looked worn and dated (fig. 133). The Michaelerplatz by then had been converted into a parking lot. For a time the space of the former tailor store served as a gallery for new art, Der Neue Raum (The New Room). The Genossenschaftliche Zentralbank purchased the building in 1968 and installed a branch and offices on the ground and mezzanine floors. Throughout this period the building continued to suffer abuse. In 1970, to accommodate a new door in the entry area leading to the upstairs apartments, one of the mirrors and its marble surround were torn out.[15]

A few years later the bank undertook the first efforts to restore the spaces, conserving and reconstructing the mezzanine, which had been destroyed after 1945.[16] Finally, in the late 1980s, the Raiffeisenbank, which had absorbed the Zentralbank, began a thorough restoration of the ground floor.

The work, overseen by Burkhardt Rukschcio, proved to be exceedingly challenging. Many details of the original design were not recorded in the surviving drawings or photographs, and the craftspeople working on the project had to

FIG. 133 The Looshaus and Michaelerplatz, c. 1960. Photo by Martin S. Kermacy. Alexander Architectural Archive, University of Texas at Austin.

rely on clues from what remained of the installations and by examining other Loos interiors. Locating materials identical to the ones Loos had used also proved to be a problem. In a remarkable stroke of luck, the restorers were able to find long sections of the same pyramid mahogany veneers. The dealer in fine woods who originally sold the veneers to Loos still had a stock of this rare material, no longer available on the market; over the years, he could find no buyer for it. Rukschcio was also able to procure three blocks of the original Greek Cipollino marble — enough to repair the façade — from the grandson of the owner of the quarry where Loos had acquired the stone more than sixty years before.[17] Some concessions to the operation of the bank proved necessary, however. A number of small changes were made, including the installation of a modern heating plant, altering somewhat the appearance from the original design.[18] What one sees now is a mostly faithful replica.

The square, too, underwent alterations around this time. The parking lot was removed, and between 1989 and 1991 an extensive archeological excavation was carried out. Portions of the Roman settlement and streets were unearthed, along with fragments of medieval, Renaissance, and later structures. After much public discussion, a small part of these ruins was left visible, and the architect Hans Hollein was enlisted to design a viewing area — a portal into two thousand years of the city's history.[19]

The painstaking restoration of the Looshaus and square, for all of the attention to historical verity, yielded a mixed result. The building is now resplendent — remade, scrubbed, gleaming (figs. 134, 135). Yet it seems almost too new, too perfect.[20]

Loos's prediction that his building would be lauded in one hundred years and that future architects would find their works unfavorably compared to it has also come to pass, though, as it happened, he was a bit off on the timing. In the mid-1980s, Vienna once more experienced a very public dispute over a new building on a prominent site: Hollein's postmodern replacement for the old Haas-Haus on the corner of the Graben opposite St. Stephen's Cathedral. Hollein's palette of deluxe materials and formal manipulation was not unlike Loos's Michaelerplatz design. And the attack from preservationists on the one side and the modernists on the other seemingly appended a new chapter to a familiar book that contains the unhappy tales of the Looshaus, Wagner's design for the city museum on Karlsplatz, the Secession, and Sicardsburg and Van der Nüll's Opera.[21]

In Vienna, continuity, as Loos suggested, may be as much about periodic eruptions of opposition as about stylistic appropriation.

FIG. 134 The Looshaus and Michaeler-platz in 2009. Photo by Wolfgang Thaler.

FIG. 135 View of the Looshaus (right) and the Hofburg from Kohlmarkt in 2009. Photo by Wolfgang Thaler.

NOTES

PROLOGUE

1 Robert Hlawatsch, "Erinnerungen an Adolf Loos und an die Loos-Schule," *Bauwelt* 46 (6 November 1981): 1893. Unless otherwise noted, all translations are my own.
2 Ernst A. Plischke, interview with the author, Vienna, 28 November 1986.

CHAPTER ONE THE COMPETITION

1 Karlheinz Gruber, Sabine Höller-Alber, and Markus Kristan, *Ernst Epstein, 1881–1938: Der Bauleiter des Looshauses als Architekt,* exh. cat. (Vienna: Jüdisches Museum der Stadt Wien/Holzhausen, 2002), 18.
2 Handels- und Gewerbekammer für das Erherzogentum Österreich unter der Enns to the Obersthofmeisteramt, 24 February 1909, Oberhofmeisteramt folder r.12/G/5/1899, Haus-, Hof- und Staatsarchiv, Vienna; Michael Goldman, application to the Oberhofmeisteramt, 1899, Oberhofmeisteramt folder r.12/G/5/ 1899, Haus-, Hof- und Staatsarchiv, Vienna.
3 Elana Shapira, "Assimilating with Style: Jewish Assimilation and Modern Architecture and Design in Vienna — The Case of 'The Out-fitters' Leopold Goldman and Adolf Loos and the Making of the Goldman & Salatsch Build-ing (1909–1911)," Ph.D. diss., Universität für angewandte Kunst, Vienna, 2004, 235–41; Leslie Topp, *Architecture and Truth in Fin-de-Siècle Vienna* (Cambridge: Cambridge Univer-sity Press, 2004), 134–36.
4 See Karl Oettinger, *Das Werden Wiens* (Vienna: H. Bauer, 1951), 1–20.
5 Richard Bösel and Christian Benedik, *Der Michaelerplatz in Wien: Seine städtebauliche und architektonische Entwicklung,* exh. cat.

(Vienna: Kulturkreis Looshaus, 1991), 10–13; Hermann Czech and Wolfgang Mistelbauer, *Das Looshaus,* 3rd ed. (Vienna: Löcker, 1984), 9–17; Margit Kohlert, "Michaelerplatz und Kohlmarkt," *Österreichische Zeitschrift für Kunst und Denkmalpflege* 40, no. 1–2 (1986): 45–50.
6 Bösel and Benedik, *Der Michaelerplatz in Wien,* 13–26; Czech and Mistelbauer, *Das Looshaus,* 10–17. See also Corradino Corradi, *Wien Michaelerplatz: Stadtarchitektur und Kulturgeschichte* (Vienna: Passagen, 1999), 99–123; Sokratis Dimitriou, "Die Entstehung des Michaelerplatzes," *Handbuch der Stadt Wien* 77 (Vienna, 1963), 326–29; and Moriz Dreger, *Baugeschichte der k.k. Hofburg in Wien bis zum XIX. Jahrhunderte* (Vienna: Anton Schroll, 1914).
7 See Ursula Prokop, *Wien: Aufbruch zur Metropole — Geschäfts- und Wohnhäuser der Innenstadt 1910 bis 1914* (Vienna: Böhlau, 1994), 13–37.
8 Carl E. Schorske, *Fin-de-Siècle Vienna: Politics and Culture* (New York: Alfred A. Knopf, 1980), 46–48.
9 "Neubauten in der Inneren Stadt," in "Der Bauinteressent," supplement to *Wiener Bauindustrie-Zeitung* 26, no. 32 (7 May 1909): 291.
10 Hans Tietze, "Der Kampf um Alt-Wien III. Wiener Neubauten," *Kunstgeschichtliches Jahrbuch der k. k. Zentralkommission für Erfor-schung und Erhaltung der Kunst- und histo-rischen Denkmale* (Vienna) 4, *Beiblatt für Denkmalpflege* (1910), 52.
11 Ibid.
12 Gruber, Höller-Alber, and Kristan, *Ernst Epstein,* 18.

13 Adolf Loos, "Mein Haus am Michaelerplatz," lecture delivered 11 December 1911, reprinted in *Parnass* (Vienna), special issue, "Der Künstlerkreis um Adolf Loos: Aufbruch zur Jahrhundertwende" (1985), ii.

14 "Carl Stephann," "AzW Architektenlexikon, Wien 1880 – 1945," www. architektenlexikon. at; Helmut Weihsmann, *In Wien erbaut: Lexikon der Wiener Architekten des 20. Jahrhunderts* (Vienna: Promedia, 2005), 383 – 84.

15 Bösel and Benedik, *Der Michaelerplatz in Wien,* 142 – 43.

16 On Epstein's early life and work, see Gruber, Höller-Alber, and Kristan, *Ernst Epstein,* 13 – 17, 49 – 72.

17 Ibid., 73 – 76.

18 "Baustiljammer," *Der Morgen,* 11 December 1911, 6. See also Bösel and Benedik, *Der Michaelerplatz in Wien,* 153 – 54; and Czech and Mistelbauer, *Das Looshaus,* 64 – 71.

19 Loos, "Mein Haus am Michaelerplatz," iv.

20 Gruber, Höller-Alber, and Kristan, *Ernst Epstein,* 73.

21 Ibid., 74.

CHAPTER TWO AN ISOLATED FIGURE IN THE FOREGROUND

1 "The Viennese knew nothing about him until the construction of his large commercial and apartment building on the Michaelerplatz," Margarete Schütte-Lihotzky, who worked with Loos in the Vienna City Housing Office in the early 1920s, remembered many years later. Margarete Schütte-Lihotzky, *Warum ich Architektin wurde* (Salzburg: Residenz, 2004), 49.

2 Richard Schaukal, "Adolf Loos: Geistige Landschaft mit vereinzelter Figur im Vordergrund," *Innen-Dekoration* 19 (August 1908): 256.

3 Burkhardt Rukschcio and Roland Schachel, *Adolf Loos: Leben und Werk* (Salzburg: Residenz, 1982), 11 – 12.

4 Elsie Altmann-Loos, *Mein Leben mit Adolf Loos* (Vienna: Amalthea, 1984), 8.

5 Rukschcio and Schachel, *Adolf Loos: Leben und Werk,* 14 – 17.

6 Dagmar Černoušková, "A Birthplace Is Not Inevitably a Destiny: Traces of Adolf Loos in Brno," in Maria Szadkowska, Leslie van Duzer, and Dagmar Černoušková, *Adolf Loos: Dílo v českých zemích/Adolf Loos: Works in the Czech Lands,* exh. cat. (Prague: Muzeum hlavní města Prahy/Kant, 2009), 56 – 57.

7 Rukschcio and Schachel, *Adolf Loos: Leben und Werk,* 17 – 21.

8 "Adolf Loos, Architekt," in Franz Planer, ed., *Das Jahrbuch der Wiener Gesellschaft* (Vienna, 1929), 10, 24.

9 Richard Neutra, *Life and Shape* (New York: Appleton-Century-Crofts, 1962), 162.

10 Robert Scheu, "Adolf Loos," *Die Fackel* 283/284 (26 June 1909): 31 – 32.

11 Ibid., 28.

12 Ibid.

13 Adolf Loos, "Der Silberhof und seine Nachbarschaft," *Neue Freie Presse,* 15 May 1898, 16.

14 See, e.g., Kurt Lustenberger, *Adolf Loos* (Zurich: Artemis, 1994), 11 – 14.

15 Rukschcio and Schachel, *Adolf Loos: Leben und Werk,* 36.

16 "Adolf Loos," *Dekorative Kunst* 4 (1899): 173.

17 On Altenberg's life and his relationship with Loos, see Andrew Barker, *Telegrams from the Soul: Peter Altenberg and the Culture of Fin-de-Siècle Vienna* (Columbia, S.C.: Camden House, 1996); Andrew Barker and Leo A. Lensing, *Peter Altenberg: Rezept die Welt zu sehen* (Vienna: Braumüller, 1995); Christian Kolser, ed., *Peter Altenberg: Leben und Werk in Texten und Bildern* (Munich: Büchergilde Gutenberg, 1981); and Heinz Lunzer and Victoria Lunzer-Talos, *Extracte des Lebens: Finem Schriftsteller auf dem Spur* (Salzburg: Residenz, 2003).

18 Harry Zohn, *Karl Kraus* (New York: Frederick Ungar, 1971), 19.

19 Elias Canetti, *The Torch in My Ear,* trans. Joachim Neugroschel (New York: Farrar, Straus and Giroux, 1982), 71.

20 Ibid., 70.

21 Barker, *Telegrams from the Soul,* 98.

22 Adolf Loos, "Ein Wiener Architekt," *Dekorative Kunst* 1 (1898): 227.

23 Adolf Loos, "Schulausstellung der Kunstgewerbeschule," *Die Zeit,* 30 October 1897; reprinted in Loos, *Ins Leere gesprochen,* 12.

24 "Adolf Loos," in *Deutsch-Österreichisches Künstler- und Schriftsteller Lexikon* (Vienna: C. Kosik, 1902), 113.

25 Rukschcio and Schachel, *Adolf Loos: Leben und Werk,* 59.

26 Adolf Loos, "Mein erstes Haus!" *Der Morgen,* 3 October 1910, 1; Topp, *Architecture and Truth in Fin-de-Siècle Vienna,* 136.

27 Dietrich Worbs, "Adolf Loos: Aesthetics as a Function of Retail Trade Establishments," *Architect's Yearbook* 14 (1974): 181.

28 Shapira, "Assimilating with Style: Jewish Assimilation and Modern Architecture and Design in Vienna," 242–46.

29 Rukschcio and Schachel, *Adolf Loos: Leben und Werk,* 412–16.

30 Ludwig Abels, "Ein Wiener Herrenmodesalon." *Das Interieur* 2 (1901): 145.

31 Ibid.

32 Adolf Loos, "Das Sitzmöbel," *Neue Freie Presse,* 19 June 1898, 16.

33 Schaukal, "Adolf Loos: Geistige Landschaft mit vereinzelter Figur im Vordergrund," 256–57.

CHAPTER THREE EXPLOSIONS OF LIGHT

1 Rukschcio and Schachel, *Adolf Loos: Leben und Werk,* 434.

2 Adolf Loos, advertisement for *Das Andere,* in *Die Zukunft* (Berlin), 30 January 1904.

3 Franz Theodor Czokor and Leopoldine Rüther, *Du silberne Dame du: Briefe von und an Lina Loos* (Vienna: Zsolnay, 1966), 16.

4 Barker and Lensing, *Peter Altenberg: Rezept die Welt zu sehen,* 423; Rukschcio and Schachel, *Adolf Loos: Leben und Werk,* 95–99.

5 Barker, *Telegrams from the Soul,* 94–99; Barker and Lensing, *Peter Altenberg: Rezept die Welt zu sehen,* 231.

6 Oskar Kokoschka, *My Life,* trans. David Britt (New York: Macmillan, 1974), 49.

7 Adolf Loos, letter to Lina Loos, reprinted in *Das Kunstwerk* 12, nos. 5 and 6 (November–December 1958): 32.

8 Rukschcio and Schachel, *Adolf Loos: Leben und Werk,* 437–38.

9 Ludwig Hevesi, "Adolf Loos," *Fremden-Blatt,* 22 November 1907, 15.

10 Ibid.

11 Many of the quotations in Hevesi's review seem to repeat precisely Loos's manner of speaking, indicating that he must have interviewed Loos at length. Rukschcio and Schachel, *Adolf Loos: Leben und Werk,* 109.

12 Hevesi, "Adolf Loos," 286.

13 Peter Altenberg, "Eine neue Bar," *Wiener Allgemeine Zeitung,* 22 February 1909, 2.

14 Adolf Loos, "Wohnungswanderungen," *Frankfurter Zeitung,* 8 December 1907, 1. Loos also reprinted the guide as a separate text, which he self-published. See *Wohnungswanderungen* (Vienna, 1907).

15 Felix Augenfeld, "Erinnerungen an Adolf Loos," *Bauwelt* 72 (6 November 1981): 1907.

16 Scheu, "Adolf Loos," 26–27.

CHAPTER FOUR THE FIRST DESIGNS

1 Loos, "Mein Haus am Michaelerplatz," ii.

2 Rukschcio and Schachel, *Adolf Loos: Leben und Werk,* 454. Hevesi, who reviewed the entries to the competition, praised Loos's entry. Ludwig Hevesi, "Der Neubau des Kriegsministeriums," *Fremden-Blatt,* 21 May 1908, 16.

3 Rukschcio and Schachel, *Adolf Loos: Leben und Werk,* 474.

4 Grundbuch Oberdöbling, Hardtgasse 27 and 29, Präs. 31 March 1909, Z. 646 B, 566, property records, Wiener Stadt- und Landesarchiv; Rukschcio and Schachel, *Adolf Loos: Leben und Werk,* 471.

5 Burkhardt Rukschcio, "Studien zu Entwürfen, Projekten und ausgeführten Bauten von Adolf Loos (1870–1930)," Ph.D. diss., Universität Wien, 1973, 79–84. See also Rukschcio and Schachel, *Adolf Loos: Leben und Werk,* 471.

6 Loos, "Mein Haus am Michaelerplatz," ii.

7 Heinrich Kulka, *Adolf Loos: Das Werk des Architekten* (Vienna: Anton Schroll, 1931).

8 Kulka, *Adolf Loos: Das Werk des Architekten,* 30.

9 Czech and Mistelbauer, *Das Looshaus,* 18.

10 Shapira, "Assimilating with Style," 300.

11 Ibid., 301.

12 Loos, "Mein Haus am Michaelerplatz," iii.

13 Shapira, "Assimilating with Style," 261.

14 Ibid., 261 – 63.

15 Loos, "Mein Haus am Michaelerplatz," ii – iii.

16 Ibid., iv.

17 Ibid.

18 Ibid.

19 Rukschcio, "Studien zu Entwürfen, Projekten und ausgeführten Bauten von Adolf Loos (1870 – 1933)," 67.

CHAPTER FIVE
THE DISCOVERY OF VIENNA

1 Loos remained in Vienna at least through the middle of August. He and Altenberg sent a postcard of the Kärntnerbar to Kraus, then traveling in the Netherlands, on the 16th. Postcard from Loos and Altenberg to Kraus, 16 August 1909, Wien Bibliothek, Vienna.

2 Loos, letter to Kraus, 9 September 1909, Wien Bibliothek, Vienna.

3 Kokoschka, *My Life,* 28 – 29; Loos's purchase of the bust, titled *Krieger* (Warrior), is confirmed in the Internationale Kunstschau records. Alfred Weidinger, "Oskar Kokoschka, Träumender Knabe und Enfant Terrible: Die Wiener Periode 1897/98 – 1910" (Ph.D. diss., Universität Salzburg, 1996 – 97), 186.

4 Kokoschka, *My Life,* 29 – 30.

5 Ibid., 31.

6 Loos, letter to Kraus, 9 September 1909.

7 Kokoschka, *My Life,* 42 – 43.

8 Ibid., 39 – 40.

9 Rukschcio and Schachel, *Adolf Loos: Leben und Werk,* 102. See also Elana Shapira, "The Pioneers: Loos, Kokoschka and Their Shared Clients," in Tobias G. Natter, ed., *Oskar Kokoschka: Early Portraits from Vienna and Berlin,*

1909 – 1914, exh. cat. (New York: Neue Galerie/ New Haven: Yale University Press, 2002), 54, 59, n. 45.

10 Kokoschka, *My Life,* 48.

11 Rukschcio and Schachel, *Adolf Loos: Leben und Werk,* 143.

12 F. Rufenacht Walters, *Sanatoria for Consumptives in Various Parts of the World* (London: Swan Sonnenschein, 1899), 293 – 94.

13 Loos, "Mein Haus am Michaelerplatz," v.

14 Ibid.

15 Ibid., vii.

16 Czech and Mistelbauer, *Das Looshaus,* 93 – 99. For an excellent discussion of the Viennese Warenhäuser, see Topp, *Architecture and Truth in Fin-de-Siècle Vienna,* 152 – 62. See also Alfred Wiener, *Das Warenhaus: Kauf-, Geschäfts-, Büro-Haus* (Berlin: Ernst Wasmuth, 1912).

17 Andreas Lehne, *Wiener Warenhäuser 1865 – 1914* (Vienna: Franz Deuticke, 1990), 144 – 49.

18 Adolf Loos, "Architektur," reprinted in Loos, *Trotzdem,* 106 – 7.

19 Adolf Loos, untitled article in *Das Andere: Ein Blatt zur Einführung abendländischer Kultur in Österreich* 1, no. 2 (15 October 1903): 2.

20 See, e.g., Stanford Anderson, "The Legacy of German Neoclassicism and Biedermeier: Behrens, Tessenow, Loos, and Mies," *Assemblage* 15 (August 1991): 63 – 87.

21 See Paul Asenbaum, Stefan Asenbaum, and Christian Witt-Dörring, eds., *Moderne Vergangenheit: Wien 1800 – 1900,* exh. cat. (Vienna: Künstlerhaus, 1981).

22 Ludwig Hevesi, "Biedermeier und Komp.," first published in the *Fremden-Blatt,* 29 November 1901, reprinted in Hevesi, *Altkunst-Neukunst: Wien 1894 – 1908* (Vienna: Carl Konegen, 1909), 188.

23 Ibid., 190.

24 On Loos's views on the persistence of classicism, see, e.g., Ludwig Münz, "Die alte und die neue Richtung in der Baukunst, von Adolf Loos," *Alte und Neue Kunst* 2, no. 3 (1953): 115 – 20.

25 Adolf Loos, "Die Entdeckung Wiens," *Fremden-Blatt,* 7 April 1907, 6.

26 Johann F. B. Walland (1875 – ?) was born in Cilli, Styria (now Celje, Slovenia), the son of a real estate speculator and developer. He moved to Vienna around the turn of the century and worked primarily overseeing construction projects. He gradually developed a reputation for his technical expertise, undertaking for G. A. Wayss a series of large-scale modern buildings. He remained active in Vienna until 1922, when he moved to Belgrade. See Ursula Prokop, *Wien — Aufbruch zur Metropole: Geschäfts- und Wohnhäuser der Innenstadt 1910 bis 1914* (Vienna: Böhlau, 1994), 50 – 53.

27 Loos, "Die Entdeckung Wiens," 6.

28 A year afterward, when asked to work on a department store in Alexandria, Egypt, for the S. Stein Company, Loos responded with a closely allied design, a studied exercise in modern structure and restrained classical elements Though it was never realized, Loos was particularly fond of his design: he hung a drawing of it, made by a student, in the living room of his apartment. See Rukschcio and Schachel, *Adolf Loos: Leben und Werk,* 484.

CHAPTER SIX IN PRAISE OF THE PRESENT

1 Adolf Loos, "Lob der Gegenwart," *März* 2 (1908): 310.

2 Harald Sterk, *Industriekultur in Österreich, 1873 – 1918: Die Wandel in Architektur, Kunst und Gesellschaft im Fabrikszeitalter* (Vienna: Christian Brandstätter, 1985), 113 – 18.

3 "It was interesting to compare the plans of the other architects with mine," Loos wrote. "Although central heating was specified, all had the same thick interior walls, which are only necessary for chimneys." Loos, "Mein Haus am Michaelerplatz," iii.

4 Ibid.

5 See Rukschcio and Schachel, *Adolf Loos: Leben und Werk,* 145 – 46, 475.

6 Jan Tabor, "Die wohlgestaltete Selbstverständlichkeit," *Wien aktuell Magazin* 2 (1985): 30. On Örley's life and work, see Otto Kapfinger

and Peter Nigst, *Robert Örley: Portraits österreichischer Architekten, Band 3,* exh. cat. (Vienna: Architekturzentrum Wien/Springer, 1996).

7 Tabor, "Die wohlgestaltete Selbstverständlichkeit," 30.

CHAPTER SEVEN ORNAMENT AND CRIME

1 Rukschcio and Schachel, *Adolf Loos: Leben und Werk,* 147; Richard von Schaukal, untitled essay in *Adolf Loos zum 60. Geburtstag am 10. Dezember 1930* (Vienna: Richard Lanyi, 1930), 46.

2 Robert Örley, "Jahresbilanz," in *Jahrbuch der Gesellschaft österreichischer Architekten 1909 – 1910* (Vienna: Gesellschaft österreichischer Architekten, 1910), 101.

3 Richard Schaukal, "Ein Haus und seine Zeit," *Der Merker: Österreichische Zeitschrift für Musik und Theater* 2 (10 December 1910): 183.

4 Telegram from Loos to Herwarth Walden, 9 September 1909, Sturm-Archiv, Staatsbibliothek zu Berlin — Preußischerkulturbesitz, Handschriftensammlung; Loos, postscript to a letter from Karl Kraus to Herwarth Walden, 18 September 1909, in George C. Avery, ed., *Feinde in Scharen. Ein wahres Vergnügen dazusein — Karl Kraus – Herwarth Walden Briefwechsel 1909 – 1912* (Göttingen: Wallstein, 2002), 62; and telegram from Kraus to Walden, 22 October 1909, in Avery, *Feinde in Scharen,* 82, 440.

5 On Walden and his place in the Berlin Modern Movement, see Freya Mülhaupt, ed., *Herwarth Walden, 1878 – 1941: Wegbereiter der Moderne* (Berlin: Berlinische Galerie, Museum für Moderne Kunst, Photographie und Architektur im Martin-Gropius-Bau, 1991); and Nell Walden and Lothar Schreyer, eds., *Der Sturm — Ein Erinnerungsbuch an Herwarth Walden und die Künstler aus dem Sturmkreis* (Baden-Baden: W. Klein, 1954).

6 George C. Avery, "Nachwort" in Avery, *Feinde in Scharen,* 615. On Kraus's and Walden's relationship, see also Peter Sprengel and Gregor Streim, *Berliner und Wiener Moderne:*

Vermittlungen und Abgrenzungen in Literatur, Theater, Publizistik (Vienna: Böhlau, 1998).

7 Letter from Kraus to Walden, 6 November 1909, in Avery, *Feinde in Scharen,* 89.

8 *Berliner Börsen-Courier,* 12 November 1909 (first supplement), 7; and *Berliner Lokal-Anzeiger,* 12 November 1909 (morning edition).

9 The writer Else Lakser-Schüler, Walden's wife, was among those in the audience. She was especially taken with Loos and his message. Afterward she composed a prose poem about the "Gorilla" — her nickname for him (in profile, she thought his face resembled a gorilla skull): "He is a palpable philosopher, for whom the adornment of architecture is the merest abomination . . . Loos wants to create order in the world here below . . . because the walls of our chambers should be a fitting dress, they should carry the imprint of our breath." Else Lasker-Schüler, "Adolf Loos," *Das Theater* 1, no. 8 (11 December 1909): 184.

10 Kokoschka, *My Life,* 49.

11 On the genesis of "Ornament and Crime," see Christopher Long, "The Origins and Context of Adolf Loos's 'Ornament and Crime,'" *Journal of the Society of Architectural Historians* 68, no. 2 (June 2009): 200 – 223.

12 As a number of scholars have noted, many of the ideas and images in "Ornament and Crime" appear in Loos's earlier writings. See, e.g., Mitchell Schwarzer, "Ethnologies of the Primitive in Adolf Loos's Writings on Ornament," *Nineteenth-Century Contexts* 18 (1994): 225 – 47; and Janet Stewart, "Talking of Modernity: The Viennese 'Vortrag' as Form," *German Life and Letters* 51 (October 1998): 455 – 70. Loos's close friends and others writing about him in this period also make similar allusions. Kraus makes repeated references to Loos's anti-ornament ideas in his publication *Die Fackel* before November 1909, and many of the basic premises of what would become "Ornament and Crime" are summarized in Robert Scheu's sketch of Loos, which appeared in *Die Fackel* in the summer of 1909. Karl Kraus, "Tagebuch," *Die Fackel* 279/280 (13 May

1909): 8. Scheu writes: "Die blankeiserne Schönheit der angelsächsischen Industrie, die glatte Fläche wird sein Idol und das Ornament sinkt ihm hinab zur 'Tätowierung.' Sein Lebensgedanke steigt herauf: Überwindung des Ornaments! Je weiter wir in der Kultur vorwärts schreiten, desto mehr befreien wir uns vom Ornament. Goldene Tressen sind heute noch ein Attribut der Hörigkeit. Die Bedürfnis zu ornamentieren durchschaut er als Indianerstandpunkt." Robert Scheu, "Adolf Loos," *Die Fackel* 283/284 (26 June 1909): 32 – 33. See also the articles by Wilhelm von Wymetal, "Ein reichbegabtes Brünner Kind (Adolf Loos 'Architekt und Schriftsteller, Künstler und Denker')," originally published in *Tagesbote aus Mähren und Schlesien,* 4 January 1908; reprinted in *Konfrontationen: Schriften von und über Adolf Loos,* ed. Adolf Opel (Vienna: Prachner, 1988), 21 – 31; and Ludwig Hevesi, "Gegen das moderne Ornament: Adolf Loos," *Fremden-Blatt,* 22 Nov. 1907, 15 – 16.

13 Adolf Loos, "Ornament und Verbrechen," in Loos, *Trotzdem 1900 – 1930* (Innsbruck: Brenner, 1931), 81 – 94.

14 "Ornament und Verbrechen," *Fremden-Blatt,* 22 January 1910, 21.

15 Ibid.

16 Adolf Loos, *Wohnungswanderungen* (Vienna, 1907).

17 Albert Ehrenstein, "Vom Gehen, Stehen, Sitzen, Liegen, Schlafen, Essen, Trinken," *Berliner Tageblatt,* 28 November 1911. Loos often employed a satirical tone in his writings and impromptu talks, lapsing at times into Viennese dialect to reinforce the humor. This sort of caustic critique was a staple of the Viennese cabarets and *feuilliton* writers. Kraus and Altenberg were both masters of the medium, and Loos, borrowing from them, had adopted the technique in his writings early on.

18 Reyner Banham, "Ornament and Crime: The Decisive Contribution of Adolf Loos," *Architectural Review* 121 (February 1957), 86.

19 Max Nordau, *Menschen und Menschliches von heute* (Berlin: Verein der Bücherfreunde, 1915), 30.

20 Adolf Loos, "Ornament und Verbrechen," in Loos, *Trotzdem,* 82.

21 Ibid., 59. On the larger ornament debate in Germany, see María Ocón Fernández, *Ornament und Moderne: Theoriebildung und Ornamentdebatte im deutschen Architekturdiskurs (1850 – 1930)* (Berlin: Reimer, 2004); and Gérard Raulet and Burghart Schmidt, eds., *Kritische Theorie des Ornaments* (Vienna: Böhlau, 1993).

22 Joseph August Lux, "Die Erneuerung der Ornamentik," *Innen-Dekoration* 18 (1907): 291.

23 Richard Schaukal, "Gegen das Ornament," *Deutsche Kunst und Dekoration* 22 (April 1908): 12 – 13, 15.

24 Schaukal writes: "Ein Tüchtiger hat schon vor Jahren den Kampf gegen das willkürliche Ornament aufgenommen: *Adolf Loos,* ein Wiener Architekt. Ihm ist die Lösung: 'Los vom Ornament!' eine Glaubens- und Gewissenssache. Er sieht in der ornamentlosen Zukunft, die er erträumt, die Menschheit von einem Fluch befreit, sieht nutzlose Arbeit abgetan, die Produktion vereinfacht, den Gewinn, zumal der Handwerker, mit geringern Mitteln erzielbar." Ibid.

25 Wilhelm Michel, "Die Schicksale des Ornaments," *Innen-Dekoration* 20 (1909): 232.

26 Loos was not the only one insisting on the removal of art from the design of utilitarian objects. The German sociologist Georg Simmel had called for the separation of art from objects of daily use in 1908: "The products of the arts and crafts," he wrote, "are intended to be integrated into daily life. For that reason, they represent the complete opposites of works of art, which belong to a world of their own." Georg Simmel, "Das Problem des Stiles," *Dekorative Kunst* 11 (April 1908): 310.

27 Czech and Mistelbauer, *Das Looshaus,* 18 – 19.

28 Ibid., 23.

29 "Bericht über die Stadtrats-Sitzung vom 8. März 1910, in *Amtsblatt der k.k. Reichshaupt- und Residenzstadt Wien* 19, no. 21 (15 March 1910): 556.

30 Ibid.

31 Letter from Kraus to Walden, 3 – 4 February 1910, in Avery, *Feinde in Scharen,* 149 – 51; card from Kraus to Otto Stoessl, 20 February 1910, in Gilbert J. Carr, ed., *Karl Kraus – Otto Stoessl: Briefwechsel, 1902 – 1925* (Vienna: Deutike, 1996), 112.

32 Kokoschka, *My Life,* 51.

33 At Walden's request, Loos also republished in the first issue of *Der Sturm* his essay "Vom armen reichen Mann" (The Poor Rich Man), which had appeared in the *Neue Freie Presse* in 1900. Adolf Loos, "Vom armen reichen Mann," *Der Sturm* 1, no. 1 (3 March 1910): 4.

34 Loos, letter to Walden, 25 February 1910, Sturm-Archiv, Berlin.

35 *Berliner Tageblatt,* 3 March 1910, second supplement.

36 "Zwanzig Zuhörer klatschen ihm gestern Beifall." *Berliner Tageblatt,* 4 March 1910, sixth supplement. Among those in attendance were Kraus, Walden, Cassirer, and Lasker-Schüler.

37 "Der Ornamentfeind," *Der Ulk: Illustriertes Wochenblatt, Beilage zum Berliner Tageblatt,* no. 11 (18 March 1910).

38 "Lieber Ulk! Und ich sage Dir, es wird die Zeit kommen, in der die Einrichtung einer Zelle vom Hoftapezierer Schulze oder Professor Van de Velde als Strafverschärfung gelten wird." (Eduard Schulz was an esteemed cabinetmaker in Potsdam; Van de Velde at the time was among the best-known design educators and reformers in Germany. Both, however, advocated the use of modern ornament, and it was on that basis that they became suitable targets for Loos.) Adolf Loos, "Ornament und Verbrechen," *Der Sturm* 1, no. 6 (7 April 1910): 44. The title of his piece, "Ornament und Verbrechen," has misled some scholars to cite this as the first or an early version of Loos's talk.

39 Letter, Walden to Kraus, 19 March 1910; letter, Kraus to Walden, 23 March 1910; letter, Kraus to Walden, 26 March 1910. All in Avery, *Feinde in Scharen,* 179, 185, 193.

40 Before leaving, Loos sent one of his essays to Walden, "Der Sattlermeister" (The Saddlemaker), to be reprinted in *Der Sturm*. Adolf Loos, "Der Sattlermeister," *Der Sturm* 1, no. 3 (17 March 1910): 20 – 21.

41 Rukschcio and Schachel, *Adolf Loos: Leben und Werk,* 148.

42 Letter, Walden to Kraus, 18 April 1910, in Avery, *Feinde in Scharen,* 217.

43 Postcard, Loos to Kraus, 17 April 1910, Wien Bibliothek, Vienna.

44 Rukschcio and Schachel, *Adolf Loos: Leben und Werk,* 148.

45 Ibid., 70.

46 "Wohn- und Geschäftshaus, Wien I., Michaelerplatz (Dreilauferhaus)," in *Bericht über die IV. ordentliche Hauptversammlung Wien, am 15. April 1912* (Vienna: Österreichischer Betonverein, 1912), 156 – 57.

47 Czech and Mistelbauer, *Das Looshaus,* 24 – 25; Gruber, Höller-Alber, and Kristan, *Ernst Epstein,* 22 – 23; Rukschcio and Schachel, *Adolf Loos: Leben und Werk,* 149.

48 "Die beanstándete Fassade des Baues am Michaelerplatz," *Illustrirtes Wiener Extrablatt,* 30 September 1910, 7.

49 Similar banding can be found on some older Viennese buildings, among them the parish house of the Lutheran church on the Doro- theergasse. See Rukschcio and Schachel, *Adolf Loos: Leben und Werk,* 149.

CHAPTER EIGHT A MONSTROSITY

1 "Der Neubau in der Herrengasse-Kohlmarkt," *Neuigkeits-Welt-Blatt,* 17 September 1910, 6.

2 Ibid.

3 See, e.g., "Der Neubau auf dem Michaeler- platz," *Neues Wiener Tagblatt,* 30 September 1910, 13; and "Sistierung des Neubaues auf dem Michaelerplatz," *Reichspost,* 30 September 1910, 5.

4 "Der Neubau auf dem Michaelerplatz," *Frem- den-Blatt,* 30 September 1910, 4.

5 "Der Neubau auf dem Michaelerplatz: Sis- tierung des Fassadenbaues," *Wiener Allge- meine Zeitung,* 4 – 5.

6 "Der Neubau auf dem Michaelerplatz," *Neues Wiener Tagblatt,* 30 September 1910, 13.

7 Adolf Loos, "Wiener Architektur Fragen," *Reichspost,* 1 October 1910, 1.

8 Ibid., 1 – 2.

9 Adolf Loos, ""Die beanstándete Fassade des Baues am Michaelerplatz," *Illustrirtes Wiener Extrablatt,* 30 September 1910, 7.

10 "Der Neubau auf dem Michaelerplatz: Sis- tierung des Fassadenbaues," *Wiener Allge- meine Zeitung,* 29 September 1910, 4 – 5.

11 On the long-running controversy, see Peter Haiko and Renata Kassal-Mikula, *Otto Wagner und das Kaiser Franz Josef-Stadtmuseum: Das Scheitern der Moderne in Wien,* exh. cat. (Vienna: Historisches Museum der Stadt Wien, 1988).

12 "Das städtische Museum," *Neue Freie Presse,* 13 January 1910 (evening edition), 3.

13 Loos, "Die beanstándete Fassade des Baues am Michaelerplatz," 7.

14 Ibid.

15 Adolf Loos, "Mein erstes Haus!" *Der Morgen,* 3 October 1910, 1.

16 Ibid.

17 *Publizistische Blätter,* 3 October 1910, quoted in Czech and Mistelbauer, *Das Looshaus,* 74.

18 "Der Getreidespeicher gegenüber der Hofburg," *Illustrirtes Wiener Extrablatt,* 26 October 1910, 4.

19 "Wiener Bausorgen," *Berliner Lokal- Anzeiger,* 9 October 1910, second supplement.

20 "Stenographischer Bericht über die öffentliche Sitzung des Gemeinderates vom 22. [*sic*] Oktober 1910," in *Amtsblatt der k.k. Reichshaupt- und Residenzstadt Wien* 19, no. 85 (25 October 1910): 2558.

21 Ibid.

22 On the rise of the Christian Socialist Party, see John W. Boyer, *Political Radicalism in Late Imperial Vienna: Origins of the Christian Social Movement, 1848 – 1897* (Chicago: University of Chicago Press, 1995).

23 When Lueger died, Loos, who had long admired his efforts to remake the city into a modern metropolis, penned a moving eulogy for *Die Fackel*. Adolf Loos, "Aufruf an die Wiener geschrieben am Totestage Luegers," *Die Fackel* 300 (9 April 1910): 13–15.

24 Boyer, *Political Radicalism in Late Imperial Vienna,* 82.

25 "Stenographischer Bericht über die öffentliche Sitzung des Gemeinderates vom 22. [*sic*] Oktober 1910," 2558.

26 Josef Strzygowski, "Wiener Bauten," *Die Zeit,* 27 October 1910, 1–2.

27 Adalbert Franz Seligmann, "V. V. W.," *Neue Freie Presse,* 1 November 1910, 2–3.

28 "'Einfache' Architektur," *Wiener Bauindustrie-Zeitung* 28 (October 1910): 21–22.

29 Helmut Weihsmann, "Hans Schneider," in *In Wien erbaut: Lexikon der Wiener Architekten des 20. Jahrhunderts* (Vienna: Promedia, 2005), 354.

30 "Der Neubau auf dem Michaelerplatz," *Neue Freie Presse,* 8 December 1910, 12; "Der Neubau auf dem Michaelerplatz," *Reichspost,* 8 December 1910, 8; "Der Neubau auf dem Michaelerplatz," *Wiener Tagblatt,* 8 December 1910, 8; "Vom Schüttkasten auf dem Michaelerplatz," *Die Neue Zeitung,* 8 December 1911, 4; Czech and Mistelbauer, *Das Looshaus,* 29; Gruber, Höller-Alber, and Kristan, *Ernst Epstein,* 26.

31 Stenographischer Bericht über die öffentliche Sitzung des Gemeinderates der k. k. Reichshaupt- und Residenzstadt Wien vom 15. December 1910," *Amtsblatt der k.k. Reichshaupt- und Residenzstadt Wien* 19, no. 102 (23 December 1910): 3209–10; Boyer, *Culture and Political Crisis in Vienna: Christian Socialism in Power, 1897–1918* (Chicago: University of Chicago Press, 1995), 65.

32 Rukschcio and Schachel, *Adolf Loos: Leben und Werk,* 153–54.

33 Ibid.

34 Kronstein [?], "Die Mistkiste am Michaelerplatz," *Die Neue Zeitung,* 7 December 1910, 5.

35 "Los von der Architektur," *Illustrirtes Wiener Extrablatt,* 1 January 1911, 7.

36. Czech and Mistelbauer, *Das Looshaus,* 75.

37 Hugo Wittmann, "Das Haus gegenüber der Burg," *Neue Freie Presse,* 4 December 1910, 1–2.

38 Ibid., 2–3.

39 Ibid.

40 Adolf Loos, "Das Haus gegenüber der Hofburg," *Neue Freie Presse,* 6 December 1910, 9.

41 Leopold Goldman, "Das Haus gegenüber der Burg," *Die Zeit,* 8 December 1910, 9.

42 Richard Schaukal, "Ein Haus und seine Zeit," *Der Merker* 2 (10 December 1910): 181–84.

43 Karl Marilaun, "Das Haus auf dem Michaelerplatz," *Reichspost,* 15 December 1910, 1–2.

CHAPTER NINE ON ARCHITECTURE

1 Czech and Mistelbauer, *Das Looshaus,* 29–30.

2 Loos, postscript to a letter from Kraus to Walden, 17 November 1910, in Avery, *Feinde in Scharen,* 275.

3 Loos, "Architektur," in *Trotzdem,* 98.

4 Ibid., 99.

5 Ibid., 99–100.

6 Ibid., 102.

7 Ibid., 109.

8 Ibid.

9 Ibid., 111–12.

10 Walden published excerpts of the talk the same week. See "Über Architektur," *Der Sturm* 1, no. 42 (15 December 1910): 334. The full text, however, did not appear in print until two decades later, in *Trotzdem.* Loos, "Architektur," in *Trotzdem,* 95–113.

11 Quoted in Dietrich Worbs, "Adolf Loos in Berlin," in *Adolf Loos, 1870–1933: Raumplan-Wohnungsbau,* exh. cat. (Berlin: Akademie der Künste, 1984), 8.

12 "Vom Neuen Verein," *Münchner Neueste Nachrichten,* 12 December 1910.

13 M.K.R., "Ornament und Verbrechen," *Münchner Neueste Nachrichten,* 17 December 1910.

14 Afterword to "Ornament und Verbrechen," *Frankfurter Zeitung,* 24 October 1929.

15 "Bausünden in Wien: Ein Gespräch mit Oberbaurat Professor Otto Wagner," *Neues Wiener Journal,* 25 December 1910, 10.

CHAPTER TEN AN ARCHITECT AT WAR

1 Loos, letter to Richard Schaukal, 22 December 1910, Wien Bibliothek, Vienna.

2 Rukschcio and Schachel, *Adolf Loos: Leben und Werk,* 155.

3 Letter, Kraus to Walden, 4 – 5 November 1910, in Avery, *Feinde in Scharen,* 129.

4 Karl Kraus, "Das Haus auf dem Michaelerplatz," *Die Fackel* 313/314 (31 December 1910): 5.

5 Kraus, "Das Haus auf dem Michaelerplatz," 6.

6 Felix Speidel, "Vom modernen Haus," *Neues Wiener Tagblatt,* 31 December 1910, 8.

7 Helmut Weihsmann, "Stefan Fayans," in *In Wien erbaut: Lexikon der Wiener Architekten des 20. Jahrhunderts,* 88.

8 Stefan Fayans, "Zur Michaelerplatzfrage," *Wiener Bauindustrie Zeitung* 28, no. 18 (3 February 1911): 145.

9 Fayans, "Zur Michaelerplatzfrage," 144.

10 Kokoschka, *My Life,* 49.

11 Loos, postcard to Kraus, 19 February 1911, Wien Bibliothek, Vienna.

12 Rukschcio and Schachel, *Adolf Loos: Leben und Werk,* 154 – 55.

13 "Die gipserne Kunst," *Wiener Mittagszeitung,* 16 February 1911, 2.

14 Rukschcio and Schachel, *Adolf Loos: Leben und Werk,* 155.

15 Otto Stoessl, "Das Haus auf dem Michaelerplatz," *Die Fackel* 317/318 (28 February 1911): 13 – 17. Stoessl had written to Kraus in early February that he had "recently seen the building again and my impression of it was so strong that I indeed want to write about it." Stoessl, letter to Kraus, 9 February 1911, in Gilbert J. Carr, ed., *Karl Kraus — Otto Stoessl: Briefwechsel 1902 – 1925* (Vienna: Deuticke, 1996), 135. Paul Engelmann, "Das Haus auf dem Michaelerplatz," *Die Fackel* 317/318 (28 February 1911): 18.

16 See, e.g., "Das Haus auf dem Michaelerplatz (Eine Polemik mit Herrn Loos)," *Wiener Montags-Journal,* 10 April 1911, 1 – 2; and Franz Servaes, "Wiener Wandlungen," *Der Tag* 57 (8 March 1911): 1 – 3.

17 "[Loos] gehört zu den interessantesten Charakterköpfen der Wiener Künstlerwelt ... [er] vertritt, wenn man so sagen darf, den Radikalismus der Sachlichkeit, ein Prinzip, das er jetzt auch praktisch, an dem vielbesprochenen Neubau auf dem Wiener Michaelerplatz anschaulich gemacht hat." [Ludwig Steiner ?], "Adolf Loos: Zu seinem heutigen Vortrag in Deutsch-Polytechnischen Verein," *Prager Tagblatt,* 17 March 1911, 7.

18 Vladimír Šlapeta, "Adolf Loos' Vorträge in Prag und Brünn," in Burkhardt Rukschcio, ed., *Adolf Loos,* exh. cat. (Vienna: Graphische Sammlung Albertina/Historisches Museum der Stadt Wien, 1989), 41 – 42. See also Vladimír Šlapeta, "Adolf Loos a česka architektura," *Památky a příroda* 10 (1983): 596 – 602.

19 Ibid. The friendly response was all the more striking given that Prague in 1911 was already in the throes of Czech Cubism, and many of the younger Czech-speaking architects were highly critical of the call for functionality in architecture and design. See, e.g., Vladimír Šlapeta, "Adolf Loos und die tschechische Architektur," in Elisabeth Liskar, ed., *Wien und die Architektur des 20. Jahrhunderts: Akten des XXV. Internationalen Kongresses für Kunstgeschichte, Wien 4.-10. September 1983* (Vienna, 1986), 88 – 89.

20 Rukschcio and Schachel, *Adolf Loos: Leben und Werk,* 155. See also "Vom Gehen, Stehen, Sitzen, Liegen, Schlafen, Essen, und Trinken," *Illustrirtes Wiener Extrablatt,* 25 March 1911, 8.

21 Adolf Loos, "Vom Gehen, Stehen, Sitzen, Liegen, Schlafen, Essen, Trinken," *Der Sturm* 2, no. 87 (November 1911): 691 – 92.

22 The published version, which appeared in Walden's *Der Sturm,* makes no direct reference to the Goldman & Salatsch Building. But when Loos repeated the lecture in Berlin in November 1911, he did so explicitly on Walden's invitation to come and speak "about his building," so he must have expanded it to include some comments about the controversy. Walden, letter to Kraus, 15 August 1911, in Avery, *Feinde in Scharen,* 348 – 49, 548.

23 Rukschcio and Schachel, *Adolf Loos: Leben und Werk,* 157.

24 "Das Haus auf dem Michaelerplatze (Eine Polemik mit Herrn Loos)," *Wiener Montags-Journal,* 10 April 1911, 1 – 2; Rukschcio and Schachel, *Adolf Loos: Leben und Werk,* 157.

25 Rukschcio and Schachel, *Adolf Loos: Leben und Werk,* 160.

26 Camillo Schaefer, *Peter Altenberg, Ein bio-graphischer Essay* (Vienna: Freibord, 1980), 122 – 27; Helene Malmberg, *Widerall des Herzens: Ein Peter Altenberg Buch* (Munich: Albert Langen/Georg Müller, 1961), 226 – 48.

27 Barker, *Telegrams from the Soul,* 141 – 42. Barker and Lensing, *Peter Altenberg: Rezept die Welt zu sehen,* 244 – 47.

28 Karl Kraus, *Sittlichkeit und Kriminalität* (Vienna: L. Rosner, 1908); Edward Timms, *Karl Kraus, Apocalyptic Satirist: Culture and Catastrophe in Habsburg Vienna* (New Haven: Yale University Press, 1986), 240 – 42.

29 Rukschcio and Schachel, *Adolf Loos: Leben und Werk,* 157.

CHAPTER ELEVEN
THE SECOND COMPETITION

1 Loos, postcards to Kraus, 19 and 25 April 1911, Wien Bibliothek, Vienna.

2 Loos, postcards to Kraus, 23 April and 1 May 1911, Wien Bibliothek, Vienna; Telegram from Kraus to Walden, 25 April 1911, in Avery, *Feinde in Scharen,* 315; Rukschcio and Schachel, *Adolf Loos: Leben und Werk,* 157.

3 "Wettbewerb zur Erlangung von Entwürfen für die Fassade des Hauses, Wien I., Michaeler-platz, der Firma Goldman & Salatsch," *Wiener Bauindustrie Zeitung* 28, no. 32 (12 May 1911): 257.

4 "Das Haus auf dem Michaelerplatz," *Neues Wiener Abendblatt,* 6 May 1911, 4.

5 Gruber, Höller-Alber, and Kristan, *Ernst Epstein,* 28.

6 "Haus am Michaelerplatz-Wettbewerb," *Wiener Mittagszeitung,* 6 May 1911, 3. See also "Am Michaelerplatz," *Der Morgen-Wiener Mon-tagsblatt,* 8 May 1911, 2 – 3; and "Das Haus auf dem Michaelerplatz," *Neues Wiener Tagblatt,* 7 May 1911, 13.

7 "Haus am Michaelerplatz-Wettbewerb," 3.

8 On Ludwig Baumann's career and work, see, e.g., Rudolf Kolowrath, *Ludwig Baumann: Architektur zwischen Barock and Jugendstil* (Vienna: Compress, 1985).

9 On Carl König, see Markus Kristan, *Carl König: Eine neubaroker Großstadtarchitekt in Wien,* exh. cat. (Vienna: Jüdisches Museum der Stadt Wien/Holzhausen, 1999).

10 Rukschcio and Schachel, *Adolf Loos: Leben und Werk,* 158.

11 Kulka, *Adolf Loos: Das Werk des Architek-ten,* 30.

12 Rukschcio and Schachel, *Adolf Loos: Leben und Werk,* 158.

13 "Das Haus am Michaelerplatz," *Fremden-Blatt,* 14 May 1911, 9.

14 Ibid.

15 See, e.g., Friedrich Pollak, "Allerlei Kunst," *Der Morgen — Wiener Montagsblatt,* 22 May 1911, 2. Gruber, Höller-Alber, and Kristan, *Ernst Epstein,* 30.

16 Jože Plečnik, letter to Jan Kotěra, undated (January or February 1911), quoted in Damjan Prelovšek, *Jože Plečnik 1872 – 1957: Archi-tectura Perennis* (New Haven: Yale University Press, 1997), 85; "Das Haus am Michaeler-platz," *Neues Wiener Journal,* 16 May 1911, 5. See Czech and Mistelbauer, *Das Looshaus,* 81.

CHAPTER TWELVE BREAKDOWN

1 "Das Haus auf dem Michaelerplatz," *Wiener Allgemeine Zeitung,* 11 July 1911, 2.

2 Adalbert Franz Seligmann, "Aus dem Wiener Kunstleben," *Neue Freie Presse,* 18 May, 1911, 1 – 2.

3 Rukschcio and Schachel, *Adolf Loos: Leben und Werk,* 159.

4 Paul Stefan, *Das Grab in Wien: Eine Chronik, 1903 – 1911* (Berlin: Erich Reiß, 1913), 92.

5 Ibid., 91.

6 Wolf Rosenberg, "Gustav Mahler's Farewell and Return Home," in Sigrid Wiesmann, ed., *Gustav Mahler in Vienna* (New York: Rizzoli,

1976), 156. Earlier, in May, Kraus had attacked the fickleness of the Viennese, who now welcomed Mahler back home. Karl Kraus, "Der Ankläger," *Die Fackel* 324/325 (May 1911): 7.

7 Stefan, *Das Grab in Wien,* 138.

8 Henry-Louis de La Grange, *Gustav Mahler, Volume 4: A New Life Cut Short (1907–1911)* (Oxford: Oxford University Press, 2008), 1275–76; Rukschcio and Schachel, *Adolf Loos: Leben und Werk,* 159.

9 "Bevorstehende Entscheidung über das Haus am Michaelerplatz," *Neue Freie Presse,* 11 July 1911, 11; "Das Haus auf dem Michaelerplatz," *Wiener Allgemeine Zeitung,* 11 July 1911, 2; "Das Loos-Haus am Michaelerplatz," *Österreichische Volks-Zeitung,* 11 July 1911, 4; Rukschcio and Schachel, *Adolf Loos: Leben und Werk,* 159.

10 "Die ornamentale Ausschmückung des Neubaues auf dem Michaelerhaus," *Neue Freie Presse,* 7 July 1911, 7; "Das Haus auf dem Michaelerplatz," *Reichspost,* 8 July 1911, 8.

11 "Das Haus am Michaelerplatz," *Deutsches Volksblatt,* 13 July 1911, 6; "Das Looshaus am Michaelerplatz," *Österreichische Volks-Zeitung,* 13 July 1911, 4; "Die Fassade des Hauses auf dem Michaelerplatz," *Neue Freie Presse,* 16 July 1911, 11.

12 Stoessl, "Das Haus auf dem Michaelerplatz," 15. See also Czech and Mistelbauer, *Das Looshaus,* 43–44.

13 "Das Haus am Michaelerplatz — Neue Fassadenpläne," *Reichspost,* 14 July 1911, 5. See also "Das Haus am Michaelerplatz," *Reichspost,* 15 July 1911, 8.

14 *Fremden-Blatt,* 15 July 1911, quoted in Czech and Mistelbauer, *Das Looshaus,* 83.

15 "Die Fassade des Hauses auf dem Michaelerplatz," *Neue Freie Presse,* 16 July 1911, 11.

16 Boyer, *Culture and Political Crisis in Vienna,* 10–11.

17 "Die Fassade des Hauses auf dem Michaelerplatz," 16 July 1911, 11. Czech and Mistelbauer, *Das Looshaus,* 34.

18 Adolf Loos, "Otto Wagner," *Reichspost,* 13 July 1911, 2.

19 Ibid., 2.

20 Arthur Roessler, "Das Haus am Michaelerplatz," *Arbeiter-Zeitung,* 18 July 1911, 8.

21 Richard Schaukal, "Noch einmal über das Haus von Adolf Loos," *Reichspost,* 18 July 1911, 6–7.

22 Kokoschka, undated letter to Walden [late July or August 1911], in Olda Kokoschka and Heinz Spielmann, eds., *Oksar Kokoschka Briefe I, 1905–1919* (Düsseldorf: Claassen, 1984), 23.

23 Loos, "Mein Haus am Michaelerplatz," x.

24 Kraus, letter to Walden [after 11 September 1911], in Avery, *Feinde in Scharen,* 344.

25 Rukschcio and Schachel, *Adolf Loos: Leben und Werk,* 159.

26 Kulka, *Adolf Loos: Das Werk des Architekten,* 30.

27 Kokoschka, undated letter to Walden [late July 1911?], in Kokoschka and Spielmann, eds., *Oskar Kokoschka Briefe I,* 21.

28 Herwarth Walden, "Schönheit! Schönheit! Der Fall Adolf Loos," *Der Sturm* 2, no. 70 (July 1911): 556.

29 See, e.g., Kraus, postcard to Walden, 3 August 1911, in Avery, *Feinde in Scharen,* 344.

30 Czech and Mistelbauer, *Das Looshaus,* 34–35.

31 Bericht über die Stadtrats-Sitzung vom 3. August 1911," *Amtsblatt der k.k. Reichshaupt- und Residenzstadt Wien* 20, no. 64 (11 August 1911): 1992; "Das Haus am Michaelerplatz," *Reichspost,* 4 August 1911, 7; Czech and Mistelbauer, *Das Looshaus,* 33–34.

32 *Neues Wiener Tagblatt,* 16 August 1911, quoted in Czech and Mistelbauer, *Das Looshaus,* 35.

33 Richard S. Geehr, *Karl Lueger: Mayor of Fin-de-Siècle Vienna* (Detroit: Wayne State University Press, 1990), 281.

34 On Bielohlawek's career and his position in Viennese politics, see Boyer, *Culture and Political Crisis in Vienna,* 65–66.

35 Geehr, *Karl Lueger: Mayor of Fin-de-Siècle Vienna,* 281.

36 "Das Dreilauferhaus: Zwei Zuschriften —

'Das letzte Wort' im Gemeinderate?" *Reichs-post,* 13 August 1911, 5. Biehlohlawek also spoke in favor of Loos's design during a meeting of the parliament in November. See "Für Adolf Loos," *Reichspost,* 8 November 1911, 6.

37 On Porzer's background and character, see Boyer, *Culture and Political Crisis in Vienna,* 499, n. 36.

38 Czech and Mistelbauer, *Das Looshaus,* 35 – 37.

39 Loos, "Mein Haus am Michaelerplatz," x; Rukschcio and Schachel, *Adolf Loos: Leben und Werk,* 159.

CHAPTER THIRTEEN MY BUILDING ON MICHAELERPLATZ

1 Kraus, postcard to Walden, 7 August 1911, in Avery, *Feinde in Scharen,* 346; Loos, postcard to Kraus, 31 August 1911, Wien Bibliothek, Vienna.

2 Loos, postcard to Kraus, 4 September 1911, Wien Bibliothek, Vienna.

3 Loos and Bessie Loos, postcard to Kraus, 8 September 1911, Wien Bibliothek, Vienna.

4 Kraus, letter to Walden [after 11 September 1911], in Avery, *Feinde in Scharen,* 361. Kokoschka, who visited Loos around this time, also confirmed that he was slowly recovering. Loos and Oskar Kokoschka, postcard to Kraus, 9 September 1911, Wien Bibliothek, Vienna.

5 Otto Stoessl, postcard to Kraus, 24 September 1911, in Carr, *Karl Kraus — Otto Stoessl: Briefwechsel,* 142.

6 Kraus, letter to Walden, 28 September 1911, in Avery, *Feinde in Scharen,* 366.

7 *Montagsblatt der Publizistischen Blätter,* 21 August 1911, quoted in Czech and Mistelbauer, *Das Looshaus,* 76.

8 Prokop, *Wien: Aufbruch zur Metropole,* 68.

9 Hans Berger, "Architektonische Auslese Wien 1910," *Neue Freie Presse,* 26 August 1911, 21.

10 See Christopher Long, "An Alternative Path to Modernism: Carl König and Architectural Education at the Vienna Technische Hochschule, 1890 – 1913," *Journal of Architectural Education* 55 (September 2001): 21 – 30.

11 Ernst A. Plischke, interview by author, Vienna, 17 November 1986.

12 Berger, "Architektonische Auslese Wien 1910," 21.

13 Ibid.

14 Ibid.

15 Georg Terramare, "Die Rücksichtslosigkeit des Gedankens," *Fremden-Blatt,* 6 October 1911, 19.

16 "Los von Fischer von Erlach!" *Kikeriki,* 19 October 1911, 3.

17 "Vandalismus in Wien," *Der Zwiebelfisch* 3, no. 4 (1911): 138 – 39. In a letter to Walden, Kraus noted with perverse pleasure that both *Die Fackel* and *Der Sturm* were mentioned in the piece. Kraus, letter to Walden, 10 October 1911, in Avery, *Feinde in Scharen,* 371, 555.

18 Karl Kraus, "Die Zuckerkandl," *Die Fackel* 334/335 (31 October 1911): 22 – 23. The woman in question, though not fully identified in the piece, was the writer, journalist, and critic Berta Zuckerkandl, daughter of the newspaper publisher Moritz Szeps. For many years she had hosted a cultural salon, attended by some of the city's leading artists and other personalities, among them Hoffmann.

19 Peter Noever and Marek Pokorný, eds., *Josef Hoffmann Selbstbiographie* (Ostfildern: Hatje Cantz, 2009), 30.

20 On the long-standing antipathy between Hoffmann and Loos, see, e.g., Rainald Franz, "Josef Hoffmann and Adolf Loos: The Ornament Controversy in Vienna," in Peter Noever, ed., *Josef Hoffmann Designs* (Munich: Prestel, 1992), 11 – 15.

21 Noever and Pokorný, eds., *Josef Hoffmann Selbstbiographie,* 30.

22 Elsie Altmann Loos, *Adolf Loos: Der Mensch* (Vienna: Herold, 1968), 46 – 47.

23 *Frankfurter Zeitung,* 17 October 1911, quoted in Rukschcio and Schachel, *Adolf Loos: Leben und Werk,* 160.

24 See, e.g., "Das verzierte Dreilauferhaus am Kohlmarkt," *Fremden-Blatt,* 26 October 1911, 12; "Das Dreilauferhaus am Kohlmarkt," *Illus-*

trirtes Wiener Extrablatt, 26 October 1911, 12; and "Das Dreilauferhaus am Kohlmarkt," *Neues Wiener Tagblatt,* 26 October 1911, 13.

25 "Das Dreilauferhaus," *Fremden-Blatt,* 27 October 1911, 13.

26 "Das verzierte Dreilauferhaus am Kohlmarkt," *Deutsches Volksblatt,* 26 October 1911, 8.

27 Rukschcio and Schachel, *Adolf Loos: Leben und Werk,* 160.

28 For a description of the building and its interiors, see Rukschcio and Schachel, *Adolf Loos: Leben und Werk,* 471, 487 – 89.

29 Ibid., 161.

30 Ibid., 160.

31 Ibid., 487.

32 Loos, Altenberg, and Bessie Loos, postcard to Kraus, 28 October 1911, Wien Bibliothek, Vienna.

33 Walden, letter to Kraus, 15 August 1911, in Avery, *Feinde in Scharen,* 348 – 49, 548.

34 Walden also published the text in the November issue of *Der Sturm.* Adolf Loos, "Vom Gehen, Stehen, Sitzen, Liegen, Schlafen, Essen, Trinken," *Der Sturm* 2, no. 87 (November 1911): 691 – 92.

35 H. H. Stuckenschmidt, *Arnold Schoenberg: His Life, World and Work* (New York: Schirmer, 1977), 150 – 51.

36 Loos, letter to Arnold Schönberg, 13 November 1911, Arnold Schönberg Archives, Vienna.

37 Rukschcio and Schachel, *Adolf Loos: Leben und Werk,* 163.

38 Ibid.

39 Philipp Berger, letter to Erhard Buschbeck, 22 November 1911, author's collection. Berger also requested that Buschbeck, who was in charge of the literary section of the society, see to it that the posters be printed and hung "as soon as possible" to publicize the event.

40 Philipp Berger, letter to Erhard Buschbeck, 22 November 1911.

41 Heinrich Nowak, "Adolf Loos — Der Feind des Ornaments," in Nowak, *Die Sonnenseuche: Das gesamte Werk 1912 – 1920* (Vienna:

Medusa, 1984), 164.

42 On the day of the lecture, *Der Morgen* ran the drawing of the twin-turreted design from the 1909 competition under the headline: "Baustiljammer" (stylistic distress). The caption explained that it was among the proposals the clients had rejected when they selected Loos's design. It was undoubtedly another attempt to fan the flames of the controversy — and to underscore the qualities of Loos's building. "Baustiljammer," *Der Morgen,* 11 December 1911, 6.

43 "Das Haus am Michaelerplatz: Adolf Loos in eigener Sache," *Reichspost,* 12 December 1911, 6.

44 Loos specifically invited Walden to come from Berlin and to bring Lasker-Schüler to hear the lecture and see the building in completed form. Adolf Loos, postscript to a letter from Kraus to Walden, 29 November 1911, in Avery, *Feinde in Scharen,* 388 – 89, 561; "Das Haus am Michaelerplatz: Adolf Loos in eigener Sache," 6.

45 "Das Loos-Haus auf dem Michalerplatze," *Neue Freie Presse,* 12 December 1911, 8.

46 Czech and Mistelbauer, *Das Looshaus,* 38.

47 The handwritten text that Loos prepared (and many of his slides from that night) have survived. In the early 1930s Loos gave the manuscript to Franz Glück, who was planning to prepare a two-volume work of his complete writings, but it was not published until 1985. See Burkhardt Rukschcio's introduction to "Mein Haus am Michaelerplatz," *Parnass,* special issue, "Der Künstlerkreis um Adolf Loos: Aufbruch zur Jahrhundertwende" (1985), ii.

48 Loos, "Mein Haus am Michaelerplatz," vi.

49 Ibid., vii.

50 Ibid., ix.

51 Ibid., x – xi.

52 Ibid., xi – xii.

53 Ibid., xiv.

54 Ibid., xv.

CHAPTER FOURTEEN TRIUMPH

1 "Das Loos-Haus," *Arbeiter-Zeitung,* 13 December 1911, 5.

2 "Das Haus am Michaelerplatze," *Deutsches Volksblatt,* 13 July 1911, 6.

3 "Das Haus am Michaelerplatz," *Fremden-Blatt,* 12 December 1911, 9; "Das Haus auf dem Michaelerplatz: Rechtfertigung des Architekten Adolf Loos," *Illustrirtes Wiener Extrablatt,* 12 December 1911, 9; "Das Loos-Haus auf dem Michaelerplatze," *Neue Freie Presse,* 12 December 1911, 7 – 8; "Architekt Loos über das Haus am Michaelerplatz," *Neues Wiener Journal,* 12 December 1911, 2 – 3; "Das Haus auf dem Michaelerplatz: Ein Vortrag des Architekten Adolf Loos," *Neues Wiener Tagblatt,* 12 December 1911, 12. See also Otto Zoff, "Adolf Loos über sein Haus (Im akademischen Verband für Literatur und Musik)," *Der Merker* 3, no. 3 (1 February 1912): 115.

4 "Das Haus am Michaelerplatz," *Wiener Mittags-Zeitung,* 12 December 1911, 2.

5 "Herr Loos und sein Haus (Eine Polemik)," *Wiener Montags-Journal,* 18 December 1911, 5 – 6.

6 *Österreichische Volks-Zeitung,* 10 December 1911; Czech and Mistelbauer, *Das Looshaus,* 38.

7 Burkhardt Rukschcio, ed., *Für Adolf Loos: Gästebuch des Hauses am Michaelerplatz* (Vienna: Löcker, 1985), 52.

8 *Zeitschrift des Niederösterreichischen Gewerbe-Vereins,* 11 April 1912, excerpts reprinted in Czech and Mistelbauer, *Das Looshaus,* 71.

9 Postcards from Loos to Kraus, 25 and 27 December 1911, Wien Bibliothek, Vienna.

10 Barker and Lensing, *Peter Altenberg: Rezept die Welt zu sehen,* 390.

11 Peter Altenberg, letter to Lilly Steiner, 12 December 1911, Wien Bibliothek — Handschriftensammlung, Vienna.

12 Peter Altenberg, *Semmering 1912* (Berlin: S. Fischer, 1913).

13 Barker, *Telegrams from the Soul,* 150 – 59.

14 Postcard from Loos and Eugenie Schwarzwald to Kraus, 2 February 1912, Wien Bibliothek; Barker, *Telegrams from the Soul,* 150 – 59.

15 Stuckenschmidt, *Arnold Schoenberg: His Life, World and Work,* 157 – 58.

16 Rukschcio and Schachel, *Adolf Loos: Leben und Werk,* 439 – 40, 489 – 92.

17 Ibid., 165.

18 Kokoschka, *My Life,* 72 – 73.

19 Karl Kraus, letter to Herwarth Walden, 18 February 1912, in Avery, *Feinde in Scharen,* 402; Rukschcio and Schachel, *Adolf Loos: Leben und Werk,* 166.

20 Karl Kraus, telegram to Herwarth Walden, 6 March 1912, in Avery, *Feinde in Scharen,* 404.

21 Rukschcio and Schachel, *Adolf Loos: Leben und Werk,* 166.

22 Czech and Mistelbauer, *Das Looshaus,* 42.

23 "Bericht über die Stadtrats-Sitzung vom 26. März 1912," *Amtsblatt der k.k. Reichshaupt- und Residenzstadt Wien* 21, no. 29 (9 April 1912): 1042; "Das Haus auf dem Michaelerplatz," *Neue Freie Presse,* 2 April 1912 (evening edition), 2.

24 Czech and Mistelbauer, *Das Looshaus,* 42 – 43.

25 See "Das Haus auf dem Michaelerplatz," *Neue Freie Presse,* 2 April 1912, 2.

CHAPTER FIFTEEN
A BUILDING AND ITS TIME

1 Karin Michaelis, "Adolf Loos: Zum 60. Geburtstag am 10. December 1930," *Neue Freie Presse,* 9 December 1930, 13.

2 Nikolaus Pevsner, *Pioneers of the Modern Movement from William Morris to Walter Gropius* (London: Faber and Faber, 1936; rpt., New York: Museum of Modern Art, 1949), 12.

3 Pevsner, *Pioneers of the Modern Movement,* 124.

4 Walter Curt Behrendt, *Der Sieg des neuen Baustils* (Stuttgart: Akademischer Verlag Dr. Fr. Wedekind, 1927), translated as *The Victory of the New Building Style,* trans. Harry Francis Mallgrave (Los Angeles: Getty Research Institute, 2000), 139.

5 Théo van Doesburg, "The Ambiguous Mentality: Factory and Home," *Het Bouwbedrijf 2 , no. 5 (May 1925),* reprinted and translated in

On European Architecture: Complete Essays from Het Bouwbedrijf, 1924–1931, trans. Charlotte I. Loeb and Arthur L. Loeb (Basel: Birkhäuser, 1986), 60–61.

6 Henry-Russell Hitchcock, Jr., and Philip Johnson, *Modern Architecture: International Exhibition,* exh. cat. (New York: Museum of Modern Art, 1932).

7 Franz Ottmann, "Adolf Loos," *Der Architekt* 22, no. 11 (1919): 167.

8 Karl Marilaun, *Adolf Loos* (Vienna: Wiener Literarische Anstalt, 1922).

9 Kulka, *Adolf Loos: Das Werk des Architekten,* 31.

10 [Ludwig Münz], "Schütz für ein architektonisches Meisterwerk," *Wiener Zeitung,* 12 December 1935, 7.

11 Alfred von Baldass, *Wien: Ein Führer durch die Stadt und ihre Umgebung, ihre Kunst und ihr Wirtschaftsleben* (Vienna: Compassverlag, 1925), 238.

12 Kulka, *Adolf Loos: Das Werk des Architekten,* 14.

13 Adolf Loos, "Josef Veillich," *Trotzdem,* 249.

14 Adolf Loos, "Adolf Loos Architekt (Selbstdarstellung), in *Meister-Archiv: Gallerie von Zeitgenossen Deutschlands* (1915); reprinted in Adolf Opel, ed., *Konfrontationen: Schriften von und über Adolf Loos* (Vienna: Prachner, 1988), 80.

15 Adolf Loos, "Vorwort," *Trotzdem,* 5.

16 See, e.g., "Adolf Loos," *Neue Freie Presse,* 25 August 1933, 9; "Adolf Loos," *Wiener Zeitung,* 25 August 1933, 8; "Adolf Loos gestorben," *Prager Tagblatt,* 25 August 1933, 5; "Adolf Loos gestorben," *Reichspost,* 25 August 1933, 6.

17 Ludwig Münz, *Adolf Loos* (Milan: Il Balcone, 1956). The work was later republished, with Münz's original German text, as *Adolf Loos: Mit Verzeichnis der Werke und Schriften* (Vienna: Georg Prachner, 1989).

18 Franz Glück, ed., *Adolf Loos: Sämtliche Schriften in zwei Bänden,* vol. 1 (Vienna: Herold, 1962).

19 Ludwig Münz and Gustav Künstler, *Der Architekt Adolf Loos: Darstellung seines Schaffens nach Werkgruppen/Chronologisches Werkverzeichnis* (Vienna: Anton Schroll, 1964), 102.

20 Ibid., 93–94, 97.

21 Ibid., 97.

22 Ibid., 98.

23 "Columns and Cubes: Review of Ludwig Münz and Gustav Künstler, *Der Architekt Adolf Loos,*" *Times Literary Supplement,* 11 February 1965, 100.

24 Ibid.

25 Reyner Banham, *Theory and Design in the First Machine Age,* 2nd ed. (Cambridge, Mass.: MIT Press, 1980), 95.

26 Leonardo Benevolo, *History of Modern Architecture: The Tradition of Modern Architecture* (Cambridge, Mass.: MIT Press, 1977), 1: 301.

27 Vincent Scully, Jr., *Modern Architecture: The Architecture of Democracy,* rev. ed. (New York: Georg Braziller, 1974), 24, plate 55.

28 Kenneth Frampton, *Modern Architecture: A Critical History* (London: Thames and Hudson, 1985), 91–93.

29 See, e.g., Thomas Weingraber, "Wem gehört Adolf Loos? Oder das Verbrechen wider den Heiligen Geist," *Parnass* 2 (1987): 6–11.

30 Czech and Mistelbauer, *Das Looshaus,* 5.

31 Ibid., 90–100.

32 Ibid., 102–3.

33 Ibid., 114.

34 Ibid., 115.

35 Burkhardt Rukschcio, "Studien zu Entwürfen, Projekten und ausgeführten Bauten von Adolf Loos (1870–1933)," Ph.D. diss., Universität Wien, 1973.

36 Yehuda Safran and Wilfried Wang, *The Architecture of Adolf Loos,* exh. cat. (London: Arts Council of Great Britain, 1985), 48.

37 Werner Oechslin, *Otto Wagner, Adolf Loos, and the Road to Modern Architecture* (Cambridge: Cambridge University Press, 2002), 116, 130, 132.

38 Dietrich Worbs, "Schweigende Rede," *Der Architekt* 47, no. 5 (May 1998): 267.

39 Hilde Heynen, *Architecture and Modernity: A Critique* (Cambridge, Mass.: MIT Press, 1999), 93. The Venetian critic and philosopher Massimo Cacciari responded in a different way: Loos's rejection of ornament and his use of disparate historical elements was a position that was "essentially constructive," he asserted. "The quest to insinuate tradition, as well as the compositional solutions of the work, into the urban fabric and into language is for the sake of *permanence*." The building's design in his view was an attempt to define "with maximum precision" the nature of history and historical change. Massimo Cacciari, *Architecture and Nihilism: On the Philosophy of Modern Architecture* (New Haven: Yale University Press, 1993), 161, 163.

40 Joseph Rykwert, "Adolf Loos: The New Vision," in Joseph Rykwert, *The Necessity of Artifice* (New York: Rizzoli, 1982), 67.

41 Panayotis Tournikiotis, *Adolf Loos* (New York: Princeton Architectural Press, 1994), 122.

42 Beatriz Colomina, *Privacy and Publicity: Modern Architecture as Mass Media* (Cambridge, Mass.: MIT Press, 1994), 279.

43 Richard Bösel, "Zur Genese eines Wiener Platzes: Topographische, historische und gestalterische Aspekte," in Bösel and Benedik, *Der Michaelerplatz in Wien*, 27–29; Corradi, *Wien Michaelerplatz: Stadtarchitektur und Kulturgeschichte;* David Leatherbarrow, "Interpretation and Abstraction in the Architecture of Adolf Loos," *Journal of Architectural Education* 40, no. 4 (Summer 1987): 2–9.

44 Benedetto Gravagnuolo, *Adolf Loos: Theory and Works* (New York: Rizzoli, 1988), 125–26.

45 Ibid., 131.

46 Topp, *Architecture and Truth in Fin-de-Siècle Vienna*, 134.

47 Ibid., 148–50.

48 Shapira, "Assimilating with Style," 5–6.

49 Ibid., 333–34.

50 Friedrich Achleitner, "Ein Haus als Kommentar," in Friedrich Achleitner, *Wiener Architektur: Zwischen typologischem Fatalismus und semantischem Schlamssel* (Vienna: Böhlau, 1996), 188.

51 Friedrich Achleitner, *Die rückwärtsgewandte Utopie: Motor des Fortschritts in der Wiener Architektur?* (Vienna: Picus, 1994), 30–36.

52 Stoessl, "Das Haus auf dem Michaelerplatz," 17.

53 During the early decades of the new century, several photographers, including August Stauda, documented the city's rapidly disappearing old buildings. Their images reveal the manifest differences between these works and the Looshaus. See, e.g., Susanne Winkler, ed., *August Stauda: Ein Dokumentarist des alten Wien*, exh. cat. (Vienna: Wien Museum/Christian Brandstätter, 2004); and also Hartwig Fischl, *Wiener Häuser* (Berlin: Benjamin Harz, 1923).

54 Achleitner, "Ein Haus als Kommentar," 188.

55 The windows Loos chose were a new type, as Hermann Czech explained: "The deep-set window is the highly developed technology of the 'Kastenfenster' (box window): both planes of the glazing open towards the inside. They were state of the art since around 1860. The Kastenfenster, with the outer plane of glazing opening towards the outside, had derived from an earlier, Baroque technology of single-glazed windows opening towards the inside, in front of which temporary outer shutters of wood or glazing were mounted in winter." Hermann Czech, note to the author, 12 December 2010.

56 Loos, "Über Architektur," in *Trotzdem*, 111.

57 Achleitner, "Ein Haus als Kommentar," 188.

EPILOGUE

1 Oskar Kokoschka, entry in the Looshaus guestbook, in Rukschcio, *Für Adolf Loos: Gästebuch des Hauses am Michaelerplatz*, 40.

2 Georg Schwalm-Theiss, *Theiss & Jaksch Architekten, 1907–1961* (Vienna: Christian Brandstätter, 1986), 95.

3 Adolf Loos, "Das Mysterium der Akustik," *Der Merker* 3, no. 1 (1 January 1912): 9–10.

4 Czech and Mistelbauer, *Das Looshaus,* 44 – 45.

5 "Loos-Haus verändert sich: Schauhaus für Wohnbautechnik oder Umwandlung in Kleinwohnungen," *Wiener Allgemeine Zeitung,* 6 April 1933, 4.

6 Czech and Mistelbauer, *Das Looshaus,* 45.

7 [Ludwig Münz], "Schutz für ein architektonisches Meisterwerk," *Wiener Zeitung,* 12 December 1935, 7. See also [Franz Glück], "Die Gefährdung des Loos-Hauses auf dem Michaelerplatz," *Wiener Zeitung,* 19 January 1936, 9.

8 Schwalm-Theiss, *Theiss & Jaksch Architekten, 1907 – 1961,* 94 – 99.

9 "Stockwerksaufbau am Palais Herberstein," *Neue Freie Presse,* 19 December 1936, 6; "Das Haus am Michaelerplatz," *Wiener Zeitung,* 11 February 1911, 8.

10 Grundbuch, EZ 635 Innere Stadt; VVSt 27186 Va (Rottenburg), Bezirksgericht, Innere Stadt (Vienna municipal property records); Tina Walzer and Stephan Templ, *Unser Wien: "Arisierung auf österreichisch"* (Berlin: Aufbau-Verlag, 2001), 125.

11 Gruber, Höller-Alber, and Kristan, *Ernst Epstein,* 57 – 59.

12 "Wien fiebert dem Führer entgegen," *Kleine Volks-Zeitung,* 9 April 1938, 6.

13 Czech and Mistelbauer, *Das Looshaus,* 46.

14 Ibid., 46 – 47.

15 Friedrich Achleitner, "Loos-Zerstörer am Werk: Weitere Demolierungen im Haus am Michaelerplatz," *Die Presse* 9/10 (January 1971): 4.

16 Czech and Mistelbauer, *Das Looshaus,* 47 – 48.

17 Burkhardt Rukschcio, "Zur Wiederherstellung des Looshauses," in *Das Looshaus: Eine Chronik, 1909 – 1989* (Vienna: Raiffeisenbank, 1989), 52 – 53.

18 See Burkhardt Rukschcio, "Zur Restaurierung des Loos-Hauses," *Österreichische Zeitschrift für Kunst und Denkmalpflege* 44, nos. 3/4 (1990): 216 – 18.

19 Jan Tabor, "Archäologische Ruinen am Michaelerplatz in Wien," *Der Baumeister* 90, no. 2 (1993): 32 – 34.

20 Tabor criticized the restoration, characterizing the result as a "modernist fantasy, a 'Kitsch-Haus.'" Ibid., 32. He may have overstated the impact of the changes, but a number of subtle alterations have undoubtedly affected how we now see the building. One of the most important of these, as Hermann Czech has observed, has to do with how the building and square meet: "What is missing — as in many urban houses of the centre — is the souterrain [i.e., basement-level] lighting by (originally circular) glass 'bricks' in the pavement along the façade around the house, which were replaced by later square glass elements. The pavement, of course, was asphalt, and the overall impression much more lucid and abstract than the present rustic pavement stones." Hermann Czech, note to the author, 12 December 2010.

21 What was very different in the controversy over the Haas-Haus is that Hollein had the official support of the mayor and city government; the negative reaction to the building came instead from architects, critics, preservationists, and much of the public. Although comparisons were made at the time with the controversy over the Michaelerplatz, many questioned the analogy because the situation and the approaches of the two architects were so different. Hermann Czech, note to the author, 12 December 2010. See also Friedrich Kurrent, *Texte zur Architektur* (Salzburg: Pustet, 2006), 225 – 26.

BIBLIOGRAPHY

ARCHIVAL SOURCES

Adolf Loos Archive, Graphische Sammlung Albertina, Vienna

Arnold Schönberg Center, Vienna

Bezirksgericht Innere Stadt, Vienna

Bildarchiv Foto Marburg, Kunstgeschichtliches Institut, Philipps-Universität, Marburg, Germany

Brenner-Archiv, Universität Innsbruck

Haus-, Hof- und Staatsarchiv, Vienna

Karl Kraus Collection, Special Collections and Archives, W. E. B. Du Bois Library, University of Massachusetts, Amherst

Österreichische Nationalbibliothek, Bildarchiv, Vienna

Plan- und Schriftenkammer der Magistratsamt (MA 37), Vienna

Sturm-Archiv, Handschriftensammlung, Staatsbibliothek zu Berlin, Preußischer Kulturbesitz

Universität für angewandte Kunst — Sammlung, Vienna

Wien Museum, Vienna

Wienbibliothek im Rathaus — Handschriftensammlung, Vienna

Wiener Stadt- und Landesarchiv

WRITINGS BY LOOS

Loos, Adolf. "Die alte und die neue Richtung in der Baukunst." *Der Architekt* 12 (March 1906): 31–32.

———. *Das Andere: Ein Blatt zur Einführung abendländischer Kultur in Österreich.* 2 issues, 1 October 1903 and 15 October 1903.

———. "Aufruf an die Wiener geschrieben am Todestage Luegers." *Die Fackel* 300 (9 April 1910): 13–15.

———. "Damenmode." *Der Sturm* 1, no. 22 (28 July 1910): 171–72.

———. "Die Entdeckung Wiens." *Fremden-Blatt,* 7 April 1907, 6.

———. *Ins Leere gesprochen 1897–1900.* Paris: Éditions G. Crès, 1921.

———. "Kultur." *März: Halbmonatschrift der deutsche Kultur* 2, no. 4 (1908): 134–36.

———. "Lob der Gegenwart." *März: Halbmonatschrift der deutsche Kultur* 2, no. 3 (1908): 310–12.

———. "Mein erstes Haus!" *Der Morgen,* 3 October 1910, 1.

———. "Mein Haus am Michaelerplatz." *Parnass,* special issue: "Der Künstlerkreis um Adolf Loos: Aufbruch zur Jahrhundertwende" (1985): ii–xv.

———. "Das Mysterium der Akustik." *Der Merker: Österreichische Zeitschrift für Musik und Theater* 3, no. 1 (1 January 1912): 9–10.

———. "Ornament und Verbrechen." *Der Sturm* 1, no. 6 (7 April 1910): 44.

———. "Ornement et Crime." Trans. Marcel Ray. *Les cahiers d'aujourd 'hui* 5 (June 1913): 247–56.

———. "Otto Wagner." *Reichspost,* 13 July 1911, 1–2.

———. "Der Sattlermeister." *Der Sturm* 1, no. 3 (17 March 1910): 20.

———. "Tristan in Wien." *Der Sturm* 1, no. 27 (1 September 1910): 216.

———. *Trotzdem 1900–1930.* Innsbruck: Brenner, 1931.

———. "Die Überflüssigen (Deutscher Werkbund)." *März: Halbmonatschrift der deutsche Kultur* 2, no. 3 (1908): 185–87.

———. "Vom armen reichen Mann." *Der Sturm* 1, no. 1 (3 March 1910): 4.

———. "Vom Gehen, Stehen, Sitzen, Liegen, Schlafen, Essen, Trinken." *Der Sturm* 2, no. 87 (November 1911): 691–92.

———. "Der Vortrag des Architekten Loos." *Neue Freie Presse*, 13 December 1911, 8.

———. "Über Architektur." *Der Sturm* 1, no. 42 (15 December 1910): 334.

———. "Ein Wiener Architekt." *Dekorative Kunst* 1 (1898): 227.

———. "Wiener Architekturfragen." *Reichspost*, 1 October 1910, 1–2.

———. *Wohnungswanderungen.* Vienna, 1907.

———. "Zuschrift." *Neue Freie Presse*, 6 December 1910, 9.

PRIMARY SOURCES

Abels, Ludwig. "Ein Wiener Herrenmodesalon." *Das Interieur* 2 (1901): 145–51.

"Adolf Loos," *Dekorative Kunst* 4 (1899): 173.

"Adolf Loos." *Neue Freie Presse*, 25 August 1933, 9.

"Adolf Loos." *Wiener Zeitung*, 25 August 1933, 8.

"Adolf Loos gestorben." *Prager Tagblatt*, 25 August 1933, 5.

"Adolf Loos gestorben." *Reichspost*, 25 August 1933, 6.

"Adolf Loos: Zu seinen heutigen Vortrag im Deutschen Polytechnischen Verein." *Prager Tagblatt*, 17 March 1911, 7.

Altenberg, Peter. "Eine neue 'Bar' in Wien." *Wiener Allgemeine Zeitung*, 22 February 1909, 2.

———. *Semmering 1912.* Berlin: S. Fischer, 1913.

Altmann-Loos, Elsie. *Adolf Loos: Der Mensch.* Vienna: Herold, 1968.

———. *Mein Leben mit Adolf Loos.* Vienna: Amalthea, 1984.

"Am Michaelerplatz." *Der Morgen — Wiener Montagsblatt*, 8 May 1911, 2–3.

"Architekt Adolf Loos." *Neues Wiener Journal*, 20 July 1911, 7.

"Architekt Loos über das Haus am Michaelerplatz: Ein Vortrag im Sophiensaal." *Neues Wiener Journal*, 12 December 1911, 2–3.

Augenfeld, Felix. "Erinnerungen an Adolf Loos." *Bauwelt* 72 (6 November 1981): 1907.

Avery, George C. *Feinde in Scharen. Ein wahres Vergnügen dazusein. Karl Kraus — Herwarth Walden Briefwechsel 1909 – 1912.* Göttingen: Wallstein, 2002.

"Baustiljammer." *Der Morgen*, 11 December 1911, 6.

"Bausünden in Wien: Ein Gespräch mit Oberbaurat Professor Otto Wagner." *Neues Wiener Journal*, 25 December 1910, 10.

"Die beanständete Fassade des Baues am Michaelerplatz." *Illustrirtes Wiener Extrablatt*, 30 September 1910, 7.

Beenfeldt, Thor. "Adolf Loos." *Architekten* (Copenhagen) 15 (5 April 1913): 266–67.

"Beim Loos-Haus auf dem Michaelerplatz." *Kikeriki*, 30 November 1911, 1.

"Der Benützungskonsens für das Michaelerhaus." *Neues Wiener Tagblatt*, 5 July 1911, 12.

Berger, Hans. "Architektonische Auslese Wien 1910." *Neue Freie Presse*, 26 August 1911, 21–22.

"Bericht über die Stadtrats-Sitzung vom 8. März 1910." *Amtsblatt der k.k. Reichshaupt- und Residenzstadt Wien* 19, no. 21 (15 March 1910): 553–56.

"Bericht über die Stadtrats-Sitzung vom 3. August 1911." *Amtsblatt der k.k. Reichshaupt- und Residenzstadt Wien* 20, no. 64 (11 August 1911): 1991–92.

"Bericht über die Stadtrats-Sitzung vom 26. März 1912." *Amtsblatt der k.k. Reichshaupt- und Residenzstadt Wien* 21, no. 29 (9 April 1912): 1041–42.

"Bevorstehende Entscheidung über das Haus am Michaelerplatz." *Neue Freie Presse*, 11 July 1911, 11.

"Der Brünner Adolf Loos über das 'Loos-Haus' — Richard Schaukal als Helfer im Streite." *Tagesbote aus Mähren und Schlesien*, 23 December 1911, 18.

Canetti, Elias. *The Torch in My Ear.* Trans. Joachim Neugroschel. New York: Farrar, Straus and Giroux, 1982.

Carr, Gilbert J. *Karl Kraus – Otto Stoessl: Briefwechsel, 1902 – 1925.* Vienna: Deuticke, 1996.

Czokor, Franz Theodor, and Leopoldine Rüther. *Du silberne Dame du: Briefe von und an Lina Loos.* Vienna: Zsolnay, 1966.

"Das Dreilauferhaus." *Fremden-Blatt,* 27 October 1911, 13.

"Das Dreilauferhaus am Kohlmarkt." *Neues Wiener Taghlatt,* 26 October 1911, 13.

"Das Dreilauferhaus am Kohlmarkt." *Illustrirtes Wiener Extrablatt,* 26 October 1911, 12.

"Das Dreilauferhaus am Michaelerplatz." *Fremden-Blatt,* 4 August 1911, 10 – 11.

"Das Dreilauferhaus am Michaelerplatz." *Neues Wiener Tagblatt,* 4 August 1911, 11.

"Das Dreilauferhaus: Zwei Zuschriften — 'Das letzte Wort' im Gemeinderate?" *Reichspost,* 13 August 1911, 5.

"'Einfache' Architektur." *Wiener Bauindustrie-Zeitung* 28 (October 1910): 21 – 22.

Engelmann, Paul. "Das Haus auf dem Michaelerplatz." *Die Fackel* 317/318 (28 February 1911): 18.

———. "Kraus, Loos, and Wittgenstein." In *Letters from Ludwig Wittgenstein, with a Memoir,* 122 – 132. Oxford: Basil Blackwell, 1967.

"Die Fassade des Hauses auf dem Michaelerplatz." *Neue Freie Presse,* 16 July 1911, 11.

Fayans, Stefan. "Zur Michaelerplatzfrage." *Wiener Bauindustrie-Zeitung* 28, no. 18 (3 February 1911): 143 – 45.

Fischel, Hartwig. *Wiener Häuser.* Berlin: Benjamin Harz, 1923.

"Für Architekt Loos." *Reichspost,* 8 November 1911, 10.

Gehlhoff-Claes, Astrid, ed. *Else Lasker-Schüler — Briefe an Karl Kraus.* Cologne: Kiepenheuer and Witsch, [1960].

"Geschichten aus dem Dreilauferhause." *Neue Freie Presse,* 17 August 1909, 9.

"Der Getreidespeicher gegenüber der Hofburg." *Illustrirtes Wiener Extrablatt,* 26 October 1910, 4.

"Die gipserne Kunst." *Wiener Mittags-Zeitung,* 16 February 1911, 2.

Glück, Franz. *Adolf Loos.* Paris: Éditions G. Crès, 1931.

———. "Die Gefährdung des Loos-Hauses auf dem Michaelerplatz." *Wiener Zeitung,* 19 January 1936, 9.

Goldman, Leopold. "'Das Haus gegenüber der Burg.'" *Die Zeit,* 8 December 1910 (morning), 9.

"Das Haus am Michaelerplatz." *Fremden-Blatt,* 13 May 1911 (evening), 5; 14 May 1911, 9; 12 December 1911, 9

"Das Haus am Michaelerplatz." *Neues Wiener Journal,* 11 July 1911, 7; 13 July 1911, 5.

"Das Haus am Michaelerplatz." *Reichspost,* 15 July 1911, 8; 4 August 1911, 7.

"Das Haus am Michaelerplatz." *Wiener Mittags-Zeitung,* 12 December 1911, 2.

"Das Haus am Michaelerplatz: Adolf Loos in eigener Sache." *Reichspost,* 12 December 1911, 6.

"Das Haus am Michaelerplatz — Neue Fassadenpläne." *Reichspost,* 14 July 1911, 5.

"Das Haus am Michaelerplatz." *Wiener Zeitung,* 11 February 1937, 8.

"Das Haus am Michaelerplatze." *Deutsches Volksblatt,* 13 July 1911, 6.

"Haus am Michaelerplatz-Wettbewerb." *Wiener Mittags-Zeitung,* 6 May 1911, 3; *Wiener Mittags-Zeitung,* 9 May 1911, 2.

"Das Haus auf dem Michaelerplatz." *Fremden-Blatt,* 14 May 1911, 9.

"Das Haus auf dem Michaelerplatz." *Illustrirtes Wiener Extrablatt,* 11 July 1911, 7 – 8.

"Das Haus auf dem Michaelerplatz, *Neue Freie Presse,* 2 April 1912 (evening), 2.

"Das Haus auf dem Michaelerplatz." *Neues Wiener Abendblatt,* 6 May 1911, 4.

"Das Haus auf dem Michaelerplatz." *Neues Wiener Tagblatt,* 7 May 1911, 13; 16 May 1911, 5; 16 August 1911, 3.

"Das Haus auf dem Michaelerplatz." *Reichspost,* 8 July 1911, 8.

"Das Haus auf dem Michaelerplatz." *Wiener Allgemeine Zeitung,* 11 July 1911, 2.

"Das Haus auf dem Michaelerplatz: Ein Vortrag des Architekten Adolf Loos." *Neues Wiener Tagblatt,* 12 December 1911, 12.

"Das Haus auf dem Michaelerplatz: Rechtfertigung des Architekten Adolf Loos." *Illustrirtes Wiener Extrablatt,* 12 December 1911, 9.

"Das Haus auf dem Michaelerplatze (Eine Polemik mit Herrn Loos)." *Wiener Montags-Journal,* 10 April, 1911, 1 – 2.

"Das Haus gegenüber der Hofburg." *Neue Freie Presse,* 6 December 1910, 9.

"Herr Loos und sein Haus." *Wiener Montags-Journal,* 25 December 1911, 11.

"Herr Loos und sein Haus (Eine Polemik)." *Wiener Montags-Journal,* 18 December 1911, 5 – 6.

Hevesi, Ludwig. *Acht Jahre Sezession (März 1897 – Juni 1905): Kritik — Polemik — Chronik.* Vienna: Carl Konegen, 1906.

———. "Adolf Loos." *Fremden-Blatt,* 22 November 1907, 15 – 16.

———. *Altkunst — Neukunst: Wien 1894 – 1908.* Vienna: Carl Konegen, 1909.

———. "Eine American Bar." *Kunst und Kunsthandwerk* 12 (1909): 214 – 15.

———. "Gegen das moderne Ornament: Adolf Loos." *Fremden-Blatt,* 22 November 1907, 15 – 16.

———. "Der Neubau des Kriegsministeriums." *Fremden-Blatt,* 21 May 1908, 15 – 16.

———. *Österreichische Kunst im neunzehnten Jahrhundert: Ein Versuch.* Leipzig: E. A. Seemann, 1903.

Hlawatsch, Robert. "Erinnerungen an Adolf Loos und an die Loos-Schule." *Bauwelt* 72 (6 November 1981): 1893.

Jaumann, Anton. "Der moderne Mensch und das Kunstgewerbe." *Innen-Dekoration* 21 (January 1910): 1 – 3, 7.

Kokoschka, Olda, and Heinz Spielmann. *Oskar Kokoschka Briefe I, 1905 – 1919.* Düsseldorf: Claassen, 1984.

Kokoschka, Oskar. *My Life.* Trans. David Britt. New York: Macmillan, 1974.

"Der 'Kornspeicher' am Michaelerplatz." *Neuigkeits-Welt-Blatt,* 1 October 1910, 1.

Kraus, Karl. "Die Ankläger." *Die Fackel* 324/325 (May 1911): 7.

———. "Das Haus auf dem Michaelerplatz." *Die Fackel* 313/314 (31 December 1910): 4 – 6.

———. "Pro domo et mundo." *Die Fackel* 300 (March 1910): 23 – 25.

———. *Sittlichkeit und Kriminalität.* Vienna: L. Rosner, 1908.

———. "Tagebuch." *Die Fackel* 279/280 (13 May 1909): 1 – 16.

———. "Die Zuckerkandl." *Die Fackel* 334/335 (31 October 1911): 22 – 23.

Kronstein, "Die Mistkiste am Michaelerplatz." *Die Neue Zeitung,* 7 December 1910, 5.

Kulka, Heinrich. *Adolf Loos: Das Werk des Architekten.* Vienna: Anton Schroll, 1931.

———. "Bekenntnis zu Adolf Loos." *Alte und moderne Kunst* 113 (November – December 1970): 24 – 26.

Lasker-Schüler, Else. "Adolf Loos." *Das Theater* 1, no. 8 (11 December 1909): 184.

———. *Mein Herz. Ein Liebesroman mit Bildern und wirklich lebenden Menschen.* Munich: Bachmair, 1912.

———. "Loos." In *Gesichte: Essays und andere Geschichten,* 69 – 71. Leipzig: Kurt Wolff, 1913.

Lehmann, Philipp. "Architektur vom Menschen her: Zur Adolf-Loos-Ausstellung im Frankfurter Kunstverein." *Frankfurter Zeitung,* 8 February 1931, 17.

Licht, Hugo, ed. *Charakteristische Details von ausgeführten Bauwerken mit besonderer Berücksichtigung der in der Architektur des XX. Jahrhunderts.* Berlin: Verlag von Ernst Wasmuth, 1914.

"Loos, Adolf." In *Wasmuths Lexikon der Baukunst.* Vol. 3. Edited by Leo Adler, 546. Berlin: Ernst Wasmuth, 1931.

"Das Loos-Haus." *Arbeiter-Zeitung,* 13 December 1911, 5.

"Das Loos-Haus am Kohlmarkt." *Illustrirtes Wiener Extrablatt,* 26 April 1911, 3.

"Das Looshaus am Michaelerplatz." *Öster-reichische Volks-Zeitung,* 11 July 1911, 4; 13 July 1911, 4.

"Das Loos-Haus auf dem Michaelerplatze." *Neue Freie Presse,* 12 December 1911, 7 – 8.

"Loos-Haus verändert sich: Schauhaus für Wohnbautechnik oder Umwandlung in Klein-wohnungen." *Wiener Allgemeine Zeitung,* 6 April 1933, 4.

Loos, Lina. *Das Buch ohne Titel: Erlebte Geschichten.* Edited by Adolf Opel and Her-bert Schimek. Frankfurt: Ullstein, 1989.

"Los von der Architektur." *Illustrirtes Wiener Extrablatt,* 1 January 1911, 7.

"Los von Fischer von Erlach. *Kikeriki,* 19 October 1911, 3.

Lux, Joseph August. "Biedermeier als Erzieher." *Hohe Warte* 1 (1904 – 5): 145 – 55.

——. "Die Erneuerung der Ornamentik." *Innen-Dekoration* 18 (1907): 286 – 92, 352 – 54.

——. "Kunst und Ethik." *Der Sturm* 2, no. 10 (10 March 1910): 13 – 14.

Marilaun, Karl. "Das Haus am Michaelerplatz." *Reichspost,* 15 December 1910, 1 – 2.

——. *Adolf Loos.* Vienna: Wiener Literarische Anstalt, 1922.

Marquardt, Ulrike. *Else Lasker-Schüler Briefe, 1893 – 1913.* Frankfurt am Main: Jüdischer Verlag, 2003.

Mebes, Paul, ed. *Um 1800: Architektur und Handwerk im letzten Jahrhundert ihrer tradi-tionellen Entwicklung.* 2 vols. Munich: F. Bruckmann, 1908.

"Meine Kämpfe." *Wiener Allgemeine Zeitung,* 5 April 1911, 2.

——. "Die Schicksale des Ornaments." *Innen-Dekoration* 20 (1909): 231 – 37.

Michaelis, Karin. "Adolf Loos: Zum 60. Geburts-tag am 10. December." *Neue Freie Presse,* 9 December 1930, 12 – 13.

Michel, Wilhelm. "Neue Tendenzen in Kunst-gewerbe." *Innen-Dekoration* 21 (1910): 127 – 28, 135.

"Moderne Innendekoration bei Luxus- und Neubauten." *Wiener Bauindustrie-Zeitung* 26 (20 August 1909): 402.

Münz, Ludwig. *Adolf Loos.* Milan: Il Balcone, 1956.

——. *Adolf Loos: Mit Verzeichnis der Werke und Schriften.* Vienna: Georg Prachner, 1989.

[Münz, Ludwig], "Schutz für ein architektoni-sches Meisterwerk!" *Wiener Zeitung,* 12 December 1935, 7.

"Der Neubau auf dem Kohlmarkt." *Neue Freie Presse,* 29 November 1910 (evening), 33.

"Der Neubau auf dem Michaelerplatz." *Frem-den-Blatt,* 30 September 1910 (evening), 4.

"Der Neubau auf dem Michaelerplatz." *Neue Freie Presse,* 30 September 1910 (evening), 29; 8 December 1910, 12.

"Der Neubau auf dem Michaelerplatz." *Neues Wiener Tagblatt,* 30 September 1910, 13; 8 December 1910, 8.

"Der Neubau auf dem Michaelerplatz." *Reichs-post,* 8 December 1910, 8.

"Der Neubau auf dem Michaelerplatz: Sistier-ung des Fassadenbaues." *Wiener Allge-meine Zeitung,* 29 September 1910, 4 – 5.

"Der Neubau in der Herrengasse-Kohlmarkt." *Neuigkeits-Welt-Blatt,* 17 September 1910, 6.

"Neubauten in der Inneren Stadt." *Der Bauin-teressent, Beilage zur Wiener Bauindustrie-Zeitung* 26 (7 May 1909): 291.

"Das neue Dreilauferhaus." *Fremden-Blatt,* 15 July 1911, 8 – 9; 23 October 1910, 7.

"Das neue Haus am Michaelerplatz: Architekt Loos für sein Werk." *Österreichische Volks-zeitung,* 12 December 1911, 2 – 3.

Neutra, Richard. *Life and Shape.* New York: Appleton-Century-Crofts, 1962.

Noever, Peter, and Marek Pokorný, eds. *Josef Hoffmann Selbstbiographie.* Ostfildern, Ger-many: Hatje Cantz, 2009.

Örley, Robert. "Jahresbilanz." In *Jahrbuch der Gesellschaft Österreichischer Architekten, 1909 – 1910,* 87 – 121. Vienna, 1910.

"Ornament und Verbrechen." *Fremden-Blatt,* 22 January 1910, 21.

"Die ornamentale Ausschmückung des Neu-baues auf dem Michaelerplatz." *Neue Freie Presse,* 7 July 1911, 7.

"Der Ornamentfeind." *Der Ulk: Illustriertes Wochenblatt für Humour und Satyree*schien, Beilage zum *Berliner Tagblatt,* no. 11 (18 March 1910).

Ottmann, Franz. "Adolf Loos." *Der Architekt* 22, no. 11 (1919): 163 – 68.

Paul, Martin, ed. *Technischer Führer durch Wien.* 2 vols. Vienna: Österreichischer Ingenieur- und Architekten Verein, 1910.

Pollak, Friedrich. "Allerlei Kunst." *Der Morgen — Wiener Montagsblatt,* 22 May 1911, 2.

Pötzl, Eduard. "Wiener Ballade." *Neues Wiener Tagblatt,* 25 December 1910, 4 – 5.

A. R-r. [Arthur Roessler]. "Das Haus am Michaelerplatz." *Arbeiter Zeitung,* 18 July 1911 (morning), 7 – 8.

Schaukal, Richard. "Gegen das Ornament." *Deutsche Kunst und Dekoration* 11 (April 1908): 12 – 13, 15.

———. "Adolf Loos: Geistige Landschaft mit vereinzelter Figur im Vordergrund." *Innen-Dekoration* 19 (August 1908): 252 – 59; reprinted in *Der Sturm* 1, no. 13 (26 May 1910): 101 – 2.

———. "Ein Haus und seine Zeit." *Der Merker: Österreichische Zeitschrift für Musik und Theater* 2 (10 December 1910): 181 – 84.

———. *Die Mietwohnung — Eine Kulturfrage — Glossen.* Munich: Georg Müller, 1909.

———. "Nochmals das Haus gegenüber dem Michaelerhof." *Reichspost,* 1 January 1911, 8.

———. "Noch einmal über das Haus von Adolf Loos." *Reichspost,* 18 July 1911, 6.

———. *Vom Geschmack.* 2nd ed. Munich: Georg Müller, 1910.

Scheffers, Otto. "Zweckform und Ornament." *Deutsche Kunst und Dekoration* 24 (1909): 234 – 38.

Scheu, Robert. "Adolf Loos." *Die Fackel* 283/ 284 (26 June 1909): 25 – 37.

Schulze-Eberfeld, Otto. "Über Ornament-Symbolik." *Innen-Dekoration* 21 (1910): 378 – 87.

Schütte-Lihotzky, Margarete. "Gedanken über Adolf Loos." *Bauwelt* 76 (6 November 1981): 1872 – 76.

———. *Warum ich Architektin wurde.* Salzburg: Residenz, 2004.

Seligmann, Adalbert Franz. "Aus dem Wiener Kunstleben." *Neue Freie Presse,* 18 May 1911, 1 – 2.

———. *Kunst und Künstler von Gestern und Heute.* Vienna: Carl Konegen, 1910.

———. "V. V. W." *Neue Freie Presse,* 1 November 1910, 1 – 3.

Servaes, Franz. "Wiener Wandlungen." *Der Tag* 57 (8 March 1911): 1 – 3.

Simmel, Georg. "Das Problem des Stiles," *Dekorative Kunst* 11 (April 1908): 310.

"Sistierung des Neubaues auf dem Michaelerplatz." *Reichspost,* 30 September 1910, 5.

Speidel, Felix. "Vom modernen Haus." *Neues Wiener Tagblatt,* 31 December 1910, 8.

"Das städtische Museum," *Neue Freie Presse,* 13 January 1910 (evening), 3 – 4.

Stefan, Paul. *Das Grab in Wien: Eine Chronik, 1903 – 1911.* Berlin: Erich Reißverlag, 1913.

"Stenographischer Bericht über die öffentliche Sitzung des Gemeinderates vom 22. [sic] Oktober 1910." *Amtsblatt der k.k. Reichshaupt- und Residenzstadt Wien* 19, no. 85 (25 October 1910): 2557 – 58.

"Stenographischer Bericht über die Stadtrats-Sitzung vom 15. Dezember 1910." *Amtsblatt der k.k. Reichshaupt- und Residenzstadt Wien* 19, no. 102 (23 December 1910): 3208 – 10.

"Stockwerksaufbau am Palais Herberstein." *Neue Freie Presse,* 19 December 1935, 6.

Stoessl, Otto. "Das Haus auf dem Michaelerplatz." *Die Fackel* 317/318 (28 February 1911): 13 – 17.

Strzygowski, Josef. "Wiener Bauten." *Die Zeit,* 27 October 1910, 1 – 2.

———. "Orientalische Abwege der Kunst." *Die Zeit,* 4 January 1912, 1 – 2.

Szittya, Emil. *Das Kuriositäten-Kabinett.* Konstanz: See-Verlag, 1923.

Terramare, Georg. "Die Rücksichtslosigkeit des Gedankens." *Fremden-Blatt,* 6 October 1911, 19 – 20.

Tietze, Hans. "Der Kampf um Alt-Wien III. Wiener Neubauten." In *Kunstgeschichtliches Jahrbuch der k. k. Zentralkommission für Erforschung und Erhaltung der Kunst- und historischen Denkmale* 4, *Beiblatt für Denkmalpflege,* 35 – 62. Vienna, 1910.

Trust [Herwarth Walden]. "Schönheit! Schönheit! Der Fall Adolf Loos." *Der Sturm* 2, no. 70 (July 1911): 556.

"Das verzierte Dreilauferhaus am Kohlmarkt." *Deutsches Volksblatt,* 26 October 1911, 8.

"Vortrag Adolf Loos." *Wiener Allgemeine Zeitung,* 4 April 1911, 2.

"Wettbewerb zur Erlangung von Entwürfen für die Fassade des Hauses, Wien I. Michaelerplatz, der Firma Goldman & Salatsch." *Wiener Bauindustrie-Zeitung* 28, no. 32 (12 May 1911): 257.

"Wien fiebert dem Führer entgegen." *Kleine Volks-Zeitung,* 9 April 1938, 6.

"Wohn- und Geschäftshaus, Wien I., Michaelerplatz (Dreilauferhaus)." In *Bericht über die IV. ordentliche Hauptversammlung Wien, am 15. April 1912,* 156 – 57. Vienna: Österreichischer Betonverein, 1912.

Wymetal, Wilhelm von. "Ein reichgegabtes Brünner Kind (Adolf Loos, 'Architekt und Schriftsteller, Künstler und Denker')." *Tagesbote aus Mähren und Schlesien,* 4 January 1908 (Feuilleton section): 1 – 2.

———. "Wiener Weihnachtsbrief." *Tagesbote aus Mähren und Schlesien,* 23 December 1911, 17 – 18.

"Vanalismus in Wien." *Der Zwiebelfisch* 3, no. 4 (1911): 138 – 40.

"Das verzierte Dreilauferhaus am Kohlmarkt." *Fremden-Blatt,* 26 October 1911, 12.

"Vom Gehen, Stehen, Sitzen, Liegen, Essen, und Trinken." *Illustrirtes Wiener Extrablatt,* 25 March 1911, 8.

"Vom Gehen, Stehen, Sitzen, Schlafen, Essen und Trinken: Vortrag des Architekten Adolf Loos." *Neues Wiener Journal,* 19 March 1911, 6.

Von Baldass, Alfred. *Wien: Ein Führer durch die Stadt und ihre Umgebung, ihre Kunst, und ihr Wirtschaftsleben.* Vienna: Compassverlag, 1925.

"Von Schüttkasten auf dem Michaelerplatz." *Die Neue Zeitung,* 8 December 1910, 4.

"Vortrag Adolf Loos." *Prager Tagblatt,* 18 March 1911, 9.

Wiener, Alfred. *Das Warenhaus, Kauf-, Geschäfts-, Büro-Haus.* Berlin: Ernst Wasmuth, 1912.

"Wiener Bausorgen." *Berliner Lokal-Anzeiger,* 9 October 1910 (2nd supplement), 6.

Wittmann, Hugo. Das Haus gegenüber der Burg. *Neue Freie Presse,* 4 December 1910 (morning), 1 – 3.

Zott, Otto. "Adolf Loos über sein Haus (Im akademischen Verband für Literatur und Musik)." *Der Merker* 3, no. 3 (1 February 1912): 115.

"Zwangsweise Herstellung einer Fassade: Das Haus gegenüber der Burg." *Illustrirtes Wiener Extrablatt,* 7 July 1911, 5.

OTHER SOURCES

Achleitner, Friedrich. "Adolf Loos: Ein Maurer, der nie Latein gelernt hat." In *Österreichische Portraits.* Edited by Jochen Jung, 86 – 98. Salzburg: Residenz, 1985.

———. "Loos-Zerstorer am Werk: Weitere Demolierungen im Haus am Michaelerplatz. *Die Presse,* 9 – 10 January 1971, 4.

———. *Die rückwärtsgewandte Utopie: Motor des Fortschritts in der Wiener Architektur?* Vienna: Picus, 1994.

———. *Wiener Architektur: Zwischen typologischem Fatalismus und semantischem Schlamassel.* Vienna: Böhlau, 1996.

Anderson, Stanford. "Architecture in a Cultural Field." In *Wars of Classification: Architecture and Modernity.* Edited by Taisto Mäkela and Wallis Miller, 9 – 35. New York: Princeton Architectural Press, 1991.

———. "The Legacy of German Neoclassicism and the Biedermeier." *Assemblage* 15 (August 1991): 67 – 87.

Asenbaum, Paul, Stefan Asenbaum, and Christian Witt-Dörring, eds. *Moderne Vergangenheit: Wien 1800 – 1900.* Exh. cat. Vienna: Künstlerhaus, 1981.

Baldass, Alfred von. *Wien: Ein Führer durch die Stadt und ihre Umgebung, ihre Kunst und ihr Wirtschaftsleben.* Vienna: Vidor, 1925.

Banham, Reyner. "Ornament and Crime: The Decisive Contribution of Adolf Loos." *Architectural Review* 121 (February 1957): 85–88.

———. *Theory and Design in the First Machine Age.* 2nd ed. Cambridge, Mass.: MIT Press, 1980.

Barker, Andrew. *Telegrams from the Soul: Peter Altenberg and the Culture of Fin-de-Siècle Vienna.* Columbia, S.C.: Camden House, 1996.

———, and Leo A. Lensing. *Peter Altenberg: Rezept die Welt zu sehen.* Vienna: Braumüller, 1995.

Becker, Sibylle. "Loos, die Wiener und ihr Michaelerplatz." *Bauwelt* 83 (January 1992): 152.

Behne, Adolf. *Der moderne Zweckbau.* Munich: Drei Masken, 1926.

Behrendt, Walter Curt. *Der Sieg des neuen Baustils.* Stuttgart: Dr. Fr. Wedekind, 1927.

Benevolo, Leonardo. *History of Modern Architecture: The Tradition of Modern Architecture.* Vol. 1. Cambridge, Mass.: MIT Press, 1977.

Bösel, Richard, and Christian Benedik. *Der Michaelerplatz in Wien: Seine städtebauliche und architektonische Entwicklung.* Exh. cat. Vienna: Kulturkreis Looshaus, 1991.

———, and Vitale Zanchettin, eds. *Adolf Loos, 1870–1933: Architettura utilitá e decoro.* Exh. cat. Milan: Electa, 2007.

Boyer, John W. *Cultural and Political Crisis in Vienna: Christian Socialism in Power, 1897–1918.* Chicago: University of Chicago Press, 1995.

———. *Political Radicalism in Late Imperial Vienna: Origins of the Christian Social Movement, 1848–1897.* Chicago: University of Chicago Press, 1995.

Bullock, Nicholas. "The Looshaus on the Michaelerplatz: Craftsmanship and Tradition." *9H* 6 (1983): 15–20.

Cacciari, Massimo. *Architecture and Nihilism: On the Philosophy of Modern Architecture.* New Haven: Yale University Press, 1993.

Colomina, Beatriz. "Intimacy and Spectacle: The Interiors of Adolf Loos." *AA Files 20* (Autumn 1990): 5–15.

———. *Privacy and Publicity: Modern Architecture as Mass Media.* Cambridge, Mass.: MIT Press, 1994.

"Columns and Cubes: Review of Ludwig Münz and Gustav Künstler, Der Architekt Adolf Loos." *Times Literary Supplement,* 11 February 1965, 100.

Czech, Hermann. *Zur Abwechslung: Ausgewählte Schriften zur Architektur.* Vienna: Löcker and Wögenstein, 1978.

———, and Wolfgang Mistelbauer. "Das Looshaus." *Der Aufbau* 19, nos. 4–5 (April–May 1964): 172–76.

———. *Das Looshaus.* 3rd ed. Vienna: Löcker, 1984.

———. "The Loos House: A History — An Analysis." *9H* 2 (1980): 2–11.

De La Grange, Henry-Louis. *Gustav Mahler, Volume 4: A New Life Cut Short (1907–1911).* Oxford: Oxford University Press, 2008.

Denti, Giovanni. *Adolf Loos: La casa in Michaelerplatz.* Florence: Alinea, 1990.

———, and Silvia Peirone. *Adolf Loos: Opera completa.* Rome: Officina, 1997.

Dimitriou, Sokratis. "Die Entstehung des Michaelerplatzes." In *Handbuch der Stadt Wien* 77: 326–29. Vienna, 1963.

Dreger, Moriz. *Baugeschichte der k.k. Hofburg in Wien bis zum XIX. Jahrhunderte.* Vienna: Anton Schroll, 1914.

Fernández, María Ocón. *Ornament und Moderne: Theoriebildung und Ornamentdebatte im deutschen Architekturdiskurs (1850–1930).* Berlin: Reimer, 2004.

Fischer, Holger. "Ein Scheusal: Das Loos-Haus am Wiener Michaelerplatz." *Deutsche Bauzeitung* 124 (May 1990): 126–133.

Frampton, Kenneth. *Modern Architecture: A Critical History.* London: Thames and Hudson, 1985.

Franz, Rainald. "Josef Hoffmann and Adolf Loos: The Ornament Controversy in Vienna." In *Josef Hoffmann Designs*. Edited by Peter Noever, 11 – 15. Munich: Prestel, 1992.

Furer, René. "Wiedersehen am Michaelerplatz." *Archithese* 20, no. 4 (July – August 1990): 54 – 57.

Geehr, Richard S. *Karl Lueger: Mayor of Fin de Siècle Vienna.* Detroit: Wayne State University Press, 1990.

Gravagnuolo, Benedetto. *Adolf Loos: Theory and Works.* New York: Rizzoli, 1988.

Gruber, Karlheinz, Sabine Höller-Alber, and Markus Kristan. *Ernst Epstein, 1881 – 1938: Der Bauleiter des Looshauses als Architekt.* Exh. cat. Vienna: Jüdisches Museum der Stadt Wien/Holzhausen, 2002.

Haiko, Peter, and Renata Kassal-Mikula. *Otto Wagner und das Kaiser Franz Josef-Stadtmuseum: Das Scheitern der Moderne in Wien.* Exh. cat. Vienna: Historisches Museum der Stadt Wien, 1988.

Harries, Karsten. "Context, Confrontation, Folly." *Perspecta* 27 (1992): 6 – 19.

Heinrich, Richard. *Wittgensteins Grenze — Essay.* Vienna: Deuticke, 1993.

Heynen, Hilde. *Architecture and Modernity: A Critique.* Cambridge, Mass.: MIT Press, 1999.

Iggers, Wilma Abeles. *Karl Kraus: A Viennese Critic of the Twentieth Century.* The Hague: Martinus Nijhoff, 1967.

Kennert, Christian. *Paul Cassirer und sein Kreis: Ein Berliner Wegbereiter der Moderne.* Frankfurt am Main: Peter Lang, 1996.

Kohlert, Margit. "Michaelerplatz und Kohlmarkt." *Österreichische Zeitschrift für Kunst und Denkmalpflege* 40, nos. 1 – 2 (1986): 45 – 50.

Kolowrath, Rudolf. *Ludwig Baumann: Architektur zwischen Barock and Jugendstil.* Vienna: Compress, 1985.

Kolser, Christian, ed. *Peter Altenberg: Leben und Werk in Texten und Bildern.* Munich: Büchergilde Gutenberg, 1981.

Kristan, Markus. *Carl König: Eine neubaroker Großstadtarchitekt in Wien.* Exh. cat. Vienna: Jüdisches Museum der Stadt Wien/Holzhausen, 1999.

———. *Adolf Loos: Villen.* Vienna: Album, 2001.

———. ed. *Adolf Loos: Laden und Lokale.* Vienna: Album, 2001.

———. *Bauten im Style der Secession: Architektur in Wien, 1900 – 1910.* Vienna: Album, 2002.

Künstler, Gustav. "Der 'traditionalist' Adolf Loos." *Österreichische Zeitschrift für Kunst und Denkmalpflege* 22, no. 2 (1968): 83 – 90.

Kurrent, Friedrich. "Das Menschenwürdige und das Schöne: Vor hundert Jahren wurden Österreichs bedeutendste moderne Architekten geboren." *Die Presse,* 12 – 13 December 1970, 3.

———. *Texte zur Architektur.* Salzburg: Pustet, 2006.

Leatherbarrow, David. "Interpretation and Abstraction in the Architecture of Adolf Loos." *Journal of Architectural Education* 40, no. 4 (Summer 1987): 2 – 9.

Lehne, Andreas. *Wiener Warenhäuser, 1865 – 1914.* Vienna: Franz Deuticke, 1990.

Locher, Hubert. "'Genug der originalgenies! Wiederholen wir uns unaufhörlich selbst!' Adolf Loos, das Neue und 'Das Andere.'" *Daidalos* 52 (15 June 1994): 76 – 85.

Long, Christopher. "An Alternative Path to Modernism: Carl König and Architectural Education at the Vienna Technische Hochschule, 1890 – 1913." *Journal of Architectural Education* 55 (September 2001): 21 – 30.

———. "The Origins and Context of Adolf Loos's 'Ornament and Crime.'" *Journal of the Society of Architectural Historians* 68, no. 2 (June 2009): 200 – 223.

Lunzer, Heinz, and Victoria Lunzer-Talos, eds. *Peter Altenberg: Extracte des Lebens: Einem Schriftsteller auf dem Spur.* Salzburg: Residenz, 2003.

Lustenberger, Kurt. *Adolf Loos.* Zurich: Artemis, 1994.

Mallgrave, Harry F. "Adolf Loos and the Ornament of Sentiment." *Midgård* 1 (1987): 79 – 87.

Malmberg, Helga. *Widerall des Herzens: Ein Peter Altenberg Buch*. Munich: Albert Langen/Georg Müller, 1961.

Mühlhaupt, Freya. *Herwarth Walden, 1878 – 1941: Wegbereiter der Moderne*. Exh. cat. Berlin: Berlinische Galerie, Museum für Moderne Kunst, Photographie und Architektur im Martin-Gropius-Bau, 1991.

Munch, Anders V. *Der stillose Stil — Adolf Loos*. Trans. Heinz Kulas. Munich: Wilhelm Fink, 2005.

Münz, Ludwig. "Die alte und die neue Richtung in der Baukunst, von Adolf Loos." *Alte und Neue Kunst* 2, no. 3 (1953): 115 – 20.

——. "Über die Grundlagen des Baustils von Adolf Loos." *Der Aufbau* 13 (October 1958): 393 – 95.

——, and Gustav Künstler. *Der Architekt Adolf Loos: Darstellung seines Schaffens nach Werkgruppen/Chronologisches Werkverzeichnis*. Vienna: Anton Schroll, 1964.

Natter, Tobias G. *Oskar Kokoschka: Early Portraits from Vienna and Berlin, 1909 – 1914*. Exh. cat. New York: Neue Galerie/New Haven: Yale University Press, 2002.

Noever, Peter, and Marek Pokorný, eds. *Josef Hoffmann Selbstbiographie*. Ostfildern, Hatje Cantz, 2009.

Nowak, Heinrich. "Adolf Loos — Der Feind des Ornaments." *Schweizer Journal* 14, nos. 7 – 8 (July – August 1948): 37, 57.

Oechslin, Werner. *Otto Wagner, Adolf Loos, and the Road to Modern Architecture*. Cambridge: Cambridge University Press, 2002.

Oettinger, Karl. *Das Werden Wiens*. Vienna: H. Bauer, 1951.

Opel, Adolf, ed. *Kontroversen: Adolf Loos im Spiegel der Zeitgenossen*. Vienna: Georg Prachner, 1985.

——. *Konfrontationen: Schriften von und über Adolf Loos*. Vienna: Georg Pracher, 1988.

——. *Lina Loos: Wie man wird was man ist. Lebens-Geschichten*. Vienna: Deuticke, 1994.

——, and Marino Valdez, eds. *"Alle Architekten sind Verbrecher": Adolf Loos und die Folgen*. Vienna: Atelier, 1990.

Pevsner, Nikolaus. *Pioneers of the Modern Movement from William Morris to Walter Gropius*. London: Faber and Faber, 1936; rpt., New York: Museum of Modern Art, 1949.

Pfäfflin, Friedrich, Eva Dambacher, and Volker Kahmen, eds. *Karl Kraus: Eine Ausstellung des Deutschen Literaturarchivs im Schiller-Nationalmuseum Marbach*. Exh. cat. Marburg: Schiller-Nationalmuseum, 1999.

Planer, Franz, ed. "Adolf Loos, Architekt." *Das Jahrbuch der Wiener Gesellschaft,* 10, 24. Vienna, 1929.

Podbrecky, Inge, and Rainald Franz, eds. *Leben mit Loos*. Vienna: Böhlau, 2008.

Posch, Wilfried. "Der Streit um Alt und Neu: Adolf Loos." In *Das grössere Österreich: Geistiges und soziales Leben von 1880 bis zur Gegenwart*. Edited by Kristian Sotriffer, 182 – 87. Vienna: Tusch, 1982.

Posener, Julius. Adolf Loos II — Das Michael-erhaus." *Arch +* 53 (1980): 30 – 35.

Prelovšek, Damjan. *Jože Plečnik, 1872 – 1957: Architectura Perennis*. New Haven: Yale University Press, 1997.

Prokop, Ursula. *Wien: Aufbruch zur Metropole. Geschäfts- und Wohnhäuser der Innenstadt 1910 bis 1914*. Vienna: Böhlau, 1994.

Raulet, Gérard, and Burghart Schmidt, eds. *Kritische Theorie des Ornaments*. Vienna: Böhlau, 1993.

Rismondo, Piero. "Vergessenes um Adolf Loos." *Die Presse,* 10 October 1975, 5.

Risselada, Max, ed. *Raumplan versus Plan Libre: Adolf Loos and Le Corbusier, 1919 – 1930*. New York: Rizzoli, 1988.

Rosenberg, Wolf. "Gustav Mahler's Farewell and Return Home." In *Gustav Mahler in Vienna*. Edited by Sigrid Wiesmann, 147 – 60. New York: Rizzoli, 1976.

Rukschcio, Burkhardt. "Ornament und Mythos." In *Ornament und Askese im Zeitgeist des Wien der Jahrhundertwende*. Edited by Alfred Pfabigan, 57 – 92. Vienna: Christian Brandstätter, 1985.

——. "Studien zu Entwürfen, Projekten und ausgeführten Bauten von Adolf Loos

(1870 – 1933)." Ph.D. diss., Universität Wien, 1973.

———. "Wien, Adolf Loos und das Haus am Michaelerplatz." In *Traum und Wirklichkeit — Wien, 1870 – 1930*. Exh. cat. Edited by Sylvia Wurm, 422 – 61. Vienna: Historisches Museum der Stadt Wien, 1985.

———. "Zur Restaurierung des Loos-Hauses." *Österreichische Zeitschrift für Kunst und Denkmalpflege* 44, nos. 3 – 4 (1990): 216 – 18.

———, ed. *Adolf Loos*. Exh. cat. Vienna: Graphische Sammlung Albertina/Historisches Museum der Stadt Wien, 1990.

———, ed. *Für Adolf Loos: Gästebuch des Hauses am Michaelerplatz, Festschrift zum 60. Geburtstag*. Vienna: Löcker, 1985.

———, and Roland Schachel. *Adolf Loos: Leben und Werk*. Salzburg: Residenz, 1982.

Rykwert, Joseph. "Adolf Loos: The New Vision." In *The Necessity of Artifice*. Edited by Joseph Rykwert, 67 – 73. New York: Rizzoli, 1982.

Safran, Yehuda, and Wilfried Wang. *The Architecture of Adolf Loos*. Exh. cat. London: Arts Council of Great Britain, 1985.

Schachel, Roland L. "Adolf Loos: Ornament kein Verbrechen, aber …" *Der Architekt* 9 (September 1994): 499 – 502.

———. "Adolf Loos, Amerika und die Antike." *Alte und moderne Kunst* 113 (November – December 1970): 6 – 10.

Schaeffer, Camillo. *Peter Altenberg: Ein biographischer Essay*. Vienna: Freibord, 1980.

Schorske, Carl. *Fin-de-Siècle Vienna: Politics and Culture*. New York: Knopf, 1980.

———. "Revolt in Vienna." *New York Review of Books*, 29 May 1986, 24 – 28.

Schwalm-Theiss, Georg. *Theiss & Jaksch Architekten, 1907 – 1961*. Vienna: Christian Brandstätter, 1986.

Schwarzer, Mitchell. "Ethnologies of the Primitive in Adolf Loos's Writings on Ornament." *Nineteenth-Century Contexts* 18 (1994): 225 – 47.

———. *German Architectural Theory and the Search for Modern Identity*. Cambridge: Cambridge University Press, 1995.

Scully, Vincent, Jr. *Modern Architecture: The Architecture of Democracy*. Rev. ed. New York: George Braziller, 1974.

Sekler, Eduard F. *Josef Hoffmann: Das architektonische Werk*. Salzburg: Residenz, 1982.

———. "Hoffmann, Loos and Britain: Selective Perspectives." *9H* 6 (1983): 2 – 8.

———. "Josef Hoffmann, Adolf Loos und die Vereinigten Staaten." In *Wien und die Architektur des 20. Jahrhunderts*. Edited by Elizabeth Liskar, 125 – 35. Vienna: Böhlau, 1986.

Shand, P. Morton. "Scenario for Human Drama." *Architectural Review* 76 (October 1934): 131 – 34.

Shapira, Elana. "Assimilating with Style: Jewish Assimilation and Modern Architecture and Design in Vienna. The Case of 'The Outfitters' Leopold Goldman and Adolf Loos and the Making of the Goldman & Salatsch Building (1909 – 1911)." Ph.D. diss., Universität für angewandte Kunst, Vienna, 2004.

———. "The Pioneers: Loos, Kokoschka and Their Shared Clients." In *Oskar Kokoschka: Early Portraits from Vienna and Berlin, 1909 – 1914*. Edited by Tobias G. Natter, 50 – 60. Exh. cat. New York: Neue Galerie/New Haven: Yale University Press, 2002.

Smith, Joan Allen. *Schoenberg and His Circle: A Viennese Portrait*. New York: Schirmer, 1986.

Sprengel, Peter, and Gregor Streim. *Berliner und Wiener Moderne: Vermittlungen und Abgrenzungen in Literatur, Theater, Publizistik*. Vienna: Böhlau, 1998.

Sterk, Harald. *Industriekultur in Österreich: Die Wandel in Architektur, Kunst und Gesellschaft im Fabrikszeitalter, 1873 – 1918*. Vienna: Christian Brandstätter, 1985.

Stewart, Janet. *Fashioning Vienna: Adolf Loos's Cultural Criticism*. London: Routledge, 2000.

———. "Talking of Modernity: The Viennese 'Vortrag' as Form." *German Life and Letters* 51 (October 1998): 455 – 70.

Stuckenschmidt, H. H. *Arnold Schoenberg: His Life, World and Work*. New York: Schirmer, 1977.

Szadkowska, Maria, Leslie van Duzer, and Dagmar Černoušková. *Adolf Loos: Dílo v českých zemích/Adolf Loos: Works in the Czech Lands.* Exh. cat. Prague: Muzeum hlavní města Prahy/Kant, 2009.

Tabor, Jan. "Archäologische Ruinen am Michaelerplatz in Wien." *Der Baumeister* 90, no. 2 (1993): 32 – 34.

———. "Loos a Vienna." *Casabella* 54, no. 565 (February 1990): 23 – 24.

———. "Die wohlgestaltete Selbstverständlichkeit." *Wien aktuell Magazin* 2 (1985): 29 – 31.

Timms, Edward. *Karl Kraus, Apocalyptic Satirist: Culture and Catastrophe in Habsburg Vienna.* New Haven: Yale University Press, 1986.

Topp, Leslie. *Architecture and Truth in Fin-de-Siècle Vienna.* Cambridge: Cambridge University Press, 2004.

Tournikiotis, Panayotis. *Adolf Loos.* New York: Princeton Architectural Press, 1994.

Van Doesburg, Théo. *On European Architecture: Complete Essays from Het Bouwbedrijf, 1924 – 1931.* Trans. Charlotte I. Loeb and Arthur L. Loeb. Basil: Birkhäuser, 1986

Vergo, Peter. "Adolf Loos zwischen Modernismus und Tradition." *Alte und moderne Kunst* 28 (1983): 38 – 39.

Walden, Nell, and Lothar Schreyer, eds. *Der Sturm — Ein Erinnerungsbuch an Herwarth Walden und die Künstler aus dem Sturmkries.* Baden-Baden: W. Klein, 1954.

Walters, F. Rufenacht. *Sanatoria for Consumptives in Various Parts of the World.* London: Swan Sonnenschein, 1899.

Walzer, Tina, and Stephan Templ. *Unser Wien: "Arisierung" auf österreichisch.* Berlin: Aufbau-Verlag, 2001.

Weidinger, Alfred. "Oskar Kokoschka, Träumender Knabe und Enfant Terrible: Die Wiener Periode 1897/98 – 1910." Ph.D. diss., Universität Salzburg, 1996 – 97.

Weihsmann, Helmut. *In Wien erbaut: Lexikon der Wiener Architekten des 20. Jahrhunderts.* Vienna: Promedia, 2005.

Weingraber, Thomas. "Wem gehört Adolf Loos? Oder das Verbrechen wider den Heiligen Geist." *Parnass* 2 (1987): 6 – 11.

Winkler, Susanne, ed. *August Stauda: Ein Dokumentarist des alten Wien.* Exh. cat. Vienna: Wien Museum/Christian Brandstätter, 2004.

Wittek, Hans. "Dokumente der Architektur des 20. Jahrhunderts: Das Michaelerhaus in Wien (Adolf Loos)." *Der Architekt* 12 (December 1988): 638.

Worbs, Dietrich. "Adolf Loos: Aesthetics as a Function of Retail Trade Establishments." *Architect's Yearbook* 14 (1974): 181 – 96.

———. "Klassizismus und Moderne — eine Entwicklung." *Deutsche Bauzeitung* 118 (November 1984): 76, 78.

———. "Schwierige Rede." *Der Architekt* 47 (May 1998): 267 – 70.

———, ed. *Adolf Loos 1870 – 1933: Raumplan — Wohnungsbau.* Exh. cat. Berlin: Akademie der Künste, 1983.

Zohn, Harry. *Karl Kraus.* New York: Frederick Ungar, 1971.

INDEX